Antony and Cleopatra

ARDEN EARLY MODERN DRAMA GUIDES

Series Editors:
Andrew Hiscock, University of Wales, Bangor, UK and Lisa Hopkins, Sheffield Hallam University, UK

Arden Early Modern Drama Guides offer practical and accessible introductions to the critical and performative contexts of key Elizabethan and Jacobean plays. Each guide introduces the text's critical and performance history and provides students with an invaluable insight into the landscape of current scholarly research through a keynote essay on the state of the art and newly commissioned essays of fresh research from different critical perspectives.

The Alchemist, edited by Erin Julian and Helen Ostovich
Doctor Faustus, edited by Sarah Munson Deats
The Duchess of Malfi, edited by Christina Luckyj
Edward II, edited by Kirk Melnikoff
Henry IV, Part 1, edited by Stephen Longstaffe
The Jew of Malta, edited by Robert A. Logan
Julius Caesar, edited by Andrew James Hartley
King Henry V, edited by Karen Britland and Line Cottegnies
King Lear, edited by Andrew Hiscock and Lisa Hopkins
Macbeth, edited by John Drakakis and Dale Townshend
A Midsummer Night's Dream, edited by Regina Buccola
Much Ado About Nothing, edited by Deborah Cartmell and Peter J. Smith
The Revenger's Tragedy, edited by Brian Walsh
Richard III, edited by Annaliese Connolly
Romeo and Juliet, edited by Julia Reinhard Lupton
The Tempest, edited by Alden T. Vaughan and Virginia Mason Vaughan
'Tis Pity She's a Whore, edited by Lisa Hopkins
Troilus and Cressida, edited by Efterpi Mitsi
Twelfth Night, edited by Alison Findlay and Liz Oakley-Brown
Volpone, edited by Matthew Steggle
The White Devil, edited by Paul Frazer and Adam Hansen
Women Beware Women, edited by Andrew Hiscock

Further titles are in preparation.

Antony and Cleopatra
A Critical Reader

Edited by
Domenico Lovascio

THE ARDEN SHAKESPEARE

THE ARDEN SHAKESPEARE
Bloomsbury Publishing Plc
50 Bedford Square, London, WC1B 3DP, UK
1385 Broadway, New York, NY 10018, USA
29 Earlsfort Terrace, Dublin 2, Ireland

BLOOMSBURY, THE ARDEN SHAKESPEARE and the
Arden Shakespeare logo are trademarks of Bloomsbury Publishing Plc

First published in Great Britain 2020
Paperback first published 2021

Copyright © Domenico Lovascio and contributors, 2020

Domenico Lovascio and contributors have asserted their right under
the Copyright, Designs and Patents Act, 1988, to be identified
as the authors of this work.

Cover image taken from the 1615 title page of
The Spanish Tragedy by Thomas Kyd

All rights reserved. No part of this publication may be reproduced or
transmitted in any form or by any means, electronic or mechanical,
including photocopying, recording, or any information storage or
retrieval system, without prior permission in writing from the publishers.

Bloomsbury Publishing Plc does not have any control over, or responsibility for,
any third-party websites referred to or in this book. All internet addresses given
in this book were correct at the time of going to press. The author and publisher
regret any inconvenience caused if addresses have changed or sites have
ceased to exist, but can accept no responsibility for any such changes.

A catalogue record for this book is available from the British Library.

A catalog record for this book is available from the Library of Congress.

ISBN: HB: 978-1-3500-4990-1
PB: 978-1-3502-1552-8
ePDF: 978-1-3500-4992-5
eBook: 978-1-3500-4991-8

Series: Arden Early Modern Drama Guides

Typeset by Integra Software Services Pvt. Ltd.

To find out more about our authors and books visit
www.bloomsbury.com and sign up for our newsletters.

CONTENTS

Series Introduction vii
Notes on Contributors viii
Timeline xi

Introduction *Domenico Lovascio* 1

1 The Critical Backstory *Daniel Cadman* 21

2 Performance History *Maddalena Pennacchia* 55

3 The State of the Art *Domenico Lovascio* 89

4 New Directions: After Decorum: Self-Performance and Political Liminality in *Antony and Cleopatra* *Curtis Perry* 113

5 New Directions: Determined Things: The Historical Reconstruction of Character in *Antony and Cleopatra* *John E. Curran Jr* 133

6 New Directions: Creative Misreadings and Memorial Constructions: The North Face of Alexandria *Julia Griffin* 155

7 New Directions: The Passion of Cleopatra: Her Sexuality, Suffering and Resurrections in *The Mummy* and *Ramses the Damned*
   Sarah Olive 177

8 Resources for Teaching and Studying *Antony and Cleopatra* Paul Innes 201

Notes 228
Bibliography 268
Index 285

SERIES INTRODUCTION

The drama of Shakespeare and his contemporaries has remained at the very heart of English curricula internationally, and the pedagogic needs surrounding this body of literature have grown increasingly complex as more sophisticated resources become available to scholars, tutors and students.

This series aims to offer a clear picture of the critical and performative contexts of a range of chosen texts. In addition, each volume furnishes readers with invaluable insights into the landscape of current scholarly research as well as including new pieces of research by leading critics.

This series is designed to respond to the clearly identified needs of scholars, tutors and students for volumes that will bridge the gap between accounts of previous critical developments and performance history and an acquaintance with new research initiatives related to the chosen plays. Thus, our ambition is to offer innovative and challenging guides that will provide practical, accessible and thought-provoking analyses of early modern drama. Each volume is organized according to a progressive reading strategy involving introductory discussion, critical review and cutting-edge scholarly debate. It has been an enormous pleasure to work with so many dedicated scholars of early modern drama, and we are sure that this series will encourage you to read 400-year-old playtexts with fresh eyes.

Andrew Hiscock and Lisa Hopkins

CONTRIBUTORS

Daniel Cadman is Senior Lecturer in English Literature at Sheffield Hallam University. His first monograph was *Sovereigns and Subjects in Early Modern Neo-Senecan Drama: Republicanism, Stoicism and Authority* (2015), and he has also published on Shakespeare, Fulke Greville and Samuel Daniel. He works as the managing editor of *Early Modern Literary Studies*, for which he has also co-edited special issues focusing on Christopher Marlowe and on the influence of ancient Rome upon early modern literature. He has also contributed to the Lost Plays Database and to *The Year's Work in English Studies*.

John E. Curran Jr is Professor of English at Marquette University and editor of the journal *Renascence: Essays on Values in Literature*. His most recent book is *Character and the Individual Personality in English Renaissance Drama* (2014). He contributed 'What Should Be in That Caesar: The Question of Julius Caesar's Greatness' for *Julius Caesar: A Critical Reader*, ed. A. J. Hartley (The Arden Shakespeare, 2016).

Julia Griffin studied Classics and then English at Cambridge and Oxford Universities and is Associate Professor of English in the Department of Literature and Philosophy at Georgia Southern University. She has published on various Renaissance authors and is particularly interested in classical influences on Renaissance literature. Among her publications are 'Shakespeare's *Julius Caesar* and the Dramatic Tradition', in *A Companion to Julius Caesar*, ed. M. T. Griffin (2009); 'Cinnas of Memory', *Shakespeare Survey* 67 (2014); and 'Cato's Daughter, Brutus's Wife: Portia Agonistes', in *Textus: English Studies in Italy*, 29 (2) (2016); her essay on Shakespeare and Plutarch is to be published in *The Cambridge Companion to Plutarch*.

Paul Innes is Professor of Shakespeare Studies and Academic Subject Leader in Literary and Critical Studies at the University of Gloucestershire. He has published widely on Shakespeare and critical theory, and has worked at the Universities of Warsaw, Edinburgh, Strathclyde and Glasgow. His primary academic interests are in Shakespeare studies and critical theory. His major publications are *Shakespeare's Roman Plays* (2015), *Epic* (2013), *Class and Society in Shakespeare* (2007), *Shakespeare: The Barriers Removed* (2005) and *Shakespeare and the English Renaissance Sonnet: Verses of Feigning Love* (1997).

Domenico Lovascio is Ricercatore of English Literature at the University of Genoa and was a visiting scholar at Sheffield Hallam University in 2016. He was awarded the AIA/Carocci Doctoral Dissertation Prize in 2014. In addition to the first English–Italian edition of Ben Jonson's *Catiline* (2011) and his monograph *Un nome, mille volti. Giulio Cesare nel teatro inglese della prima età moderna* (2015), his articles have been published in *English Literary Renaissance*, *The Ben Jonson Journal*, *Renaissance Studies*, *Early Theatre* and elsewhere. He is the Italian adviser for the Oxford edition of *The Complete Works of John Marston* and contributes to the Lost Plays Database. He has recently edited an issue of *Textus* on 'The Uses of Rome in English Renaissance Drama' (with Lisa Hopkins); the Arden Early Modern Drama Guide to *Antony and Cleopatra*; and a special issue of *Shakespeare*, 'Shakespeare: Visions of Rome'; and he is currently editing the collection *Roman Women in Shakespeare and His Contemporaries* for Medieval Institute Publications, and *The Householder's Philosophy* for *The Collected Works of Thomas Kyd*. Other current work in progress includes a monograph on the Roman plays in the Fletcher canon.

Sarah Olive is Senior Lecturer in English in Education at the University of York. Additionally, she is a visiting lecturer at the Shakespeare Institute, University of Birmingham. Her monograph, *Shakespeare Valued*, was published in 2015. She is the founding editor of the British Shakespeare Association's triannual *Teaching Shakespeare*. Her interest in Shakespeare in popular culture is reflected in her publications on Shakespeare in reality television, the ITV detective drama series *Lewis*, BBC Shakespeare seasons and young adult vampire fiction. She also publishes on Shakespeare in East Asian education. Her co-authored monograph *Shakespeare in East Asian Education* is forthcoming.

Maddalena Pennacchia is Professore Associato of English Literature at Roma Tre University. She was a member of the steering committee of the Italian Association of Shakespearean and Early Modern Studies (2009–12) and is currently a member of the editorial and advisory board of the *Journal of Adaptation in Film and Performance*. She is also Project Director of the Silvano Toti Globe Theatre Archive. Among her recent publications on Shakespeare are *Shakespeare intermediale. I drammi romani* (Editoria e Spettacolo, 2012); 'Shakespeare's Puppets: *The Tempest* and *The Winter's Tale* in *The Animated Tales from Shakespeare*', in *Shakespeare on Screen: The Tempest and Late Romances*, ed. S. Hatchuel and N. Vienne-Guerrin (2017); and 'Roman Shakespeare and Adaptation: A Short Survey of the Silent Films', in *Rome in Shakespeare's World*, ed. M. Del Sapio Garbero (2018). She co-edited *Questioning Bodies in Shakespeare's Rome* (2010) and authored a bio-fiction for children, *Shakespeare e il sogno di un'estate* (2009), which was translated into Spanish (2013) and Romanian (2016).

Curtis Perry is Professor of English at the University of Illinois at Urbana-Champaign, where he also holds courtesy appointments in the Department of the Classics, the Program in Medieval Studies, and the Unit for Criticism and Interpretive Theory. In addition to his single-author books – *The Making of Jacobean Culture* (1997) and *Literature and Favoritism in Early Modern England* (2006) – he has edited or co-edited several volumes and published numerous articles and book chapters on early modern literature and culture. Current projects include a book-length study of Shakespeare and Senecan drama and the editorship of the Roman plays volume in a forthcoming reissue of *The Narrative and Dramatic Sources of Shakespeare*.

TIMELINE

100 BCE	Birth of Gaius Julius Caesar.
83 BCE	Birth of Mark Antony.
69 BCE	Birth of Cleopatra.
54 BCE	Antony starts serving under Caesar in Gaul.
49 BCE	Caesar crosses the Rubicon, thereby instigating civil war against his former ally, Pompey.
48 BCE	Caesar defeats Pompey at the battle of Pharsalus. Pompey flees to Egypt, where he is killed. Caesar meets Cleopatra in Egypt, and the two start an affair.
47 BCE	Caesar defeats Ptolemy XIII's army at the Battle of the Nile and installs Cleopatra as ruler. Birth of Ptolemy Caesar, Caesar and Cleopatra's son, known as Caesarion. Cleopatra and Caesarion go to Rome, where they live as Caesar's guests. Antony marries Fulvia.
44 BCE	Caesar is killed by a conspiracy of aristocratic senators led by Marcus Brutus and Caius Cassius. Cleopatra flees back to Egypt with Caesarion. Mark Antony forms an alliance ('the Second Triumvirate') with Marcus Aemilius Lepidus and Octavian, Caesar's great-nephew and adopted son.
42 BCE	Mark Antony and Octavian defeat Brutus and Cassius at the Battle of Philippi. Antony is assigned Rome's eastern provinces.
41 BCE	Antony meets Cleopatra in Tarsus, and the two start an affair.
40 BCE	Death of Fulvia. Birth of Antony and Cleopatra's twin children, Alexander Helios and Cleopatra Selene. Antony marries Octavia, Octavian's sister.

	Sextus Pompey's admiral Menas seizes Sardinia from Octavian's governor Marcus Lurius.
39 BCE	Sextus Pompey and the members of the Second Triumvirate sign the Pact of Misenum.
37 BCE	Antony leaves Rome and goes back to Cleopatra.
36 BCE	Birth of Antony and Cleopatra's third child, Ptolemy Philadelphus.
31 BCE	The Roman Senate declares war on Cleopatra and proclaims Antony a traitor. Octavian defeats Antony at the Battle of Actium.
30 BCE	Battle of Alexandria. Antony and Cleopatra commit suicide.
27 BCE	Octavian is granted the title of Augustus and becomes the first Roman emperor.
1550	Alessandro Spinello's tragedy *Cleopatra* is published.
1552	Cesare de Cesari's tragedy *Cleopatra* is published.
1553	Étienne Jodelle's tragedy *Cléopâtre captive* is published.
1558	Elizabeth I becomes queen of England.
1564	Birth of William Shakespeare in Stratford-upon-Avon.
1576	Don Celso Pistorelli's tragedy *Marc'Antonio e Cleopatra* is published.
1578	Robert Garnier's tragedy *Antoine* is published.
1579	*The Lives of the Noble Grecians and Romanes Compared Together by That Graue Learned Philosopher and Historiographer, Plutarke of Chæronea; Translated out of Greeke into French by Iames Amyot ... and out of French into Englishe*, by Thomas North, Shakespeare's primary historical source for *Antony and Cleopatra*, is published.
1582	Diego López de Castro's tragedy *Marco Antonio y Cleopatra* is performed.
1583	Giovan Battista Giraldi Cinthio's tragedy *Cleopatra* (first performed in 1543) is published.
1592	*Antonius*, Mary Sidney's translation of Garnier's play, is published. Nicolas de Montreux's tragedy *Cléopâtre* is published.

1594	The first edition of Samuel Daniel's tragedy *Cleopatra* is published.
1595	The second edition of North's *Plutarch* is published.
1598	Samuel Brandon's tragedy *The Virtuous Octavia* is published.
1601	Fulke Greville burns the manuscript of his tragedy *Antony and Cleopatra* for fear that the action of the play might be seen as paralleling the fall of Robert Devereux, 2nd Earl of Essex.
1603	Death of Queen Elizabeth I. King James VI of Scotland becomes King James I of England. The third edition of North's *Plutarch* is published.
1605	Gunpowder Plot.
1606	The anonymous *Tragedy of Caesar's Revenge* is published.
c. 1606–7	Shakespeare writes *Antony and Cleopatra* for the King's Men.
1607	A heavily revised edition of Daniel's *Cleopatra* is published, probably influenced by Shakespeare's play.
1614	One line from Scene 12 is quoted in *A Horrible, Cruel, and Bloody Murder*, printed by George Eld for John Wright
1616	Death of Shakespeare.
c. 1620	John Fletcher and Philip Massinger's Roman play *The False One* is staged by the King's Men.
1623	*Antony and Cleopatra* appears in print in the First Folio of Shakespeare's plays.
1626	Thomas May's tragedy *Cleopatra* is performed.
1667	The Duke's Men first perform John Dryden's *All for Love* at the Drury Lane.
1669	A note in the Lord Chamberlain's records for 1669 states that *Antony and Cleopatra* had been 'formerly acted at the Blackfriars'.
1759	David Garrick revives *Antony and Cleopatra* at the Drury Lane with a heavily trimmed text. It is not as successful as expected.

1813	*Antony and Cleopatra* is staged by John Philip Kemble at the New Covent Garden with processions, fights and triumphs in full display. The text is heavily cut and interpolated with passages from Dryden's *All for Love*. The production is not successful.
1833	John Macready directs *Antony and Cleopatra* at the Drury Lane. The production is praised for Clarkson Stanfield's painted marine scenes of Misenum and Actium. The text is heavily cut and interpolated with passages from Dryden's *All for Love*. The production is not a box-office success.
1849	Samuel Phelps stages *Antony and Cleopatra* at the Sadler's Wells Theatre, leaving most of the scenes complete and omitting a few entirely, without interpolations from Dryden's *All for Love*. It is the first successful production of *Antony and Cleopatra* since the seventeenth century, playing for as many as twenty-two nights. Isabella Glyn is acclaimed as the best Cleopatra ever.
1890	Lily Langtry produces *Antony and Cleopatra* at the Princess's Theatre. The audience's interest is mainly stirred by the fact that Langtry, who also plays Cleopatra, is one of the Prince of Wales's mistresses.
1906	Herbert Beerbohm Tree directs *Antony and Cleopatra* at His Majesty's Theatre. A triumph of oriental lavishness, it can be regarded as the swan song of archaeological spectacle.
1908	Charles Kent directs the first silent movie adaptation of *Antony and Cleopatra*, which is now lost.
1913	Enrico Guazzoni's silent movie *Marcantonio e Cleopatra* is released. Though advertised as related to Shakespeare's play, it has very little Shakespeare in it.
1921–2	William Bridges-Adams and Robert Atkins both direct *Antony and Cleopatra* at the Shakespeare Memorial Theatre in Stratford-upon-Avon and

at the Old Vic in London respectively. Both productions achieve remarkable success by presenting an almost uncut text and applying the 'continuous staging' principle, with a virtually bare scenography and very simple costumes.

1930 John Gielgud and Dorothy Green play the title roles in Harcourt Williams's production of *Antony and Cleopatra* at the Old Vic. It is the first production to adopt Harley Granville-Barker's suggestion to dress the actors in costumes inspired by Paolo Veronese's painting *Alexander and the Wife and Daughter of Darius*.

1951 Showcasing an innovative use of the revolving stage, Michael Benthal's production of *Antony and Cleopatra* at the St James's Theatre stars the most glamorous couple of British show business, Laurence Olivier and Vivien Leigh.

1953 Glen Byam Shaw directs Michael Redgrave and Peggy Ashcroft in a production of *Antony and Cleopatra* at the Shakespeare Memorial Theatre in Stratford-upon-Avon. The two protagonists are especially praised for their performance.

1963 Joseph Mankiewicz directs *Cleopatra*, with Richard Burton and Elizabeth Taylor as Antony and Cleopatra. It is not, however, an adaptation of Shakespeare's play. It nearly bankrupts Twentieth Century Fox. The BBC broadcasts a black-and-white miniseries of nine fifty-minute episodes, *The Spread of the Eagle*, produced and directed by Peter Dews. It adapts *Coriolanus*, *Julius Caesar* and *Antony and Cleopatra* with Keith Michell as Antony and Mary Morris as Cleopatra.

1972 Trevor Nunn directs a spectacular modernist *Antony and Cleopatra* for the Royal Shakespeare Company at the Royal Shakespeare Theatre. Janet Suzman as Cleopatra is made up as bronze-coloured and with black hair. Charlton Heston directs a cinematic

	adaptation of Shakespeare's *Antony and Cleopatra* with himself as Antony and Hildegarde Neil as Cleopatra. The world premiere is so disastrous that virtually no commercial release of the film follows.
1974	Trevor Nunn's film adaptation of *Antony and Cleopatra* airs on ITV. Based on the 1972 stage production for the Royal Shakespeare Company and starring the same cast, it is largely considered the best screen version of the play.
1978	Peter Brook directs a consciously avant-garde and minimalist *Antony and Cleopatra* at the Royal Shakespeare Theatre in Stratford-upon-Avon starring Glenda Jackson as Cleopatra.
1981	Jonathan Miller directs *Antony and Cleopatra* for the BBC Television Shakespeare project.
1982	The Royal Shakespeare Company performs *Antony and Cleopatra* at Stratford-upon-Avon's most intimate theatre, The Other Place, under the direction of Adrian Noble and with Helen Mirren as Cleopatra.
1986	Michele Shay is the first ever black Cleopatra on stage in the American production of *Antony and Cleopatra* by Shakespeare & Company of Lenox, Massachusetts.
1989	The first British black Cleopatra, Pauline Black, plays the role in a production titled *Cleopatra and Antony* by the Actors Touring Company at the Lyric Studios in Hammersmith.
1999	Giles Block directs *Antony and Cleopatra* at Shakespeare's Globe in London with an all-male cast, starring Mark Rylance as Cleopatra.
2006	Gregory Doran directs a successful production of *Antony and Cleopatra* for the Royal Shakespeare Company at the Swan Theatre with Patrick Stewart and Harriet Walter in the leading roles. Dominic Dromgoole directs *Antony and Cleopatra* at Shakespeare's Globe in London as part of the

	'Edges of Rome' season. The production is not particularly successful.
2007	Ivo van Hove directs an intermedial production of Shakespeare's *Roman Tragedies* for Toneelgroep Amsterdam. The heavily mediatized six-hour show, combining in the same immersive experience *Coriolanus*, *Julius Caesar* and *Antony and Cleopatra* rewritten in Dutch, with surtitles in the language of the hosting country, is highly acclaimed by critics and will be revived many times in the ensuing years.
2013	Joaquina Kalukango is the first black Cleopatra to appear in a Royal Shakespeare Company co-production of *Antony and Cleopatra*.
2014	The *Antony and Cleopatra* directed by Jonathan Munby at Shakespeare's Globe in London with Clive Wood and Eve Best in the title roles receives general critical acclaim. Best's performance is especially praised.
2017	The Royal Shakespeare Company launches the 'Rome MMXVII' season under the direction of Angus Jackson, with Robert Innes Hopkins as the designer for the sets of all the four plays. *Antony and Cleopatra* is directed by Iqbal Kahn, with Josette Simon as Cleopatra and Antony Byrne as Antony. The critics particularly praise the music score created by Laura Mvula and the spectacular staging of the Battle of Actium.
2018	Simon Godwin directs Ralph Fiennes and Sophie Okonedo in *Antony and Cleopatra* for a National Theatre production that is broadcast live in cinemas worldwide.

Introduction

Domenico Lovascio

Accustomed as we are to movies, TV series – and, to a lesser extent, books – being repeatedly advertised as intrinsically valuable for their nature of sequels, prequels, reboots, remakes, crossovers or spinoffs, it is hard from an early twenty-first-century perspective to resist the temptation to view *Antony and Cleopatra* (1606–7) as a sequel to *Julius Caesar* (1599). To be sure, the two plays share considerable common ground: both have a Roman setting; the main source for both is Plutarch's *Lives*; both focus on politics, power and honour; the second dramatizes what happens to the triumvirs Antony, Octavius and Lepidus after the events of the first one; so that, in a sense, one could regard *Antony and Cleopatra* as a sequel to *Julius Caesar*, 'in that it is a chronological extension of its dramatic plot with recognizable characters from one play to the next within the same historical context'.[1]

Yet, it is also true that the two tragedies belong to two different periods in William Shakespeare's career and that they were not placed side by side in the 'Catalogue of the Several Comedies, Histories and Tragedies' included in the 1623 Folio edition of his plays; besides, the role of Antony was probably assigned in early performances of the two tragedies to two different players, since Richard Burbage, who definitely played the title role in *Antony and Cleopatra*, is very likely to have acted Brutus in *Julius Caesar*.[2] Even more importantly, the intertextual links between the two plays do not establish a linear connection between them, but actually 'rais[e] doubts on what is said and what is shown' by means of 'narrative revisions that question the earlier play' (e.g., *AC*, 3.11.35–40, 3.254–60).[3]

Accordingly, Sarah Hatchuel persuasively argues that there is 'no reason to believe that, in Shakespeare's time, *Antony and Cleopatra* was presented [or perceived] as *Julius Caesar*'s consistent sequel'.[4] Admittedly, however, there are interesting potentialities in what Hatchuel labels an '"enforced" sequelization' of the two plays as forming a narrative continuum encompassing the events from the Lupercalia of 44 BCE to the lovers' suicides in 30 BCE, potentialities that – at least since the second half of the twentieth century – have been exploited several times on stage in various 'Roman Seasons', the latest having taken place in Stratford-upon-Avon in 2017.[5] For example, directors can feel legitimized in magnifying the friction between Antony and Octavius at the end of *Julius Caesar*, thereby replacing formal closure of that play with the harbingers of new political strife; they can emphasize the similarities between the brief reconciliation of Octavius and Antony on the one hand and that between Brutus and Cassius on the other; they can play on the differences between Brutus's dignified death and Antony's failure to perform a decorous suicide; or they can stress the resemblances and dissimilarities between Antony's elegy over Brutus and Octavius's obsequies over Antony.

Irrespective of the later play being a sequel to the earlier one or not, my sense is that it is not really possible to grasp the full potential of *Antony and Cleopatra* without either having read or seen *Julius Caesar* or being acquainted with the facts of Caesar's life. And it is the ghostly presence of Caesar in *Antony and Cleopatra* that I want to make my preponderant concern in this introduction rather than provide the reader with a more traditional survey of the most prominent thematic strands of the play and its main critical interpretations, since as many as three chapters in this collection ('The Critical Backstory' [21–53], 'The State of the Art' [89–111] and 'Resources for Teaching and Studying *Antony and Cleopatra*' [201–27]) do deal, to varying degrees, with the pre-eminent thematic concerns of the play and the leading critical perspectives about it.

As is plain to see, the characters in *Antony and Cleopatra* seem obsessed with Julius Caesar. Many of them mention him at least once, and his spirit seemingly still 'walks abroad' (*JC*, 5.3.95) to haunt *Antony and Cleopatra* just as it haunted the second half of *Julius Caesar*.[6] More specifically, all the major characters appear to be dealing, as it were, with some form of comparison anxiety with the great Roman *dictator* – the present apparently unable to measure up to the recent past. As a matter of fact, although Rome's physiognomy has dramatically changed since the events depicted in *Julius Caesar*, little time has actually elapsed between the Ides of March and Antony's 'dotage' (*AC*, 1.1.1), and the memory of Caesar and the other protagonists of the previous historical phase feels very much alive in the Romans' and the Egyptians' minds.

Before turning to the exploration of this comparison anxiety, I think it is important to make clear that while Antony (and the other protagonists of *Antony and Cleopatra*) may conform to a deficit model by being less than Caesar, the play itself certainly does not. If anything, Shakespeare seems in this respect to have learned much in the seven or eight years since *Julius Caesar*, which 'span the most creative period in Shakespeare's life and mark the height of his poetic development'.[7] For one thing, *Antony and Cleopatra* can boast an inventiveness of language that *Julius Caesar*, for all its focus on rhetorical construction and oratorical persuasion, almost completely lacks. Besides, a more mature and even more assured sense of playwriting seems to transpire from Shakespeare's choice to get as far as possible from any semblance of Aristotelian precepts by utterly disregarding the three unities; by alternating extremely long and excessively short scenes as a way to convey a succession of dynamism and stasis that contributes to endowing the play with its peculiar shape and texture; by blending comedy and tragedy more organically and consistently than ever before throughout the play, thus instilling in it an uninterrupted undercurrent of humour that would be completely out of place in the overly serious world of *Julius Caesar* but paradoxically appears to heighten the tragic potential of *Antony and Cleopatra*; and by expanding his Roman world outside the Urbs and into Egypt, thereby creating a structural contrast that lays the foundation for a more nuanced sense of *romanitas* and a much more immediate sense of the intrinsic slipperiness of human situations, ideals and selves. And since clearly *Antony and Cleopatra* cannot be seen as inferior to *Julius Caesar*, the inferiority complex of Antony and the others towards Caesar ends up acquiring even deeper resonance.

That Antony may suffer from comparison anxiety with Caesar – and not just with Octavius, as is more commonly remarked – is hardly surprising.[8] The parallels are striking. Antony is a Roman general, and so was Caesar. He is part of a triumvirate, and so was Caesar. He travels to Egypt, and so did Caesar. He falls in love with Cleopatra, and so did Caesar. He cheats on his wife with Cleopatra, and so did Caesar. He has children from Cleopatra, and so had Caesar. He has a formidable opponent, Octavius, as Caesar had one in Pompey. Antony would even re-enact that rivalry by fighting Octavius at Pharsalus, and in single combat to boot (*AC*, 3.7.30–2). Though not at Pharsalus, Antony eventually fights against his rival, and so did Caesar, but he is defeated, and here Antony's emulation fails. Caesar had routed Pompey at Pharsalus and had become – at least in the medieval and early modern imagination – the first Roman emperor, in substance though not in form. The historical Caesar is remembered to this day as the epitome of the conqueror, the winner, to the point that the asyndetic, ascending tricolon *veni, vidi, vici* could easily be used as a substitute for his name – a consideration that, incidentally, alone belittles the play's Antony and Octavius, who, Ventidius states, 'have ever won / More in their officer than person' (*AC*, 3.1.16–17). Only treason, deceit and envy could defeat Caesar. Fortune never parted from him (at least until the day of his assassination), while it does abandon Antony in the play after Cleopatra's flight from the sea battle: 'Fortune and Antony part here; even here / Do we shake hands' (AC, 4.12.19–20). In sum, Caesar's greatness was indisputable.

Antony – the later play seems to suggest – can never attain that greatness: defeated by Octavius, he becomes the emperor who never was. He does display a charming grandeur, a boundless generosity, a majestic benevolence, a charismatic courage, a passionate eloquence, an enthralling vitality, an aspiring mind, a decorous nobility in suffering and carries what John Roe describes as a Machiavellian *grandezza dello animo*.[9] At the same time, however, as David Bevington points out, 'Shakespeare repeatedly allows Antony to be deflated by a humorous or ironic touch', something he never does with Caesar; in addition, 'Shakespeare takes pains to expose the more imperfect side of [Antony's] career as well. Antony has lost at Modena, loses Actium, and loses his last battle; he has only one land victory to his credit.'[10] Nonetheless, Antony probably 'is, despite his manifest failures, the greatest man in the world' – at least in the world of the play.[11] And yet, he is never great in the sense that Caesar was. And he never even becomes a Caesar. Put rather cynically, *Antony and Cleopatra* somehow seems to prove the earlier play's Brutus right: Antony 'is but a limb of Caesar' (JC, 2.1.164).

'I dreamt there was an emperor Antony. / O, such another sleep, that I might see / But such another man!' (AC, 5.2.75), Cleopatra cries to Dolabella as the play progresses towards its tragic conclusion. Cleopatra's lament appears to echo the highly emotionally charged conclusion of Antony's funeral elegy in *Julius Caesar*: 'Here was a Caesar: when comes *such another?*' (JC, 3.2.243, my emphasis). The juxtaposition of the two passages contributes to exposing more clearly the dissonance between the world of the play as it is and as Cleopatra would like it to be: only in her dreams can Antony achieve imperial greatness. Very few lines further on, Cleopatra remarks that Antony's 'legs bestrid the ocean' (AC, 5.2.81), again seemingly quoting from the previous play, in which a disgruntled Cassius had described Caesar as one who 'doth bestride the narrow world / Like a colossus' (*JC*, 1.2.134–5). Both Cassius and Cleopatra envision a colossal figure that can span vast spaces with its very physical presence. Yet, while it is easy to credit Cassius's description of a Caesar so magnified that he could become dangerous – as Brutus ultimately does – it is harder to believe Cleopatra, who is again projecting outside of herself her inner, imaginary version of reality, which appears significantly augmented by the dimension of remembrance: for all his positive qualities, Antony has never given the audience such an impression of greatness in the play as the one she seems to recognize. As Ernst Honigmann sums up, 'allusions to Julius Caesar' in the play 'remind us that a giant's robe now hangs upon a much smaller man'.[12]

That Antony is never as great as Caesar – and, possibly, as Cleopatra – may even be seen as reflected in the fact that he is, as an early modern English stage character, inextricably linked to either of them or both, and that with either he invariably has to share the spotlight. There is no early modern English play centring on Antony alone – not even Mary Sidney's *Antonius* (1592), in spite of its title – and there are two instances of plays – the anonymous *Caesar's Revenge* (c. 1595, publ. 1606) and John Fletcher and Philip Massinger's *The False One* (c. 1620) – altering the historical record by having Antony fall in love with Cleopatra earlier than he actually did (that is, as soon as he gets to Egypt with Caesar) in order to have the three characters on stage all together so as to increase the impression of the power of Cleopatra's allure, while at the same time belittling Antony in Caesar's presence. In early modern English drama, so to speak, Antony is necessary but not sufficient. He must either be played against someone, serve as foil to someone or reckon with someone else. Yes, in *Julius Caesar* he does momentarily steal the scene in the aftermath of Caesar's murder. True, his funeral elegy is among the best pieces of oratory ever delivered on a stage: his performance is rhetorically incisive, emotionally gripping, passionately delivered. And yet, *momentarily* is the key word here: after the oration, Octavius gradually gains more and more space and authority, eventually taking away from Antony, the senior figure, both 'the right hand' of the army (*JC*, 5.1.18) and the concluding lines of the play (*JC*, 5.5.77–82).

Antony's comparison anxiety occasionally results in palpable unease at the mention of Caesar, as occurs with Sextus Pompey's attempt to ascertain the truthfulness of the mattress anecdote:

> POMPEY ... I have heard that Julius Caesar
> Grew fat with feasting there.
> ANTONY You have heard much.
> POMPEY
> I have fair meanings, sir.
> ANTONY And fair words to them.
> POMPEY
> Then so much have I heard.
> And I have heard Apollodorus carried –
> ENOBARBUS
> No more of that! He did so.
> POMPEY What, I pray you?
> ENOBARBUS
> A certain queen to Caesar in a mattress.
> (*AC*, 2.6.64–70)

Neither Antony nor Enobarbus can deny that all this actually happened; yet their reticence, their refraining from openly naming Cleopatra and their ill-concealed desire quickly to transition to a different topic betray their discomfort in being directly confronted with the memory of Caesar and his relationship with the Egyptian queen. As John E. Curran Jr remarks, Sextus 'must be stopped, for the love-play of Caesar and Cleopatra is too humiliating to bear for too long'.[13] Cleopatra had managed to exert some influence on Caesar – 'She made great Caesar lay his sword to bed. / He ploughed her, and she cropped' (*AC*, 2.2.237–8), Agrippa recalls – but she had never succeeded in engulfing him completely as she is now doing with Antony. Apart from highlighting 'both Cleopatra's oft-used mercenary skill at alluring Romans and Caesar's capacity to combine business with pleasure', as Curran again points out, Enobarbus's account here objectifies Cleopatra, who is said to have been brought to Caesar as an item of bedding, thereby putting the Roman general in a position of superiority to the Egyptian queen.[14] That, unlike Antony's, the emasculation and loss of discernment that Caesar had experienced by dint of his inability to resist Cleopatra's sensual offers had only been temporary – and that he had indeed been 'able to absorb her influence rather than be depleted and defeated by it' – seems to have been quite clear to early modern English people, as the sparkling dramatization the King's Men themselves would offer little more than a decade later in *The False One* demonstrates.[15] Fletcher and Massinger's play offers a playfully ironic re-enactment of the mattress scene (which represents the starting point of Caesar's temporary emasculation) and ends with Caesar's blazing victory over the Egyptians and the recovery of his full manly splendour.

Memories of Caesar's superiority also creep into *Antony and Cleopatra* in a much more subtle guise. This happens, for example, when the couple are discussing preparations for their ill-advised sea battle. Antony is amazed at Octavius's rapidity in crossing the Ionian Sea to arrive at Toryne, which prompts the following exchange:

CLEOPATRA
    Celerity is never more admired
    Than by the negligent.
ANTONY   A good rebuke,
    Which might have well becomed the best of men,
    To taunt at slackness.

(*AC*, 3.7.24–7)

Cleopatra's use of the Latinate noun 'celerity' – which had earlier been used by Enobarbus to underline her speed in reaching orgasm (*AC*, 1.2.151) – might be construed as an oblique nod to the historical Caesar, who was especially admired for his *celeritas* in his military expeditions.[16] Seemingly catching on to Cleopatra's allusion, Antony replies that such a reproach might as well have come from 'the best of men', an admittedly generic noun phrase that in this context may, however, feasibly shadow a reference to Caesar and, accordingly, an unconscious admission of inferiority on Antony's part.

Further examples of oblique allusions to Caesar can be provided. Cleopatra once calls her lover with the Italian form 'Antonio' (*AC*, 2.5.26), just as Caesar does in *Julius Caesar*, in which that form of the name is used as many as five times (*JC*, 1.2.3, 4, 6, 189, 1.3.37). As David Daniell argues, 'Since [four] of the "Antonio" uses are from Caesar (and the [fifth], from Caska, is reporting Caesar's words) they could be intentional, Caesar using a jocular, almost pet, name for someone close to him.'[17] Hence, even in a moment of affection between the couple can Caesar creep his way between them, and he does so also when the lovers quarrel. Readily conjured up by Antony's famous insult 'Triple-turned whore!' (*AC*, 4.12.13) – the three men implied here being Caesar, Pompey and Antony himself – Caesar had been also explicitly recollected after Cleopatra's unexpected and hardly explicable flight from the battle: 'I found you as a morsel cold upon / Dead Caesar's trencher – nay, you were a fragment / Of Gnaeus Pompey's' (*AC*, 3.13.121–3). Antony's affront is rather crude and hurtful for Cleopatra, but it ends up reflecting badly on himself as well, in so far as his lines imply that he settled on Caesar's (and even Pompey's elder son's) half-chewed leftovers, which again places Antony below Caesar.

In any event, Caesar seems to be a touchstone for all the major characters of the play, not only Antony. Cleopatra herself is apparently unable completely to get over Caesar. After first receiving news from Rome regarding Antony, she has a telling exchange with Charmian:

CLEOPATRA   ... Did I, Charmian
  Ever love Caesar so?
CHARMIAN   O that brave Caesar!

CLEOPATRA
  Be choked with such another emphasis!
  Say, the brave Antony.
CHARMIAN   The valiant Caesar!
CLEOPATRA
  By Isis, I will give thee bloody teeth,
  If thou with Caesar paragon again
  My man of men!
CHARMIAN   By your most gracious pardon,
  I sing but after you.
CLEOPATRA   My salad days,
  When I was green in judgment: cold in blood,
  To say as I said then!

                                    (*AC*, 1.5.69–78)

Here, the name 'Caesar' is significantly repeated an impressive four times in a mere ten lines, thus providing Caesar with a sort of corporeal presence that eerily feels more tangible than Antony's. Besides, Cleopatra interestingly employs the word 'paragon', which may be especially revealing in this case, inasmuch as 'paragon' both means 'To compare or equate with or to' (as a verb) and 'A person of outstanding merit; a person who serves as a model of some quality' (as a noun).[18] Though 'paragon' is here evidently used as a verb, the proximity between the two words may nevertheless subtly trigger the notion of Caesar as a 'paragon' of all the qualities that make a man manly, a feasible interpretation considering that Cleopatra similarly plays on the ambiguity between noun and verb towards the end of the play, when she scornfully envisions hypothetical future theatrical performances of the events of her life in which 'scald rhymers / *Ballad* us out o'tune' and 'Some squeaking Cleopatra *boy* my greatness' (*AC*, 5.2.215, 219, my emphasis). Cleopatra's uneasy and piqued reply to Charmian's mimicking recollection of her sighing over the 'brave' and 'valiant' Caesar reveals that she has trouble wrestling with the memory of Caesar, 'for Antony cannot', as Curran suggests, 'as his beloved's overprotesting here proves, ever truly compete' with Caesar.[19] It is arduous for Cleopatra to liberate herself from such a cumbersome and awkward presence as Caesar's shadow is, and the compulsion to set up a comparison between him and Antony – which hardly ever proves to be in the latter's favour – is hard to avoid. As Curran again points out, the memory of Caesar is one that 'Shakespeare's Cleopatra must erase, forget, and rewrite, as it nullifies the splendour she lavishes on the present'.[20] Deep down, she seems to be aware that the all-too-human Antony can never truly compete with the deified Julius. To be sure, Cleopatra had already used Caesar as a paragon fewer than thirty lines earlier, again during a conversation about Antony. While she imagines her current Roman lover on horseback thinking about her, her mind is struck by the memory of her former paramours:

> Broad-fronted Caesar,
> When thou was here above the ground, I was
> A morsel for a monarch; and great Pompey
> Would stand and make his eyes grow in my brow;
> There would he anchor his aspect, and die
> With looking on his life.
>
> (*AC*, 1.5.30–5)

Caesar (and Pompey) had found her tempting enough to bite; hence, Antony cannot be expected to behave any differently. Once again, this does not seem to reflect very flatteringly on Antony, who invariably comes after Caesar (and even Pompey), whose superiority is also signalled by his apparently non-coincidental association with the word 'monarch'.

Literally, the 'Pompey' Cleopatra mentions is not Pompey the Great but his elder son Pompey the Younger (who was also defeated by Caesar at Munda in 45 BCE in the victory celebrated by the commoners at the beginning of *Julius Caesar*); yet it is inevitable for most audiences or readers immediately to think of Caesar's great adversary, who is also repeatedly conjured up in the other characters' speeches. The play very early clarifies that Pompey's name still signifies power and commands the enemies' fear on the battlefield: 'Pompey's name strikes more / Than could his war resisted' (*AC*, 1.4.55–6), the Messenger warns Octavius. In addition, the very presence on stage of his younger son Sextus further strengthens the onstage ghostly presence of Pompey, whom Sextus does not hesitate openly to recall in front of the assembled triumvirs:

> I do not know
> Wherefore my father should revengers want,
> Having a son and friends, since Julius Caesar,
> Who at Philippi the good Brutus ghosted,
> There saw you labouring for him. What was't
> That moved pale Cassius to conspire? And what
> Made the all-honoured, honest Roman, Brutus,
> With the armed rest, courtiers and beauteous freedom,
> To drench the Capitol; but that they would
> Have one man but a man? And that is it
> Hath made me rig my navy, at whose burthen
> The angered ocean foams, with which I meant
> To scourge th'ingratitude that despiteful Rome
> Cast on my noble father.
>
> (*AC*, 2.6.10–23)

It would appear that Sextus means to follow in the steps of Pompey, Brutus and Cassius, the virtuous Romans he puts forward as symbols of that republic that is now gone – and gone forever, as the audience is aware. As Andrew Hadfield remarks, in

> *Antony and Cleopatra*, the representative of the republic is the son of its great warrior hero, Pompey, the defeated opponent of Julius Caesar in the Pharsalia. He has his chance to influence the future of the world, but fails to take it and instantly disappears to the dust heap of history.[21]

Rather than waging war against the triumvirs, bringing back the republic and turning history around, Sextus is content with their offers and just drinks the night away with them. This cannot but make him look painfully small in the shadow of his father: 'Thy father, Pompey, would ne'er have / Made this treaty' (*AC*, 2.6.82–3), Sextus's admiral Menas resentfully comments after the signing of the Pact of Misenum.

Pompey is also recalled explicitly together with Caesar in the words of Octavius's Messenger:

> Thy biddings have been done, and every hour,
> Most noble Caesar, shalt thou have report
> How 'tis abroad. Pompey is strong at sea,
> And it appears he is beloved of those
> That only have feared Caesar.
>
> (*AC*, 1.4.34–8)

Lines like these take advantage of the very confusion and slipperiness they simultaneously contribute to creating between personalities active during different historical phases. Is this 'Caesar vs Pompey' again, one might wonder? When names are used like this, it is virtually impossible not to think of the two greater rivals, all the more so because, when they eventually fight, (Sextus) Pompey loses, and (Octavius) Caesar wins. *Mutatis mutandis*, history repeats itself, and names seem to be endowed with the power decisively to influence individual destinies. With this in mind, it may not be coincidental that Antony's ultimate defeat is largely due to a poor decision just as Pompey's was: in the play, Antony agrees to fight at sea though aware that Octavius is stronger there; historically, Pompey had given in to the pressures of the senators and his officers and agreed to fight at Pharsalus, even though he knew that the best course of action would have been just to surround and starve Caesar's outnumbered army instead. In this sense, the play seems to liken Antony to Pompey rather than Caesar, to the loser rather than the winner, and the fact that Antony now lives in Pompey's house in Rome (*AC*, 2.6.26–9), not in Caesar's, becomes sneeringly ironical.

Not even the character that history acknowledges as the winner, Octavius, ever really manages to escape comparison with

Caesar. This most blatantly materializes in Octavius's seizing of Caesar's name for himself as a title and despising Caesar's true – albeit illegitimate – son Caesarion (*AC*, 3.6.6), who seems especially guilty of displaying 'Caesar' as part of his own name: as Enobarbus scoffingly remarks, 'Would you praise Caesar, say "Caesar". Go no further' (*AC*, 3.2.13). The text offers only three instances of the future emperor being referred to as 'Octavius': one in the 'List of Roles'; one in a stage direction at the beginning of 1.4; and only one in dialogue, when Charmian calls him 'Octavius Caesar' (*AC*, 1.2.31). Concurrently, only twice is Julius Caesar referred to as 'Julius', and never by the three major characters – only Sextus and Agrippa do so (*AC*, 2.6.12, 3.2.54). The relentless repetition of the name 'Caesar' further increases the confusion among characters, periods and events (even more consistently so in reading, because of the added reiteration of 'CAESAR' as a speech heading). Nonetheless, appropriating Caesar's name and becoming Caesar prove to be two very different things. Andrew Hiscock remarks upon 'the derivative nature of [Octavius's] political career whose narrative will, he hopes, be inscribed within and cited from the existing corpus of heroic Roman lives ... and establish a continuity of heroic rule with Julius Caesar'.[22] And even though the audience knows that Octavius will eventually become Augustus and start the *pax romana* that will witness the birth of Jesus Christ – 'The time of universal peace is near' (*AC*, 4.6.5) – the feeling the play radiates is that whereas Octavius does become *a* Caesar, he can never be like *that* Caesar.

In particular, clemency, fortune and women seem to be areas in which the two of them sharply differ. When the Egyptians Pothinus and Achillas had beheaded Pompey with a view to pleasing and befriending Caesar, Caesar had cried. Historians identified in those tears various degrees of sincerity; yet, while he certainly benefited from his rival's death, Caesar never approved the Egyptians' initiative and would in due course punish the murderers. On the contrary, in *Antony and Cleopatra*, Octavius openly states that he would like Cleopatra 'from Egypt [to] drive her all-disgraced friend [i.e. Antony] / Or take his life there' (*AC*, 3.12.22–3). No *clementia* – a trait commonly associated with Caesar – and no respect for his rival seem to harbour at this point in Octavius, who appears interested exclusively in magnifying himself and his victory through a glorious triumph, to the point that his offer of imperial *clementia* to Cleopatra in Act 5 comes off as ultimately hypocritical and self-serving. As to fortune, Cleopatra observes that, 'Not being Fortune, [Octavius]'s but Fortune's knave, / A minister of her will' (*AC*, 5.2.3–4). On the face of it, this statement might simply look like a loser's scornful remark addressed to the winner – after all, Antony elsewhere acknowledges that 'The very dice obey him [i.e. Octavius]' (*AC*, 2.3.32) – yet it may also shadow an indirect comparison between Octavius and Caesar. No one in the Renaissance would have either dreamt of calling Caesar 'Fortune's knave' or ever doubted the support of Fortune in his favour: Caesar was regarded as the epitome of the *fortunatus*, as the darling of Fortune. Characterizing Octavius as a simple instrument of Fortune rather than her favourite seems to connote him as inferior to Caesar. Concerning women, even though historically Octavius was already in his third marriage at the time the events of the play take place, there is no mention in Shakespeare's play of any wife or love interest in his life. There is just no woman around him apart from his sister Octavia, whom he unscrupulously uses as a disposable pawn on the chessboard of politics – and his wife Livia is mentioned only once in passing by Cleopatra (*AC*, 5.2.168). This certainly contributes to Octavius's oft-discussed coldness – which also makes him emerge, in John Wilders's phrasing, as 'a lesser person' than Antony in his '[in]capacity for extreme and spontaneous feeling', thus adding up to the sharp contrast between the two rivals, who can be viewed as 'merely two extremes of the same moral spectrum: if Antony embodies passion without reason, [Octavius] embodies reason without passion, lacking in consequence the pity, mercy, and humaneness in which justice depends', as Barbara L. Parker helpfully sums up.[23] Yet Octavius's isolation from women may also be aimed subtly to prompt a further dimension to his comparison with Caesar, in so far as the latter had managed to win and gain power in spite of having women (and especially Cleopatra) around him. In other words, the play may imply that Octavius's final victory owes considerably to his ability to keep Cleopatra at arm's length, thus avoiding the potential danger of her ensnaring charms. As Bevington contends, 'In his cynical remark that "want will perjure / The ne'er-touch'd vestal" (*AC*, 3.12.30–1) we see a glimpse of a personal need to demean women and control them because they are, in his mind, both inferior and dangerous'; in this sense, it is possible to see Octavius as 'the voice inside the play for those male readers who cannot entertain the wholeness of Cleopatra and are threatened by the challenge she represents to a male desire for control'.[24] While undoubtedly exhibiting political shrewdness, Octavius's decision to keep his distance from Cleopatra might consequently also be construed as prompted by a certain weakness, inasmuch as – to put it rather crudely – it is easier not to give in to temptation when one keeps it far away from oneself.

When Sextus attacks Antony for living in his father's house, Lepidus interrupts them observing that 'this is from the present' (*AC*, 2.6.29), meaning that petty feuds are beside the point, irrelevant for the business at hand, namely the treaty. Yet, Lepidus's utterance may be taken as carrying a deeper meaning about the play as a whole. One way or another, all the key characters of the play try to shake off Julius Caesar's shade, but they never succeed. The past repeatedly interrupts their progress towards the future by casting large shadows over the present, and Caesar's ghostly *presentia in absentia* incessantly comes back to haunt the world of the play, influencing the main characters' personalities, *Weltanschauungen* and decisions. *Antony and Cleopatra* may not be a sequel to *Julius Caesar*, but 'Julius Caesar, thou art mighty yet' does seem a perfectly fitting tagline for it.

***

The chapters that follow approach the text from a broad array of perspectives both in literary critical and theatrical terms. The volume starts off with Daniel Cadman's chapter surveying the most important trends and contributions in the critical history of the play from the seventeenth century to the end of the twentieth; it moves to Maddalena Pennacchia's study of the evolution of *Antony and Cleopatra* in performance from the seventeenth century onwards in London and Stratford-upon-Avon, supplemented by an exploration of the rich intermedial potential made available for staging the play by the latest technological innovations; it then offers an overview of the current state of *Antony and Cleopatra* scholarship that also identifies some innovative approaches.

The four ensuing chapters tackle the play from several different angles. Curtis Perry considers *Antony and Cleopatra*'s concern with the problem of consistent self-performance in a time of political transition, suggesting that this is closely bound up with the liminal nature of the historical story it explores: it begins just after the end of the republic – and thus at the moment when ideas about self-performance enshrined in Cicero's influential discussion of decorum in *De officiis* no longer make sense – and ends with the ascendancy of Augustus, which brought with it a radically new model for public self-performance. In Perry's view, the play explores precisely this liminality, staging the nature of public self-performance after decorum as contested, at least until Act 5. Here, as Augustus displays his *clementia* – the characteristic public virtue of empire – Cleopatra counters with a bravura self-staging that references Senecan closet drama as a form of self-dramatization for the politically abject.

The way Shakespeare explores the specific psychologies of Antony, Octavius and Cleopatra, and how they and their combustion with each other cause the momentous events portrayed in the play are at the core of John E. Curran Jr's analysis, which helpfully complements ideas put forward in this introduction. Curran's essay especially diagnoses Antony, touching on his self-dramatizing, and doomed, effort to align two of his obsessions, his descent from Hercules and his subjection to fortune. This aspect of Antony is in contrast to the characters of Octavius, with his comfort with fortune's sway, and of Cleopatra, who is entirely comfortable with self-dramatization and unaffected by fortune. In the interplay between the forces of these three individual psychologies, argues Curran, Shakespeare locates the cause of world-altering history – character is determined, and determines mighty things.

Julia Griffin focuses on the fact that some particularly inspirational details of Thomas North's *Plutarch* used with powerful effect by Shakespeare were either misleading translations or actual inventions by North himself. Griffin discusses three passages from the play: Cleopatra's remark about her birthday (3.13), Caesar's reaction to Antony's challenge to single combat (4.1), and the conversation between the dying Charmian and the anonymous Roman soldier after Cleopatra's death (5.2). In each case, Griffin contends that Shakespeare draws on North's not-quite-Plutarchan scenes to create dramatic moments that epitomize something important about his characters and the structure of the play itself.

The 'passion' of Cleopatra in Anne Rice's *The Mummy* (1989) and its belated sequel *Ramses the Damned: The Passion of Cleopatra* (2017) by Anne and Christopher Rice is the main concern of Sarah Olive's essay on *Antony and Cleopatra* in popular culture. The two novels, suggests Olive, can be seen as 'passion' texts both in describing Cleopatra's passionate sexuality and in giving an account of her death and suffering. Interestingly, a significant share of Cleopatra's suffering in the novels stems from confronting her own pre- and early-twentieth-century artistic and critical representations. As Olive argues, portraying the bulk of Cleopatra's suffering as that of a woman whose reputation has been slandered enables the characters of both novels to explore critically a range of Cleopatra narratives, including but not confined to Shakespeare, who is on occasion invoked through a direct reference, but more commonly through characterization. By blending notions from literary criticism and scholarship into their fictional narratives to tackle pejorative representations of Cleopatra in literature and culture, Olive concludes, the Rices eventually provide a sympathetic account of the Egyptian queen's sexuality and suffering.

The final chapter of the collection is Paul Innes's assessment of the potentialities and difficulties of *Antony and Cleopatra* as a classroom text, which comes along with a survey of the most relevant paper and online resources to teach and study the play. There is also a complete bibliography at the end of the volume that will help students interested in further research.

Given the amount of material published on Shakespeare and on *Antony and Cleopatra* every year, this volume too ran the risk of suffering from comparison anxiety. Yet we believe that all the contributors together have managed to produce a useful guide for students and scholars alike, a collection that can take stock of the past and current situation of scholarship while simultaneously contributing to widening and complicating our understanding of a play that – by virtue of its quasi-Tamburlainesque geographic span; its bewildering disregard for the unities; its innovative cinematic quality; its matchless female lead; its uncompromising depiction of the pleasures and pitfalls of love and passion; its daring exploration of notions of infinity and overflowing of the limits; its disenchanted outlook on politics; its sophisticated treatment of conflicts and polarities; as well as its complex tackling of such delicate issues as race, gender and empire – still makes hungry where most it satisfies.

1

The Critical Backstory

Daniel Cadman

In Janet Adelman's book *The Common Liar*, *Antony and Cleopatra* is famously described as a play that 'consists of a few actions and almost endless discussion of them'.[1] This play is notable for the ways in which it continually opens up space to analyse actions, to present contested accounts of events, and to interrogate the representative strategies of the various characters and even the play itself. Such processes culminate in the final scene, in which Cleopatra speculates upon the ways that she and her lover, Antony, will be remembered by posterity. She fears that their 'Alexandrian revels' will be burlesqued upon the public stage; Antony will 'be brought drunken forth', whilst she will be presented on stage by a 'squeaking Cleopatra', who will 'boy my greatness / I'th' posture of a whore' (5.2.217–20).[2] In this extraordinary moment of metatheatre, Cleopatra confronts the probability that she and her lover will continue to be subjects of representations in ways they will be unable to control. This play is acutely aware of the extent to which characters will be presented and re-presented, and even confronts the prospect that the play itself will be subject to such re-presentation. Beyond the theatre, literary criticism would be the key mode in which such processes would take place.

As we shall see below, some critics would indeed condemn Antony for his excessive appetite and indulgence, while others would remark upon Cleopatra's histrionics and her challenges to gender boundaries. Commentators would debate upon a wide variety of other issues provoked by the play, including, amongst other things, its treatment of history; its dramatic structure; its depictions of individuals negotiating sweeping political changes; and its complex challenges to conventional notions of morality, genre and identity. In what follows, I seek to present an account of the directions that critical responses to this play have taken. Because of their volume and range, however, my aim is to be selective and representative rather than exhaustive. The critical interventions discussed below are included to provide a sense of how the reputation of this play has developed and how our understanding of it has been shaped by broader trends in literary and cultural criticism. I hope to show that, over the best part of four centuries, this play has constantly provoked questions and debates and has inspired a diverse range of readings which, taken together, have produced a rich critical tradition to which commentators continue to contribute.

From the Seventeenth Century to the Victorian Era

In the two centuries following Shakespeare's death, his elevation to the status of 'natural' genius and exemplary national poet was a slow process, and various critics, actors and editors found themselves going to great lengths to excuse or adapt various elements of his works that did not align to the tastes or literary conventions of those eras. In 1642, amidst the onset of civil war, the public theatres were closed and would not reopen until after the Restoration of Charles II in 1660. The theatrical culture that emerged at this time was radically different from that of the late sixteenth and early seventeenth centuries. Whereas Shakespeare and his contemporaries had been relatively untroubled by the classical conventions of drama, the literature of the Restoration period was undergoing a radical realignment of taste. Fashioning themselves, self-consciously, as the key participants in a revitalized era of literary innovation and as the practitioners of a new 'Augustan' age of literature, the major writers of this period sought to emulate classical models of literary practice in a manner characterized by taste, decorum and imitation of the ancients. Shakespeare's works, along with those of his contemporaries, could not easily be accommodated within this tradition, and *Antony and Cleopatra*, with its expansive time frame, its plurality of locations and its often radical shifts in tone, proved particularly problematic in relation to precepts regarding unity and decorum. The reception of *Antony and Cleopatra* therefore provides an especially useful case study for viewing the development of Shakespeare's reputation from the ambivalence or outright hostility of the Restoration period through to his gradual rehabilitation and eventual elevation to his status as national poet through the nineteenth century. During this period, critics, authors, performers and editors often approached this work with a mixture of enthusiasm, ambivalence and outright hostility in their responses to the play's structure, its treatment of history and the complexities in its characterizations.

Shakespeare, and indeed *Antony and Cleopatra*, certainly generated their share of admirers during the Restoration period and the early eighteenth century, yet this admiration was somewhat tainted by Shakespeare's fundamental incompatibility with the literary tastes of the period. Many writers and dramatists, including William D'Avenant and Nahum Tate, were prompted to rewrite certain Shakespearian dramas in order to bring them more into line with the contemporary literary tastes and conventions. In this way, theatrical adaptation became, effectively, a mode of literary criticism, with dramatists correcting or removing elements of Shakespeare's plays that proved problematic for Restoration tastes. Two notable reworkings of *Antony and Cleopatra* were to emerge during this era: Sir Charles Sedley's play of the same name (1677) and John Dryden's *All for Love; or, The World Well Lost* (1677–8). Both of these plays compress the action into the final twenty-four hours of the protagonists' lives and locate the action entirely in Alexandria following the Battle of Actium in order to conform to the Aristotelian unities. In his preface to *All for Love*, Dryden himself confirms that he has observed 'the unities of time, place, and action more exactly ... than, perhaps, the English theatre requires' and that 'the action is so much one that it is the only of the kind without episode or underplot, every scene in the tragedy conducing to the main design, and every act concluding with a turn of it', thus confirming his adherence to the unity of action.[3] Dryden also admits that in terms of style he had 'professed to imitate the divine Shakespeare' and, in doing so, had 'disencumbered' himself from the heroic rhyming couplets in which his previous plays had been written.[4] In spite of the necessary adaptations, though, Dryden ends his preface by asserting that 'by imitating [Shakespeare] I have excelled myself throughout the play'.[5] This mixed view on Shakespeare's relative liberty from the neo-classical conventions that characterized literary taste is also evident in the work of Nicholas Rowe, Shakespeare's biographer and first editor. Rowe pointed out that if one were to survey Shakespeare's work in the light of his adherence, or otherwise, to the classical models of drama outlined by Aristotle, then 'it would be no very hard Task to find a great many faults'.[6] Rowe attempts to indulge such oversights on the grounds that, 'as Shakespeare liv'd under a kind of mere Light of Nature, and had never been made acquainted with the Regularity of those written Precepts, so it would be hard to judge him by a law he knew nothing of'.[7] In the case of *Antony and Cleopatra*, he suggests that one compensation for Shakespeare's failure to adhere to the Aristotelian unities is that the 'Scene travels over the greatest Part of the Roman Empire ... in Recompence for his Carelessness' in this respect.[8] He also praises the verisimilitude of the historical dramas on the grounds that one can find in them 'the Character as exact in the Poet as the Historian', thus identifying another compensation for the lack of adherence to the unity of time.

Dryden's *All for Love* continued to cast its shadow over critical responses to *Antony and Cleopatra* well into the eighteenth century. Such responses tended to be framed in terms of weighing up the relative values between Dryden's decorum and Shakespeare's 'natural', though undisciplined, genius as demonstrated in the play. Such was the case with one anonymous commentator, writing in 1747, who invited the reader to 'Read *Antony and Cleopatra*, from which [*All for Love*] is taken, tho' one of the most incorrect and careless of Shakespeare's Plays, and you will soon feel the Difference', before suggesting that a reader's inevitable conclusion would be that 'Dryden's Play is most correctly poetical with the Unities; Shakespeare's is most pathetically Natural without 'em.'[9] The author concludes that Dryden's play is the 'finish'd Performance of a great Poet', whilst Shakespeare's is 'the hasty Production of a true Dramatick Genius'.[10] William Dodd's 1752 *The Beauties of Shakespeare*, a compendium of quotations with commentaries, also considered *Antony and Cleopatra* alongside Dryden's play. Dodd highlights Enobarbus's famous barge speech, which Dryden imitates in *All for Love* but with the speech being delivered by Antony. When comparing the two versions, Dodd confesses that 'Partiality, perhaps, may incline me to think Shakespeare's the greatest; tho' I am greatly pleas'd in hearing it from Antony's own mouth, in Dryden's play.'[11] Comparisons with Dryden were also evident in responses to Shakespeare in the eighteenth-century theatre. Writing in response to a revived and abridged version of Shakespeare's play produced by David Garrick, who was one of the most active proponents of Shakespeare's cultural legacy in this period, John Hall asserted that *Antony and Cleopatra* 'is inferior to most of Shakespeare's productions' and 'even gives way to Dryden's *All for Love*'.[12] Hall even struggles to find the historical authenticity that other commentators had found as a compensation for the other perceived defects; a particularly egregious anachronism for Hall was that, even following the abridgement of the play, Cleopatra 'still talks of playing at Billiards, a game utterly unknown at that period, as well as many years after'.[13] There is, however, a hint of deliberate and self-conscious provocation when Hall speculates that his comments will no doubt be regarded as 'blasphemy by the Garicians and Shakespeare-bigots, who imagine no piece of this poet can be less than perfection's-self', a remark that indicates his attack is targeted just as much at what G. B. Shaw would later label the culture of 'Bardolatry' as at the play itself.[14] Hall closes his attack by complimenting the staging, albeit in decidedly pithy and backhanded terms, as the 'scenery, dresses, and parade strike the eye and direct one's attention from the poet'.[15]

Garrick's influential efforts to re-establish Shakespeare on the stage were complemented by those of his friend, Samuel Johnson, to ensure that Shakespeare's works remained on the page. Such efforts culminated in the publication of *The Plays of William Shakespeare*, an influential edition of Shakespeare's complete dramatic works, in 1765. In an end note to his commentary on *Antony and Cleopatra*, Johnson presents a somewhat ambivalent view on the play, particularly regarding its construction and characterization. He notes that the events represented in the play are 'described according to history' but 'are produced without any art of connection or care of disposition'.[16] He also comments that the 'power of delighting is derived principally from the frequent changes of the scene', largely because 'no character is very strongly discriminated' from the others.[17] The one exception to this is Cleopatra who stands out because of her association with 'the feminine arts, some of which are too low'.[18] These kinds of comments upon Cleopatra are not uncommon. A similar response was suggested by William Duff, who highlights how the reader's 'sympathy for the wretched though worthless Cleopatra is strongly excited by a single image', the application of the asp to her breast.[19] For Duff, the pathos and poignancy of this image can be found in its mingling of suicide and maternity.

These two commentators therefore indicated how judgemental patriarchal views on Cleopatra were frequently translated into ambivalence through the acknowledged power of her poetry.

In spite of Johnson's somewhat mixed comments on the play, *Antony and Cleopatra* was becoming recognized as part of a body of works which was gaining increased currency as a staple of national literature and whose reputation was continuing to grow in stature. This process continued into the nineteenth century thanks, in part, to the work of a number of notable and influential commentators, including Samuel Taylor Coleridge and William Hazlitt. Coleridge's comments on *Antony and Cleopatra* are relatively brief but have been subject to frequent quotation and reiteration. Although he did not regard the play as being in the same class as what he regarded as the four major tragedies – *Hamlet, Othello, King Lear* and *Macbeth* – he still saw *Antony and Cleopatra* as 'a formidable rival' to them.[20] However, his most notable intervention in the critical history of the play is his application of the motto *Feliciter audax* to it, a phrase through which he aims to emphasize the 'happy valiancy' of the play's style, which 'is but the representative and result of all the material excellencies so exprest'.[21] Coleridge also goes on to praise the realization of Shakespeare's Cleopatra, particularly the way in which 'the sense of criminality in her passion is lessened by our insight into its depth and energy', as well as the complementary relationship between the 'flashes of nature' in the poetry and the close adherence to history. Whilst Coleridge approaches Shakespeare from the point of view of a poet, Hazlitt's comments are informed by his experiences as a theatre reviewer and his particular interests in characterization. Hazlitt's style, along with the image of Shakespeare as a natural genius and exemplary poet that he sets out to promote, is very much in evidence in his final remark on *Antony and Cleopatra* that 'Shakespeare's genius has spread over the whole play a richness like the overflowing of the Nile.'[22] He also praises the representation of Cleopatra, whose 'whole character is the triumph of the voluptuous, of the love of pleasure and the power of giving it, over every other consideration'.[23] At the same time, he also voices the now commonplace view that, although she 'had great and unpardonable faults', the 'grandeur of her death almost redeems them'.[24] While Hazlitt comments on the elevated nature of Cleopatra's suicide, he also notes that grandeur and violence are not always so easily linked in the play, which, in the midst of the scenes of 'extreme magnificence', presents 'pictures of extreme suffering and physical horror', particularly the description of Antony's endurance following the Battle of Modena.[25] Such positive readings on the parts of Coleridge and Hazlitt may not have elevated the play to the same status as the greatest of Shakespeare's tragedies, but they did play a considerable part in stimulating further discussion of the play and in contributing to the wider campaign to elevate the reputation of Shakespeare.

Towards the end of the nineteenth century, however, studies of Shakespeare's play were steered in a particularly innovative direction by the Irish critic Edward Dowden. Instead of following earlier emphases upon the 'natural' genius of Shakespeare, Dowden's *Shakspere: A Critical Study of His Mind and Art* presented a sustained critical narrative that saw the development of Shakespeare's works in relation to his life and background, thereby marking an important step in biographical criticism. In his chapter on the Roman plays, Dowden notes a pronounced shift in tone between the austerity of *Julius Caesar* and the exoticism of *Antony and Cleopatra*, a transition that 'produces in us the change of pulse and temper experienced in passing from a gallery of antique sculpture to a room splendid with the colours of Titian and Paul Veronese'.[26] Such an effect is compounded by the figures of Antony and Cleopatra themselves, who 'insinuate themselves through the senses, trouble the blood, ensnare the imagination, invade our whole being like colour or like music'.[27] Such a rapturous response to the play, however, is hardly unqualified, as Dowden goes on to moralize about the sinister elements being shrouded by such an intoxicating outward show. He is particularly condemnatory towards Cleopatra and how, 'in her complex nature, beneath each fold or layer of sincerity, lies one of insincerity, and we cannot tell which is the last and innermost', features that are complemented by her 'beauty and witchcraft'.[28] Yet Dowden also highlights that behind his initial rapturous response to the play lies a recognition of the artistic insight that Shakespeare brings: he shows that this 'sensuous infinite is but a dream, a snare', and that, whilst 'the glory of the royal festival is not dulled ... or diminished ... he shows us in letters of flame the handwriting upon the wall'.[29] Dowden thus departs from critics like Hazlitt who emphasize the admirable grandeur of Cleopatra's death by highlighting that such regal glory is decidedly finite and does not compensate for what he sees as Cleopatra's unforgivable feminine duplicity.

The Twentieth Century, 1900–79

During the early twentieth century, a range of important developments were taking place in the establishment of literary studies as a distinctively professional discipline. Thanks to his established status as a key part of canonical English literary tradition, Shakespeare was very much at the centre of these movements. One of the earliest, and arguably the most monumental, of early twentieth-century studies of Shakespeare was A. C. Bradley's *Shakespearean Tragedy*, a book that signals these developments in the increasing professionalization of the field of Shakespeare studies and, indeed, the continuing rise of literary criticism more broadly as an academic discipline. First published in 1904 and based upon a series of lectures delivered during his tenure as professor of poetry at the University of Oxford, Bradley's book is most significant for its character-based approach to Shakespeare's tragedies. *Antony and Cleopatra* is not one of the four plays upon which Bradley's book primarily focuses – indeed, Bradley, in another lecture, follows Coleridge in asserting that regarding this play 'as a rival of the famous four, whether on stage or in the study, is surely an error' – but he nevertheless highlights a number of points of comparison with the other tragedies featured in the study.[30] Bradley identifies the 'intractable nature' and 'undramatic' qualities of its historical source material as one of the major flaws in the construction of the play, and singles out the rapid flitting between scenes and groups of characters in the middle of the play as a symptom of its 'defective method', leading to its becoming 'the most faultily constructed of all the tragedies'.[31] One of the repeated emphases in Bradley's asides on *Antony and Cleopatra* is his identification of the play as one of the 'love-tragedies', in which 'the heroine is as much at the centre of the action as the hero'.[32] Bradley did, however, elaborate upon many of his comments in a separate lecture on the play. He further distances it from the 'great' tragedies on the grounds that in the 'famous four' the 'greatness' stems from the tragedies themselves, whereas *Antony and Cleopatra* provokes the reader or spectator to marvel at 'the artist and his activity' rather than the work itself.[33] In contrast to Hazlitt, he also comments that, for a tragedy, the play 'is not painful' and that it contains 'hardly one violent movement; until the battle of Actium is over we witness scarcely any vehement passion; and that battle, as it is a naval action, we do not see'.[34] Shakespeare reserves any 'tragic impressions of any great volume or depth' for the concluding scenes of the play and, prior to that, tends to prioritize in equal measure 'the political aspect of the story' and 'the personal causes' that lead to the play's conclusion.[35] Bradley concludes that, although the tragedy never reaches the heights of the 'famous four', an observer will inevitably end up 'lost in astonishment at the powers which created it'.[36]

While Bradley advocated character as the central lens through which to study Shakespearian drama, other critics turned towards the intellectual contexts that influenced Shakespeare's plays, especially his engagement with classical history. One of the principal exponents of this approach was Mungo William MacCallum in his lengthy study *Shakespeare's Roman Plays and Their Background*. One of MacCallum's principal innovations was to regard Shakespeare's trilogy of Roman plays (*Julius Caesar, Antony and Cleopatra* and *Coriolanus*) as a coherent genre of their own, with an approach and tone that distinguish them from the rest of his tragic dramas. In his analysis of *Antony and Cleopatra*, MacCallum notes the 'distinctive place' it holds in the Shakespearian canon.[37] Part of the reason for this is its ability, simultaneously, to be historically authentic and a remarkable literary achievement: 'there is no play that springs more spontaneously out of the heart of its author, and into which he has breathed a larger portion of his inspiration', and at the same time 'there is none that is more purely historical'.[38] For these reasons, the 'angelic strength' observed by Coleridge is all the more remarkable given Shakespeare's 'close adherence to his authority' in relating the historical events.[39] Such close adherence to the historical events outlined in Plutarch is complemented, according to MacCallum, by the development of the love story, and he compares the play with *Romeo and Juliet* and *Troilus and Cressida*, noting the common feature of including the names of both lovers in the titles. He also highlights how 'three aspects' of the play – 'chronicle history ... personal tragedy ... love poem' – all 'merge and pass into each other'.[40] MacCallum then goes on to develop lengthy chapters, analysing, by turns, the political leaders, the associates of Antony, the characters of Antony and Cleopatra themselves, and the representation of the love affair between the protagonists. One of the conclusions MacCallum draws on the latter of these topics is that Shakespeare harnesses various elements in Plutarch to emphasize the common attributes of the two lovers: 'they correspond in their experiences. Neither is a novice in love and pleasure ... They are alike in their emotionalism, their impressibility, their quick wits, their love of splendour, their genial power, their intellectual scope, their zest for everything.'[41] Shakespeare also follows Plutarch in presenting 'a picture of the completest camaraderie in things serious and frivolous, athletic and intellectual, decorous and venturesome, with memories of which the play is saturated'.[42] Whilst Bradley expressed some scepticism upon the extent of Shakespeare's 'fidelity to his historical authority', MacCallum makes a sustained, prolonged and spirited effort to highlight the play as a work of art that combines historical authenticity with remarkable literary accomplishment.[43]

Bradley's emphasis upon character proved to be a key influence upon a number of subsequent studies, including Harley Granville-Barker's famous *Prefaces to Shakespeare*, which provided a range of distinctive critical responses to Shakespeare's play due to the influence of Granville-Barker's experiences as a theatre practitioner. Such experience is evident in his interests in imagery, costume and performance options, combined with a Bradleyan focus on character. Numerous aspects of Granville-Barker's interests in theatricality are evident in his reading of *Antony and Cleopatra*, particularly relating to the play's perspectives and uses of space. It is Shakespeare's 'most spacious' play, possessing 'a magnificence and a magic all its own, and Shakespeare's eyes swept no wider horizon'.[44] He also notes the 'broad picturesque contrast' between Rome and Egypt, an opposition that 'braces the whole body of the play, even as conflict between character and character will sustain each scene'.[45] The most notable of such conflicts is the rivalry between Antony and Caesar, commenting particularly upon Antony's tragic downfall which culminates in his botched suicide attempt: it is a play in which 'Shakespeare spares him no ignominy.'[46] Granville-Barker's sensitivity to performance conditions is especially evident in his comments upon the representation of Cleopatra, particularly the extent to which this portrayal is influenced by the conditions of the early modern theatre: 'Shakespeare's Cleopatra had to be acted by a boy, and this did everything to determine, not his view of the character, but his presenting of it.'[47] For this reason, Shakespeare 'does not shirk her sensuality, he stresses it time and again; but he has to find other ways than the one impracticable way of bringing it home to us'.[48] Yet, in the same way that he spares Antony no ignominy, Shakespeare, in his characterization of Cleopatra, 'shirks nothing about her', and he notes the detrimental effect upon the audience's impression of her 'womanly charm when we see her haling the bringer of the news of Antony's treachery up and down by the hair of his head, and running after him, knife in hand, screaming like a fish-fag'.[49] Whilst Shakespeare 'allows her here no moment of dignity, nor of fortitude in grief', Granville-Barker asserts that such apparent breaches in her feminine decorum 'reveal, not inconsistency, but that antithesis in disposition which must be the making of every human equation', thus contributing to the richness of the characterization.[50]

Along with Bradley and Granville-Barker, another name that would dominate the critical landscape of Shakespeare studies was that of G. Wilson Knight. Knight's approaches to Shakespeare differed significantly from those of Bradley, adhering as they did to the Anglo-American branch of formalist, or 'New', criticism, which aimed to view literary texts on their own terms without falling back on such elements as biographical details or the historical and cultural contexts. It also privileged close reading as its critical practice. This is evident in Knight's tendency to treat each of the plays as a 'poem' or 'expanded metaphor', concentrating upon the ways in which imagery provides unity and coherence to the text.[51] *Antony and Cleopatra* features prominently in his book *The Imperial Theme*, as the subject for three chapters and a short note. The first of these chapters, 'The Transcendental Humanism of *Antony and Cleopatra*', is a good representative of Knight's typical way of approaching the text and his somewhat idiosyncratic writing style. His principal argument in this chapter relates to the ennobling qualities of poetry. *Antony and Cleopatra* is a play, he argues, in which 'nature itself is here transfigured, and our view is directed not to the material alone, nor to the earth alone, but rather to the universal elements of earth, water, air, fire, and music, and beyond these to the all-transcending visionary humanism which endows man with a supernatural glory'.[52] Such an effect is achieved by an 'ascending scale' of poetic transcendence, which 'views its world as one rising from matter to spirit, and hence, seeing all things in terms not of their immediate appeal, but rather their potential significance, we find that all here is from the first finely gilded with the tinct of spiritual apprehension'.[53] This is evident, particularly, in the recurrence of imperial imagery, which serves a 'dual purpose' by 'suggesting both the material magnificence which Antony loses, and shadowing symbolically the finer spiritual magnificence of love for which he sacrifices it'.[54] In the following chapter, though, Knight reminds us that there is a 'stern realism' about the play and that it is 'fired by an intenser realism than any play from *Hamlet* to *Timon of Athens*. There is pain, failure, hate, and evil. The poet never shirks the more sordid aspect of things divine. The play's visionary transcendence marks not a severance from reality but a consummation of it.'[55] He also devotes a subsequent chapter to comparing *Antony and Cleopatra* to *Macbeth* in its representations of gender and power. 'Both plays are clearly dominated by a woman ... Lady Macbeth and Cleopatra each possess a unique power and vitality which are irresistible and, in both, expressly feminine: their mastery is twined with their femininity.'[56] Knight's approach therefore aims to highlight recurring motifs or images to present the play as a unified poem.

Ernest Schanzer also strived to underline the coherence and unity of the text in his chapter on the play in *The Problem Plays of Shakespeare*. Schanzer's book is unusual in considering *Antony and Cleopatra* as one of the so-called problem plays, a label most commonly associated with *Measure for Measure*, *All's Well That Ends Well* and *Troilus and Cressida*, as plays whose resolutions present considerable difficulty in terms of generic classification. The elevated representation of Cleopatra's death is the key element that Schanzer identifies as problematic when he comes to viewing this play as a tragedy. He asks rhetorically, 'if such words as "triumph", "exultation", "delight" really express our feelings at the close, if we experience wonder but no woe, if pity and terror are both lacking in our experience, can we still speak of the play's ending as belonging to the realm of tragedy?'[57] Such a conclusion anticipates later romances, like *Cymbeline* and *The Winter's Tale*, 'where tragic suffering is succeeded by a serene and harmonious close'.[58] The other 'problematic' element of the play can, according to Schanzer, be discerned by examining the play's 'structural pattern', which 'becomes a silent commentator, a means of expressing the playwright's attitudes and concerns'.[59] The two major structural patterns he identifies include 'a series of contrasts between Rome and Egypt' and 'a series of parallels between Antony and Cleopatra'.[60] The latter of these is, in turn, divided into three groups: first, 'echoes of each other by the lovers, both in words and actions', including their employment of images of the dissolution of empires, their eroticization of death, and, in terms of actions, affinities between Cleopatra's beating of a messenger in 2.5 and Antony's order for Caesar's messenger, Thyreus, to be whipped in 3.13; second, 'similarities in descriptions of them', including recurring images of stars and the recurrent use of the term 'fancy'; and, third, 'parallels in relations with them'.[61] With the first 'structural pattern', Schanzer identifies a number of elements that complicate any straightforward contrasts between Rome and Egypt; the two values for which they stand (honour and love) are placed in tension with one another, rather than any moralistic privileging of the one over the other taking place. Similarly, the two worlds also share certain qualities, including 'cruelty and deceit'.[62] Such parallels point towards the 'dualistic structure' that is the key element contributing to its status as 'Shakespeare's problem play par excellence'.[63] Such dualism presents its audience with 'opposed evaluations' of events 'in such a way as to exclude – at least in those open to the play's full imaginative impact – a simple or consistent response'.[64] For Schanzer, then, the play's multivalence serves to disrupt any comfortable generic classification of it.

Whilst Schanzer's interest is in complicating any straightforward labelling of the play, numerous other critics continued, throughout the century, to follow MacCallum's precedent in placing *Antony and Cleopatra* together with Shakespeare's other Roman works as part of a coherent group. Derek Traversi's *Shakespeare: The Roman Plays* contains an analysis of *Antony and Cleopatra* that subjects the play to similar methods of close reading to those employed by Knight, though Traversi goes as far as to provide, effectively, a running scene-by-scene commentary of the play. Traversi's objectives and preoccupations are very much in line with those of the so-called 'New Criticism', aiming as he does to analyse ambiguities and to find unity within the text. This is evident from his introduction to the chapter in which he sets out to resolve the problem of reconciling two competing views on the play as, by turns, 'a tragedy of lyrical inspiration, presenting the relationship of its central figures as triumphant over adverse circumstance', or as 'a pitiless exposure of human frailties, of the dissipation of spiritual energies through wilful surrender to passion'.[65] At the same time, though, 'the contrast between Rome and Egypt, two worlds embodying contrary attitudes to life and bound to seek one another's destruction, gives variety and a kind of structural unity', and viewing the fates of 'the central protagonists as embedded in this presentation of a world in conflict is to maintain the balance which Shakespeare's conception requires'.[66] At the centre of this reading, then, is an emphasis upon the individuals caught up in the bitter global power struggles taking place around them. Traversi concludes by returning to the fates of Antony and Cleopatra and to the question of resolving the play's conflicting elements into a kind of unity. The play achieves this unity by presenting how 'The emotions of Antony and Cleopatra have been built upon "dungy earth", upon "Nilus' slime", and so upon the impermanence which the nature of these elements implies'; however, 'just as earth and slime can be quickened into life ... by the action upon them of fire and air, so the very elements of waste and vanity which nurtured this tragedy have become, by the time it reaches its necessary conclusion, constituent ingredients in the creation of an intuition of immortality'.[67] The conclusion Traversi reaches therefore has clear echoes of that reached by Knight as he presents a play in which the earthy is elevated into something transcendent.

Maurice Charney's similarly titled *Shakespeare's Roman Plays* places its emphasis upon style, seeing the plays, in similar terms to Knight, as 'poetry of the theater' and arguing that an appreciation of the language should be viewed alongside the performance or dramaturgical features.[68] Charney also emphasizes the contrast between *Julius Caesar* and *Antony and Cleopatra*, with the Roman setting being '"overarched" by the world of Empire and the perils of Egypt. Antony abandons the Roman style and values of Octavius Caesar – they are public, political, and objective as in *Julius Caesar* – and enters into the Egyptian style and values of Cleopatra.'[69] In this way, he preserves the traditional comparison between the austerity of the earlier play with the exoticism of the later one. The majority of Charney's analysis is concerned with identifying groups of oppositions which frame the contrast between Rome and Egypt. These are organized into groups of images: references to the Nile and its serpents, food and drink, heat and cold, and Egypt's association with indolence. Charney does, however, warn against an overly reductive understanding of the opposition between the two cultures as a lens for examining the play; one needs 'to hold both the Egyptian and Roman themes in the play together in the mind as a tragic unity. Either without the other makes for distortion and incompleteness.'[70] One must avoid reducing it to either 'the Roman point of view', which 'simplifies the tragedy into a morality play', or to 'the Egyptian one' that 'transforms the tragedy into a paean of transcendental love. If the tragic choices in this play are between kinds of rightness, then we need both of these views to understand the meaning of the action.'[71] Charney therefore shares an emphasis with Schanzer in his attempt to unify competing imperatives into a coherent vision of genre.

Two other studies of the Roman plays, appearing the following decade, emphasize not so much coherence as continuity and change in the development of the Roman genre. J. L. Simmons's *Shakespeare's Pagan World* presents the coherent property of these plays as the 'historically pagan environment out of which each tragedy arises'.[72] This means that, unlike in the other tragedies, 'the conflict of opposing sides does not ... involve the struggle between characters associated with the clarifying absolutes of good and evil'; in other words, there are no clear villains, nor are there any 'characters whose goodness intimates absolute and transcending value', and whilst the plays may 'deal with the conflict of extremities, the extremities are not those of good and evil'.[73] Another of Simmons's emphases is the problematic nature of tragic subjectivity for the central protagonists in the context of the pagan societies from which they emerge; their 'vision never reaches the level of our moral perspective'; such a lack of a moral compass results in Antony fluctuating 'between a condemnation of his effeminacy and a glorification of his love'.[74] This is complemented by a sense of alienation that links the Roman protagonists, whose actions result in their exile from Rome and a situation in which 'the Roman heroes must therefore, in the falling action of their tragedies confront their city. There is no world elsewhere.'[75] This results in a lack of reconciliation for them which Simmons suggests has a knock-on effect upon the experience of the audience: 'the closing scenes of these plays, while satisfying our moral expectations, leave us more painfully aware of the limited nature of the world', a point accentuated by the fact that 'there is no evil to purge' and there are 'no villains to punish'.[76] When it comes to *Antony and Cleopatra*, Simmons emphasizes the liminal position of the play's action in relation to the development of Western history and the establishment of Christianity because of its historical proximity to the nativity 'that will clarify the significance of man's ability to love and his desire for honor'.[77] Simmons concludes his reading by revisiting the vexed questions relating to the moral dimension of the protagonists' relationship and eventual suicide: the protagonists are 'pre-Christians', who live 'in a world where the lovers can have no other means to rise but the flesh and earthly glory'.[78] Simmons's conclusion is therefore notable for the extent to which he departs from Knight's and Traversi's emphases upon the 'transcendent' qualities of the play; their inability to achieve Christian salvation makes such a conclusion unavailable to them. Paul A. Cantor's *Shakespeare's Rome: Republic and Empire* looks at the transition towards Rome's imperial phase rather than towards the onset of Christianity. His study takes the form of an extended contrast between *Coriolanus* and *Antony and Cleopatra*, representing, respectively, the beginnings and the decline of Rome as a republic. As Cantor explains, 'for Shakespeare, Roman as a term of distinction means primarily Republican Roman, and ... with the death of the Republic, true Romanness in Shakespeare's view begins to die also'.[79] The contrast is also present in *Antony and Cleopatra*'s representation of the 'dissolution of the Roman world' in comparison to the state of Rome as imagined in *Coriolanus* in all its 'rocklike and stubborn solidity'.[80] The effect of this historical setting also means, for Cantor, that what has often been seen as a straightforward choice for Antony between love and duty must be framed by the play's position in Roman history, especially in terms of the transition from republic to empire, highlighting the contrast between the 'narrow horizons of the early Roman Republic and the "infinite variety" offered by the cosmopolitan world of the Empire'.[81] Cantor therefore clearly demonstrates the extent to which the protagonists are caught up in the changes to the political landscape rather than rising above them.

One of the key books of the 1970s focused upon *Antony and Cleopatra* alone. The main focus of Adelman's *The Common Liar* is upon the question of 'what constitutes meaning in a Shakespeare play' and how that meaning is achieved.[82] For Adelman, '*Antony and Cleopatra* is fundamentally about the action it presents and the various efforts of the characters to understand that action.'[83] Such an endeavour is also extended towards the audience and reader of the play, through the way that the 'presentation of character and the dramatic design ... force us to question virtually everything in it'; it is a play in which 'Shakespeare exploits the conflicts of opinion which are built into the traditional accounts of the lovers.'[84] Adelman's study progresses by touching upon a number of areas, including the play's representation of uncertainty and judgement, and the effects of framing Antony and Cleopatra's affair in relation to narratives of other mythical figures, including Dido and Aeneas and Mars and Venus, as well as the effects of language, particularly the slippery and deceptive qualities of poetry; in the end, 'we can neither believe nor wholly disbelieve the claims made by the poetry'.[85] Adelman concludes by underlining the play's evasive qualities and the difficulties it poses for the application of critical systems to it. Nevertheless, as we shall see below, commentators continued to turn towards the play to produce a range of innovative readings in the final decades of the century.

The Late Twentieth Century, 1980–99

The closing decades of the twentieth century saw a marked increase in both the volume and range of readings of *Antony and Cleopatra*. While there were numerous continuities with earlier critical debates and many of the same topics – including the complexities of the characterizations, the political impact of the events on stage and the range of locations employed by Shakespeare, along with questions relating to genre and Shakespeare's engagement with Roman history – critics were continuing to find new ways of approaching the play. The increasing influence of various critical theories upon literary scholarship can be seen in approaches to literary texts that prioritize their representations of various kinds of identities (including gender, race and sexuality), along with particular interests in the relationships among theatrical representation, ideology and power relations. The overview that follows highlights how *Antony and Cleopatra* continually figured in the debates provoked in relation to these topics.

As well as taking advantage of this increasing range of critical lenses, Shakespeare scholars also continued to develop existing models, and the monograph on Shakespeare's Roman works remained a consistent means through which to analyse *Antony and Cleopatra*. One of the most significant of these books to be published at this time was Robert S. Miola's *Shakespeare's Rome*. Following the precedent of MacCallum, amongst others, Miola's book focuses upon Shakespeare's engagement with his sources and his engagement with an idea of Rome throughout these works. In his introduction, Miola comments upon the relatively wide range of sources that influenced Shakespeare and his relatively flexible approach to them. According to Miola, he 'did not insist on any exclusive, dogmatic interpretation, but drew upon various attitudes, stories, and traditions as he pleased'.[86] At the same time, though, Rome itself 'maintains a distinct identity. Constructed of forums, walls, and the Capitol, opposed to outlying battlefields, wild, primitive landscapes, and enemy cities, Rome is a palpable though ever-changing presence. The city serves not only as a setting for action, but also as central protagonist.'[87] There is also a consistency of approach in Shakespeare's Roman works, with a common feature of them being an interrogation of 'the thematic implications of three Roman ideals: constancy, honor, and *pietas* (the loving respect owed to family, country, and gods)'.[88] Such preoccupations are brought to bear in his chapter on *Antony and Cleopatra*, which is identified as a play that interrogates the 'Roman code of honor, shame, and fame; the paradoxes implicit in Roman ceremony and ritual; the political motifs of rebellion and invasion', as well as analysing 'the predicament of the living human beings who must define themselves against the oppressive background of Roman tradition and history'.[89] One of the key elements identified in Miola's reading is the play's continual representation of the superficiality of Roman values as they emerge in practice. Miola highlights the role of Sextus Pompey, whose pacification by the triumvirate reveals how 'the vision of Roman military heroism quickly fades to reveal a sordid world of self-interested bargaining' in which 'the battlefield yields to the marketplace', and notes that the 'scenes with Pompey and Ventidius cast a qualifying irony over the renewed hostilities between Antony and Octavius', especially in their cynical depictions of Roman honour.[90] Such emphases are also reflected in the fact that, throughout the play, Rome comes to figure less as a 'city of definite dimensions and familiar landmarks' than as 'an Empire that spans vast spaces'. However, following a similar line to Charney, Miola concludes by complicating the traditional practice of seeing Rome and Egypt in binary opposition to one another by highlighting that the 'dichotomy between these places and these values does not remain absolute and unqualified', particularly through Shakespeare's depiction of Rome as an empire 'in spiritual conflict with itself, caught between its profession of honorable ideals and its sordid, self-serving practice'.[91]

Miola's was one of a wide range of monographs to appear in these decades that continued to view Shakespeare's Roman works as a coherent group. Published towards the end of the 1980s, Vivian Thomas's *Shakespeare's Roman Worlds* argued that this coherence among the plays could be found in their consistent presentation of 'a changing Rome' marked by 'the collision of values or the divergence between personal aspirations and obligations to the society'.[92] Thomas also aimed, in similar terms to Miola, to present a coherent idea of 'Romanness' as a system of values, which included 'service to the state, constancy, fortitude, valour, friendship, love of family and respect for the gods'.[93] At the same time, though, such values inevitably become intermingled with such features as 'political ambition, friendship and favouritism'.[94] In *Antony and Cleopatra*, the values underpinning Roman identity come to clash with those of the antithetical society of Egypt. Thomas underlines the irony in the fact that Antony, 'the great Roman general who turns his back on Roman values and becomes Egyptianized is extolled, retrospectively, by the abstemious and puritanical Octavius as the embodiment of the greatest Roman virtues', becoming the 'fallen angel' of Romanness.[95] Thomas's main chapter on the play looks in detail at Shakespeare's adaptation of Plutarch's narrative when developing his characters, noting at the outset that one is 'immediately struck by the extent to which the dramatist omits several important references to their actions and attitudes in order to maintain sympathy for them'.[96] Such omissions comprise several unsavoury details about Antony recorded in Plutarch, as well as a notable marginalization of the role of Octavia, including a compression of the years they spend together and no mention of their children. Thomas also notes several key alterations to Plutarch's account of Caesar's treatment of Cleopatra and her mourning of Antony.

Whilst the idea of constancy had figured in both of these studies as part of a broader picture of exemplary Roman qualities, it is at the centre of Geoffrey Miles's *Shakespeare and the Constant Romans*, which traces the influence of this idea and its association with Roman Stoic philosophy throughout Shakespeare's Roman works. For Miles, each of the plays demonstrates the ambiguous and untenable nature of this virtue, represented particularly by Antony's movement between the two cultures and his outright refusal to make a definitive choice between them: 'He is not satisfied to be bound to either Rome or Egypt, but wants to combine both: to be both soldier and lover, have both honour and pleasure, be great both in public and in private life.'[97] By doing so, Antony attempts to turn inconstancy into a positive *modus vivendi*. However, this is ultimately untenable, as shown by the representations of the protagonists' suicides. Miles argues that 'Antony's Stoic death seems like a tragicomic attempt to attain stability in a world whose chaotic mutability undercuts any such attempt.'[98] By contrast, Cleopatra manages to succeed where Antony fails, as although 'she claims to renounce the fleeting moon in favour of marble-constancy, Cleopatra in her death unites the two' in a way that still retains 'her un-Roman, un-Stoic qualities – emotionalism, sensuality, frivolity, capriciousness, changeableness – but combines them with a new Stoic dignity and resolution', thereby achieving a kind of synthesis between constancy and inconstancy that Antony failed to attain.[99]

Questions surrounding the play's genre continued to resonate into this era, and its status as a tragedy is interrogated in a book-length study by J. Leeds Barroll. Barroll's starting point is an idea of tragedy as a tradition that 'pitted itself against man's sense that the universe was chaotic, random, amoral' and that tragic occurrences should be seen as emanating 'not from a blemished universe but from the blemished person whose stricken life must curiously give us hope'.[100] Barroll goes on to argue that Shakespeare participates in a tradition of tragedy that 'received its shape and ideological form from that bent which thus did not condemn the heavens that destroyed men but scrutinized those who perished'.[101] The choice of *Antony and Cleopatra* as the book's case study is justified by the idea that it is a play in which 'Shakespeare achieved that most difficult of tragic effects which neither demeans human beings nor evades those deeper questions urged by our life around us.'[102] The first two of the main chapters on the play focus upon the two protagonists, with Barroll presenting a reading of Antony as a character whose 'private feeling of self lives away from all those judging notions of his duties which others in the play are always so ready to envisage for him'.[103] The chapter on Cleopatra also interrogates the extent to which she can be regarded as a tragic protagonist; such ambiguity is registered in the representation of her 'all-embracing triumph' in the suicide, in which 'she stands magnificent, triumphant. But hardly tragic'.[104] Barroll concludes that the emphasis in views on Shakespeare's tragic protagonists should not be upon their 'disintegration', but upon 'their efforts to stay whole', and that 'the stuff of tragedy is not only man's incipient deafness to the harmony of the ordered universe ... but the paradoxical strength of that uniquely human aspiration which seeks control but brooks no order'.[105]

While numerous readings highlighted the importance of genre and history, critics in these decades also promoted topical approaches to Shakespeare that illuminated the ways in which the plays responded to the specific circumstances of their historical moment. Such approaches were marked by an outright rejection of older scholarship that had tended to see Shakespeare as a proponent of order and political orthodoxy; such a view is outlined, most notably, in E. M. W. Tillyard's 1942 *The Elizabethan World Picture*. The tradition of New Historicism, along with that of Cultural Materialism, its characteristically British counterpart, flourished in the 1980s and set out to present literary texts in a far more complex, and much less acquiescent, relationship with political power. New Historicists tended to regard the literary text as part of a network of discourses in which power relations were perpetuated, whilst Cultural Materialists would present literary texts as the sites of continuing ideological tensions. Arguably the most important Cultural Materialist analysis of early modern drama was Jonathan Dollimore's *Radical Tragedy*. This book is predicated upon the idea that early modern dramas were not mouthpieces for authority but were sites in which institutions of state 'and their ideological legitimation were subjected to sceptical, interrogative and subversive representations'.[106] In his section on *Antony and Cleopatra*, Dollimore highlights that it is the concepts of honour and *virtus* that are subject to such an interrogation. Antony, like Coriolanus, may 'appear innately superior and essentially autonomous, their power independent of the political context in which it finds expression', yet 'as they transgress the power structure which constitutes them both their political and personal identities – inextricably bound together if not identical – disintegrate'.[107] This process is evidenced in the way that 'Antony's conception of his omnipotence narrows in proportion to the obsessiveness of his wish to reassert it; eventually it centres on the sexual anxiety – an assertion of sexual prowess – which has characterised his relationship with Cleopatra and Caesar from the outset.'[108] Dollimore outlines how Antony becomes preoccupied with the youth of Caesar in contrast to his own advancing age, as well as the military prowess which is deflated by the defeat at Actium. The futility of Antony's assertions of *virtus* outside of the ideological parameters of Caesar's Rome lead towards his suicide, leading to the conclusion that this quality, 'divorced from the power structure, has left to it only the assertion of a negative, inverted autonomy'.[109] This also leads to a radical ambiguity when his relationship with Cleopatra is considered, as 'the heroic *virtus* which he wants to reaffirm in and through Cleopatra is in fact almost entirely a function of the power structure which he, again ambivalently, is prepared to sacrifice for her'.[110]

Appearing two years after the first edition of Dollimore's study, Leonard Tennenhouse's *Power on Display: The Politics of Shakespeare's Genres* stems from the New Historicist tradition and is an excellent example of the ways in which this critical practice aimed to analyse the intersections among culture, discourse and political power. Tennenhouse's analyses are largely based upon a perceived transition during the Jacobean era towards a model of tragedy that took particular interest in the 'representation of aristocratic community, in the prevalence of scenes of punishment, and in the radically altered powers attached to the female body'; the latter of these is particularly notable in his reading of *Antony and Cleopatra*.[111] Tennenhouse begins by complicating the traditional assumption that Antony's dalliance with Cleopatra is an abandonment of politics, as the 'very desire to have sovereignty over one's sexual relations and therefore to construct a private world within the public domain is an inherently political act'.[112] This is especially important in relation to what is highlighted as a marked shift in the significance of the aristocratic female body in Jacobean drama. According to this view, in 'the Elizabethan plays, union with the aristocratic female was always a political act. In fact, desire for the female and desire for political power could not be distinguished one from the other', whilst in Jacobean drama, 'the iconic bond between the aristocratic female and the body politic is broken. No longer conceived as a legitimate means for access to membership in the corporate body, the aristocratic female has the potential to pollute.'[113] Tennenhouse sees in the deaths of Antony and Cleopatra a reinscription of characteristically Roman rule and the re-establishment of patriarchal power over the aristocratic female body; however, such closure is presented with considerable ambiguity and the play itself ends up as 'Shakespeare's elegy for the signs and symbols which legitimized Elizabethan power.'[114]

Antony and Cleopatra has also revealed itself to be a play that is responsive to more directly topical readings, of which H. Neville Davies's article, 'Jacobean *Antony and Cleopatra*', is an outstanding example. Davies sees *Antony and Cleopatra* as a transitional play, reflecting upon the accession of James I, and one that can be viewed on the same terms as *King Lear*: as a union play, responding to James's efforts to draw together the various nations of the British Isles. Especially significant in terms of this context is the figure of Octavius Caesar, the future Augustus, given that James sought to establish a 'new order' modelled upon 'the Augustan era of peace'.[115] Speculating upon Shakespeare's possible response to James's union project, Davies suggests that the 'myriad-minded creator of the serpent of old Nile might reasonably be expected to have adopted a highly ambiguous attitude toward the policies and person of his unattractive sovereign'. Such a view forms the basis for the main reading in this article, which is based upon a contextualization of the play in relation to an account of a visit by James's brother-in-law, Christian IV of Denmark, highlighting that if 'Shakespeare looked for a modern Antony to compare with neo-Augustus, he could have found no better likeness than the king of Denmark.'[116] The contrast between the two is demonstrated in reports about prolonged banqueting and drinking aboard Christian's vessel, the *Tre Kroner*, which Davies suggests are parodied in the scenes of revelry set aboard Pompey's galley.

While we have seen that criticism of these decades opened up considerable space for debates about the topicality of the play, the rise of a range of critical theories also enabled an array of readings responding to various kinds of identity politics, relating especially to gender, sexuality and race. The approach in Ania Loomba's important book *Gender, Race, Renaissance Drama* combines methods characteristic of feminist scholarship with those of increasingly prominent post-colonial theories and interests in literary representations of race. In a short section analysing *Antony and Cleopatra*, Loomba highlights the ways in which many of the play's key themes are reflected in the representations of space (both geographical and theatrical). As Loomba puts it, 'issues of imperial expansion, political power and sexual domination are dramatically compressed into spatial and geographical shifts and metaphors'.[117] This reading begins by revisiting many of the critical commonplaces regarding the play, particularly the representations of Rome and Egypt and what Loomba describes as the 'almost cinematic' effect triggered by the various shifts in location. Loomba departs from the conventional views on such shifts by highlighting how 'different characters strive to rise "above" their earlier turbulence and assert an inner unity of being'; any 'harmony' they might establish, however, is 'precarious' and 'the various sets of oppositions noted by critics are not subscribed to but eroded by the play'. One of the ways this is achieved is in the representation of the geographical spaces: 'in each setting we are reminded of another. In Egypt, Rome is evoked, and vice versa.'[118] The play's representation of this tension between Rome and Egypt highlights the political implications of these oppositions. According to Loomba, 'Roman patriarchy demonises Cleopatra by defining her world as private (Antony is no longer a serious general by entering it); as female (Egypt robs Antony and his soldiers of their manhood); and as barbaric (Antony is now a slave of gypsies).'[119] At the same time, though, 'both Antony and Caesar are aware that Egypt is not merely a private space and that its female, non-European nature only intensifies its challenge to imperial Rome'.[120] Such a challenge is embodied most readily by Cleopatra, yet Loomba highlights that this brings to the surface a number of contradictions, 'which are inherent in the position she occupies as a sexually active non-European female ruler' and in the level of control she has over her own spaces: 'as the ruler of Egypt her space is threatened by the expansionist designs of the Roman empire, and as a woman, by the contradictions of heterosexual love'.[121] Equally ambiguous is Cleopatra's characteristically

'Roman' suicide which marks an end to both the 'vacillations of Antony and the unruly theatricality of Cleopatra'.[122] Such shifts in character see the play taking a marked dramaturgical turn by abandoning 'the cinematic montage that so adequately expressed the discontinuity of character, the dialectic between inner and outer, political and personal, male and female spaces'.[123] The stability of setting, however, serves to belie the 'false resolutions' that underpin Cleopatra's actions, leading to a 'final performance' that 'not only cheats Caesar but denies any final and authoritative textual closure'.[124] For Loomba, then, the oppositions and contradictions that characterized the play remain unstable and unresolved in spite of what the shift in staging techniques may be suggesting.

Similar tensions generated by the relationship between gender and authority over the stage are at the heart of two readings that relate the play to contemporary discourses of antitheatricality. The earlier reading is provided by Jyotsna G. Singh, who begins from the premise that Cleopatra's much-noted and 'varied histrionic moments' are linked to anxieties around 'the blurring of gender boundaries'.[125] The most notable example of this is Cleopatra's account of the cross-dressing between herself and Antony, which is related to the frequent voicing of fears of Antony's emasculation. In such performances, 'the theatrical queen puts into question the very notion of a unified, stable identity'.[126] Laura Levine also highlights the ways in which similar questions generated by Cleopatra's histrionics relate to the same kinds of anxieties promulgated in anti-theatrical discourse. The chapter on *Antony and Cleopatra* in her *Men in Women's Clothing* highlights the play's implication that the emphases upon the apparently emasculating effects of theatre in fact register anxieties and inconsistencies in the upholding of masculine selfhood. Such anxieties are voiced, in particular, in Caesar's laments about the decline of Antony which, Levine argues, echo the trope of the effeminized warrior frequently evoked in anti-theatrical literature. Levine sees *Antony and Cleopatra* as a 'vision of a world in which masculinity not only must be enacted, but simply cannot be enacted, his vision of a world in which this particular performance has broken down' and a play which 'casts anti-theatricality itself as a walking contradiction' because of its recognition of the performative nature of the very masculinity that theatricality is supposed to threaten.[127] The inconsistencies in Caesar's outlook are also evident in 3.6, in which he condemns reports about Antony and Cleopatra's audacious public enthroning of themselves in the Alexandrian marketplace. According to Levine, Caesar's 'attack springs from a conviction that it is the representation which Antony and Cleopatra generate that is itself threatening: what goes on in the "public eye"'.[128] Levine sees in Caesar's austere attacks upon Antony's performative excesses 'a secret glorification of appetite' and 'an intense longing for theatricality'.[129] Such representations highlight the fault lines in the wider contemporary anti-theatrical discourse and its privileging of exemplary masculine selfhood.

The tensions in upholding an ideal of masculine selfhood are also the subject of Janet Adelman's *Suffocating Mothers*. Whilst her earlier book, *The Common Liar*, focused upon *Antony and Cleopatra* alone, *Suffocating Mothers* incorporates the play into a much broader discussion of Shakespeare's later plays that explores the relationship between that ideal of masculine selfhood and the 'occluded' figure of the mother, particularly in her return 'with a vengeance' in the plays that follow *Hamlet*.[130] Masculine selfhood, which is 'grounded in paternal absence and in the fantasy of overwhelming contamination at the site of origin', is something which 'becomes the tragic burden of Hamlet and the men who come after him', a burden that 'is passed on to the women, who pay the price for the fantasies of maternal power invested in them'.[131] In a chapter that focuses on the representation of maternal bounty in both *Timon of Athens* and *Antony and Cleopatra*, Adelman takes as her starting point Cleopatra's suicide, seeing it, like many other commentators, as a fragile moment in which 'Cleopatra reigns triumphant on stage' and observing that this triumph 'turns crucially on her capacity not to destroy but to recreate Antony, remaking him from her own imaginative amplitude'.[132] This association between Cleopatra and bounteous generation in her views of Antony is further accentuated by comparing 'two memorializing portraits' delivered, respectively, by Caesar in 1.5 and by Cleopatra in 5.2.[133] Caesar's portrait emphasizes Antony's rugged endurance in 'a landscape of absolute deprivation', which 'figures his heroic masculinity as his capacity to survive in this wintry landscape'. Cleopatra's, on the other hand, 'locates him in a landscape of immense abundance with no winter in it; and it figures his heroic masculinity as his capacity to participate in the bounty of its self-renewing autumn'.[134] Adelman concludes by highlighting how this play marks a turning point in the depiction of the crisis in masculine selfhood in Shakespeare's plays upon which she has been focusing. Through Antony, 'Shakespeare restages the loss of idealized masculinity' which had been a key trope in his plays since dramatizing the passing of Old Hamlet, 'and in his recovery of Antony through Cleopatra's dream of bounty, Shakespeare brings that masculinity back to life'.[135] By staging this recovery in such a way, he 'returns masculinity to its point of origin, the maternal body', and 'rewrites that body as the source of male bounty'.[136]

Similar questions about masculinity, Roman identity and the marginalization of femininity are applied to Shakespeare's Roman works as a whole in Coppélia Kahn's *Roman Shakespeare: Warriors, Wounds and Women*. The central objective of this book is to highlight how 'Shakespeare's Roman works articulate a critique of the ideology of gender on which the Renaissance understanding of Rome was based.'[137] These works also show that, in spite of apparent antagonism towards the feminine, women 'are nonetheless basic to the construction of male subjects as Romans' and that 'some of Shakespeare's Roman women provide, in effect, an alibi for the heroes with whom they are paired – in that, when impulses inimical to manly virtue are associated with women, such impulses can be disavowed'.[138] Her chapter on *Antony and Cleopatra* underlines this play as Shakespeare's 'most daring and original' experiment in Roman drama, constituting as it does 'an attempt to transmute Roman matter and style into a glittering if unstable new alloy of mettle and mutability, a Rome drawn to, repelled by, and finally fused with what is Other to it'.[139] Yet Kahn also highlights that focusing upon the love story tends to obscure what she regards as the central rivalry of the play: the struggle between Antony and Caesar. By dramatizing this story, Kahn argues, Shakespeare is working within a tradition that was

> organized by and centering on the mythic construction of Octavius Caesar as the destined victor in a prolonged power struggle who instituted the *pax romana* that ushered in the Christian era. Virgil sees Octavius's victory as decreed by the gods; we can see it as exemplifying a pattern of agonistic rivalry already familiar in both Roman history and Shakespeare's Roman works.[140]

For Kahn, their conflict comes to emblematize 'the homosocial bonding that is Rome's hallmark'.[141] Kahn remarks, in particular, on Caesar's lament following Antony's death: 'Caesar calls him brother, competitor ... mate, friend, companion, the arms of his body, even his very heart ... in short, the person above all others to whom Caesar considers himself bound by intimate, affectionate ties.'[142] The sincerity, or otherwise, of such an outpouring is largely immaterial; Kahn instead sees this speech as typical of the nature of Roman male relations, characterized simultaneously by rivalry and 'intense identification'.[143]

The idea of memorializing, with which Kahn's chapter concludes, is at the centre of Linda Charnes's *Notorious Identity*, in which *Antony and Cleopatra* is one of three plays, along with *Richard III* and *Troilus and Cressida*, which put 'notorious' figures on the stage. Charnes is interested, primarily, in the 'representational politics, strategies, and fantasies that make a certain kind of fame productive in a certain way', along with the ways in which the plays 'explore what it is like to be subjected to and by the extraordinary determining force of infamous names'.[144] Her chapter on *Antony and Cleopatra* looks at how the extent to which the protagonists 'play to, and against, competing representational apparatuses determines the degree to which they become the successful subjects or entrapped objects of spies and whispers'.[145] This is figured in the contrast between Antony and Cleopatra and the ways in which their authority over locations has a considerable bearing upon their abilities to exert control over their representations. Antony is the '"displaced" or uprooted agent who moves between the locations ... of Rome and Egypt' and is forced into a 'literal displacement which finally does him in'.[146] Cleopatra, on the other hand, takes advantage of her association with her own space in a campaign of self-identification that is based upon 'the constitution of her "identity" as Egypt, which consists precisely of being "unidentifiable" in the discursive terms of Roman narration'.[147] This allows her to take advantage of the marginalization of Egypt in Roman culture in order to 'constitute herself in ways not available to Antony'.[148]

In *The Common Liar*, Adelman outlines the challenge this play poses to critics. Attempts to impose a single and coherent interpretation upon the play are bound to fail and none 'can hope to account for the complexity of its experience: certainly no interpretation which demands that it conforms to a purely tragic model'.[149] Any attempt to accommodate it within a system of images or oppositions is similarly futile for a play that 'achieves a fluidity of possibility far more akin to our experience than any of our systems can be' and, therefore, if 'an act of criticism can be imagined as a struggle between the critic and the author, then it must be conceded that the author has won, hands down'.[150] Nevertheless, as we have seen, numerous attempts have been made, and continue to be made, to offer interpretations of this play. The result has been a rich and diverse range of readings that have illuminated numerous aspects of it. As we shall see in the third chapter, the quality of elusiveness Adelman identifies in relation to the interpretation of *Antony and Cleopatra* continues to stimulate a variety of approaches and critical interventions into the twenty-first century.

2

Performance History

Maddalena Pennacchia

Antony and Cleopatra is notoriously one of the most challenging plays to stage in Shakespeare's canon, and for many reasons. To begin with, it is among Shakespeare's longest plays and is also completely free from the restraints of the Aristotelian dramatic unities. Great actors are needed for the title roles, and the stagecraft must be able to handle the change of locations at a dizzy pace while time is compressed or expanded at the playwright's will. Space, in particular, is managed with such elasticity in Shakespeare's playtext that it seems to 'overflow the measure' of the stage – the action shifting from one corner of the Mediterranean to the other – as if heralding its future treatment in a medium yet unborn: cinema.

In this chapter, I will outline the most meaningful trends in *Antony and Cleopatra*'s stage history and the way different eras and stylistic approaches reshaped the play depending on the cultural and ideological context of the different productions. The fascinating performance history of *Antony and Cleopatra* is indicative of the ways in which approaches to performing Shakespeare developed in the course of over four centuries.[1]

An Experimental Celebrity Bio-Drama

Shakespeare wrote *Antony and Cleopatra* at the end of his main tragic period, after *Othello*, *Macbeth* and *King Lear*, but can one say that the play thoroughly belongs to that phase of his career? John Heminges and Henry Condell, when arranging the list of plays in the catalogue of the First Folio, placed *Antony and Cleopatra* among the tragedies but they positioned it before the last one, *Cymbeline*, which at the time would have been called a tragicomedy (and is now commonly referred to as a romance). Odd as it may sound, they probably knew what they were doing, for the irregular form of *Antony and Cleopatra*, as well as its fondness for excess and transgression, seems to pave the way for the new, experimental phase in Shakespeare's later career.

Antony and Cleopatra's first entrance on stage in 1.1 is famously introduced by two Roman soldiers, Philo and Demetrius – of whom we never hear again in the play – announcing their captain's 'dotage' (1.1.1) for a powerful woman who does not belong to their culture, a 'gypsy' (1.1.10) with a 'tawny front' (1.1.6). These few lines frame the ensuing dialogue between the eponymous characters, thus foregrounding its play-within-the-play quality.[2] In their conversations we find an open statement of the characters' – and hence the play's – irresistible drive defiantly to trespass all set boundaries in order to find 'new heaven, new earth':

CLEOPATRA
   If it be love indeed, tell me how much.
ANTONY
   There's beggary in the love that can be reckoned.
CLEOPATRA
   I'll set a bourn how far to be beloved.
ANTONY
   Then must thou needs find out new heaven, new earth.
                                                  (1.1.14–17)

These words, which echo the Book of Revelation, have been variously interpreted as a reference to the geographical discoveries that were opening up the confines of the old world ('new earth'), spurring explorers to go further beyond (*plus ultra*), or as a cryptic hint to the concept of the infinite universe being introduced at the time in selected circles by Giordano Bruno ('new heaven').[3] At the same time, however, they can be also read as a powerful meta-theatrical statement about the exceptional form of the show that the audience is going to experience – because *Antony and Cleopatra* consciously transgresses all classical theatrical rules, pushing the boundaries of the medium to find new, undiscovered territories of representation, in which time, space, action, genre and gender are tested to their limits.

Indeed, *Antony and Cleopatra* may well be considered an early example of 'celebrity biographical drama', in which Shakespeare adapts for the stage his main source, Plutarch's *Life of Antony*, displaying great empathy with the Greek writer's anecdotal approach to history, on the one hand, but a less judgemental attitude, on the other. Plutarch's biographical writing is politics seen from private rooms: rooms that are, as Shakespeare shows, always overcrowded with servants, messengers, soldiers and people of lower social status who observe celebrities under the spotlight and, if given the opportunity, comment on their behaviour, thus balancing, when not deflating, their tendency to theatricalize and mythologize their own lives. Shakespeare mobilized the informative attractiveness of Plutarch's *Life of Antony* by adding an exceptional co-star to his stage adaptation, Cleopatra, who survives Antony's death in Act 4 and goes on to stage her own spectacular suicide, which ends the play. Shakespeare thus concocts a mesmerizing spectacle and possibly even invents a genre that has fully thrived in today's celebrity-oriented culture.[4] To see celebrities in their 'undress', to go beyond their public personae and peep into their private lives in search of 'unpublished' details, looking for a privileged access into their inward emotional responses, is what appeals the most to today's celebrity culture. In this respect, *Antony and Cleopatra* does appear to be the play for the new millennium.[5]

As almost all commentators have observed, the play can activate its full meaning only if the polarization between Romans and Egyptians is made evident (through setting, costume, lighting, music, acting style and so forth). However, it is also true that the action does not simply shift from Rome to Alexandria and set there: it rather moves incessantly between the two cities. More importantly, the trajectory of characters across space presents unexpected detours: from Sicily to Cape Misenum, from Parthia to Athens, from Actium to the Peloponnesus. The whole globe is the stage on which this political drama is played out. This is a play 'on the road', in which it is not clear where 'home' is, or what the final destination will be, if not death. *Antony and Cleopatra* catches our interest today more than ever precisely for its intercultural potential (perhaps not always fully exploited in performance), which defies and problematizes the binary logic opposing Rome to Egypt: a potential that the text activates as soon as Antony, as conqueror of Egypt, meets Cleopatra, who, as vanquished queen, sets out to deconstruct the opposition, claiming instead 'her right to give hospitality as a possible means to maintain her majesty', as Maria Del Sapio Garbero remarks.[6] As a female politician, Cleopatra questions all given polarities as well as the gendering itself of geopolitics – with its 'male conqueror appropriating feminized land' logic – and succeeds in constructing new hybrid spaces by performing seductiveness in a script of her own design, which in turn appropriates Roman concepts of femininity and masculinity, bending them to her purpose and eventually passing from *tableau vivant* (on the river Cydnus) to *tableau mort* (in her monument) in an apotheosis of performativity.[7]

Yet this is also a play of military and political action, as Harley Granville-Barker first observed, remarking that 'Antony, the once triumphant man of action, is hero' and 'we are to watch his defeat by his subtler sometime pupil'. The sequel-like nature of the play was clear to him too, for Shakespeare shows the audience what happens between two former political allies after they have defeated their enemies;

of course, Plutarch is there to foster the narrative, but the psychological consistency of the characters of Antony and Octavius as they are introduced in *Julius Caesar* and then developed in *Antony and Cleopatra* is all Shakespeare's, and, Granville-Barker continued, 'we may even read into passages of *Julius Caesar* a foreshadowing of the breach between the two'.[8] Moreover, two battles are fought on stage, by sea and land, at Actium and Alexandria; but whereas in *Julius Caesar*, at the Battle of Philippi, it was clear that Romans were fighting against Romans, here the presence of Cleopatra introduces a crucial element of discontinuity and perhaps even enables Octavius Caesar to present the war under the guise of a clash of civilizations, through the argument that Antony has gone 'native' and betrayed Roman *virtus*.

But let us now move to examine how this complex play has been actually performed over the centuries.

A Curiously Uneventful Early Stage History

Very little information is available about the staging of *Antony and Cleopatra* in the Jacobean period. The play's title was first entered in the Stationers' Register on 20 May 1608; however, some scholars are persuaded that its debut happened at least a year earlier, in 1607, because of echoes of the play to be found in Samuel Daniel's *Cleopatra* and Barnabe Barnes's *The Devil's Charter*, which were printed in that year. As has been noted, the former – a revised edition of a play Daniel had originally published in 1594 – inserted a new description of the way in which Antony is laboriously hoisted to Cleopatra's monument, while the latter referenced asps being used to kill two young princes in their sleep, calling them 'Cleopatra's birds'.[9] Such an immediate response in print would seem to suggest that *Antony and Cleopatra* must have caused quite an impact not only on the regular audience but also on Shakespeare's fellow playwrights, who, significantly enough, appropriated two spectacular theatrical moments instead of borrowing linguistic items: in other words, the visual staging of the play may have been what caused the longest lasting impression on the audience. But does that also imply that the play was successful? According to some critics, it may well have been: this would be confirmed by the fact that the record in the Stationers' Register was not followed by publication, which may mean that the registration was a 'blocking entry' by the King's Men to try and protect their dramatic property.[10] The compliant printer in the registration was Edward Blount, who would in 1623 receive a licence, shared with Isaac Jaggard, to print sixteen unpublished plays by Shakespeare in folio format: if Blount had actually been complaisant in 1608, the King's Men certainly repaid the favour fifteen years later.

Be that as it may, the fact is that no written record of any performance prior to the Restoration is extant, and there is no certainty that the play was actually staged even then. As it was originally conceived as continuous action on a bare stage, there is no scene division in the First Folio text, and it must have seemed almost impossible to attune such an unruly dramatic structure to the conventions of the proscenium arch stage as it had been imported from France with the return of the Stuarts on the British throne in 1660. Moreover, the title roles must have seemed more than challenging, especially because there was a revolution in casting under way. The exclusive royal patent bestowed in 1660 on Thomas Killigrew (King's Men) and William D'Avenant (Duke's Men) had created a duopoly, thereby also legitimating the professional figure of the actor-manager. More importantly, however, in the ensuing warrant of April 1662 to Killigrew the king granted that 'all the women's part ... may be performed by women', a fact for which there was no local tradition.[11] What neophyte would have dared to impersonate Shakespeare's Cleopatra and her 'infinite variety' (2.2.246)? Some actresses must have tried their fortune at that, since in his *History of Restoration Drama* Allardyce Nicoll transcribes a document listing a number of 'plays allotted to Killigrew' in 1668–9, 'as they were formerly acted at the Blackfryars', including 'Anthony & Cleopatra'.[12] Yet there is no record of any specific productions; consequently, we cannot be entirely sure that the play was indeed performed. From such scanty information we can at least infer that *Antony and Cleopatra* was 'formerly acted at the Blackfryars', but the hypothesis that it might have been written for this smaller indoor theatre cannot disregard the date of composition, 1606–7 or 1608. If we consider that the Blackfriars became the King's Men's winter venue only in 1608, this possibility does not seem very likely.[13]

Rescuing the 'Unruly' Play: John Dryden's Domestication

The only way to stage a play that so blatantly 'o'erflows the measure' (1.1.2) of theatrical conventions was to adapt it rigorously to the classical rules celebrated by Restoration theatre, as John Dryden did in *All for Love* (1677). Dryden's sources, notwithstanding what he states in the Letter to the Reader, were not limited to Shakespeare's play, but since the Bard's name was already turning into valuable cultural currency he understandably made the most of it. Dryden's *All for Love* enjoyed such a success as a revision of Shakespeare's *Antony and Cleopatra* that it was paradoxically performed instead of the original playtext not only in the seventeenth but also through the eighteenth century; furthermore, it served through the nineteenth century as a textual basis with which Shakespeare's original playtext could be interpolated. This is why it indisputably 'belongs to the stage history of *Antony and Cleopatra*', as Lamb remarks.[14] Dryden transformed the epic scope of Shakespeare's play into a domestic drama that could plausibly be represented on stage according to the classical unities. He radically 'confined' the action to one place only, Alexandria, and a precise time, after the defeat of Actium, thus almost entrapping the protagonists in the last stage of their journey through the Mediterranean: Antony and Cleopatra can speak and reflect on their past, but there is no movement forward, if not towards death. Dryden rewrites Shakespeare's generically hybrid play into what was considered the finest example of English 'classical' tragedy in the seventeenth century. Moreover, the opening scene of *All for Love* shows Dryden's skill in resetting the character relationships: while in *Antony and Cleopatra* two Roman soldiers introduce the audience to Antony's overflowing 'dotage' (1.1.1), thus preparing the prodigal atmosphere in which the formidable couple is going to appear, Dryden's *All for Love* begins with two Egyptian priests who comment with Alexas on Cleopatra's absurd 'doting' on a 'vanquished man', while also introducing, in a mix of admiration and impatience, Ventidius, a side character in Shakespeare's play who takes centre stage in Dryden's.[15] Ventidius only appears twice in *Antony and Cleopatra*: he is silent in 2.2, when Antony orders him to go to Parthia, but he is given an important though very short scene later on (3.1), which shows him as finally victorious against the Parthians but also very careful in handling a victory he has gained in Antony's name. In Dryden's version, Ventidius, in whom 'the plainness, fierceness, rugged virtue / Of an old true-stamped Roman lives', becomes the better part of Antony and a constant reminder of Roman military duties and values as opposed to Cleopatra's all-consuming and destructive love: the question of duty vs love is thus embodied in two characters who contend their proximity on stage to the general's body.[16]

The puzzling ethics of Shakespeare's play is domesticated for generations to come by Dryden even to the present day, if one thinks that many directors conflate the roles of a number of minor characters in the figure of Ventidius. In other words, Dryden turned the potential fascination of the audience with the grandiose boldness of an unfaithful husband and his mistress into a more palatable and decorous feeling of 'pity' for the fall of the 'triple pillar of the world' (1.1.12) who, like Hercules, has strayed from the path of virtue and made the wrong choice. The restrained Antony and the dignified Cleopatra played by Thomas Betterton and Mrs Barry after 1684 are the acting counterpart of Dryden's desire to reduce the excess of the two protagonists to the classical measure, an extremely successful decision for a long time. There is an even more permanent legacy Dryden left to future productions of *Antony and Cleopatra*: as Lamb noticed, 'the hierarchical seated pose of Egyptian funerary sculpture' in which Cleopatra dies – even in present-day performances – 'instead of on her Jacobean daybed' is due to *All for Love*.[17] Critics writing about Dryden's play at the beginning of the eighteenth century praised Cleopatra's death scene in terms of 'statuesque beauty' and 'marble countenance', marking the long-lasting affective impression of the final scene.[18]

Pictorial Revivals of Egypt and Rome from Garrick to Beerbohm Tree

The first director who tried to revive *Antony and Cleopatra* on the English stage in the eighteenth century was David Garrick, who produced it at the Drury Lane in 1759. Garrick critically edited and adapted the play with the collaboration of well-known scholar Edward Capell, who heavily trimmed the text, reducing the forty-two scenes in which it had been divided by eighteenth-century editors to twenty-seven and the list of named characters from thirty-four to twenty-six.[19] The enterprise was bold and was made, notwithstanding the cuts, in the name of a more scholarly approach to Shakespeare. Ten years later, Garrick was to organize the first Jubilee in Stratford-upon-Avon, an event that marked a more general trend reversal in Shakespearian performance and a tendency to return to 'original' Shakespeare as the national genius who had not conformed to the neo-classical rules imported from France (at the time England's principal political opponent);

from the Jubilee onwards, rewritings, such as Dryden's, were gradually driven from the stage while early scholarly editions, such as Nicholas Rowe's, became texts to be studied by theatre practitioners. Despite Garrick's scholarly approach, however, his playtext still worked along the lines of Dryden's revision, thereby downplaying the political aspect of the story by excising scenes like those set in Rome, Misenum and Athens, and consequently minimizing the imperial theme to focus instead almost exclusively on Antony as a hero in love.[20] Adding to this, the production showed the increasing preference of the English stage for the Italian illusionist tradition of set design made of 'changeable scenes painted in perspective on flats'.[21] No wonder the most striking feature of Garrick's *Antony and Cleopatra* was its opening, in which the protagonists first entered the stage each followed by a cortège that must have made a very colourful and exotic spectacle if Garrick's detailed account of *Antony and Cleopatra*'s parade for the Jubilee was reminiscent of it.[22] The cortège was accompanied by the Cydnus speech (2.2.200-36), which was therefore brought forward and assigned to Thyreus, an obsequious soldier, instead of Enobarbus, an experienced military man of unrelenting realism, thus turning the famous lines into a sort of long sycophantic caption to the opulent scene set up before the audience. The device was reprised by several later productions. Pictorialism, the tendency to illustrate the words in a play with a large use of *tableaux vivants*, had started its course; for all his laudable efforts, however, Garrick did not obtain the success he hoped for, and the production ran for six nights only.

Fifty-four years had to pass until someone else ventured to stage the play again. In the meantime, theatres had undergone significant changes with regard to both the architecture and stagecraft. London was growing into a gigantic metropolis with its population 'quadrupling from 959,310 in 1800 to 4,536,267 in 1900', and the number of theatres increased considerably, their size growing accordingly to accommodate very large audiences, which were socially much more diversified than in the previous century.[23] All this, of course, affected the way in which Shakespeare was performed. The intimacy between actors and audience had been lost because of the scale of the playhouses and the new arrangement of the auditorium, so that, in order to be heard, actors had to howl and rant. The fact that many spectators could only look at the stage from a distance and follow the action as if it were a dumb-show had to be taken into account by the great actors, who were often also theatre managers, and hence financially responsible for the artistic enterprise. Technology was improving enormously and contributed to the development of a theatre of illusion and wonder; stages grew in size to host all kinds of sophisticated machinery, while in terms of artificial lighting, gaslight was introduced in 1817, limelight in 1855 and electricity in 1881, thus making a wide range of new optical effects available.

A strong antiquarian interest in classical civilization also characterized this period, which saw the rise and consolidation of the British empire; as a consequence, as Dennis Kennedy points out, 'the stage saw the plays as opportunities to illustrate the past'.[24] *Antony and Cleopatra* could finally be exploited as a window opened on enthralling historical landscapes, and this approach was adopted in the productions of the Romantic and Victorian age until the beginning of the twentieth century: the splendour of the setting, lighting, costumes and music became inversely proportional to the importance of the acting, while the text suffered all kinds of heavy cuts and manipulations.

At least five productions must be mentioned within this time span: John Philip Kemble's (1813), John Macready's (1833), Samuel Phelps's (1849), Lily Langtry's (1890) and Herbert Beerbohm Tree's (1906).

After Garrick's experiment, Kemble was the first to revive the play at the New Covent Garden, one of the patent theatres, followed by Macready, who mounted his version of the play at the Drury Lane, the other patent theatre. Both venues could accommodate as many as 3,000 spectators (the Drury Lane even more). Kemble and Macready therefore shared the challenging task of staging a play in such colossal spaces.

They both prepared an acting version with heavy cuts and interpolations taken from *All for Love*, and they both staged processions, fights and triumphs. Kemble, who was determined to rescue the play from oblivion, made careful researches for both costumes and setting, and astonished the audience by adding a spectacular onstage sea-fight and a magnificent closing funeral procession. In contrast to Kemble, Macready was not enthusiastic about staging *Antony and Cleopatra*; he was forced to undertake the endeavour by the theatre manager Alfred Bunn: no wonder the production was mainly praised for Clarkson Stanfield's painted marine scenes of Misenum and Actium. Notwithstanding the magnificence of their *mise en scène*, neither production was a box-office success. Kemble's was on only for nine nights and Macready's just for three.

In 1843, Parliament passed the Regulation Act, which ended the monopoly of patent theatres. The actor-manager Samuel Phelps bought Sadler's Wells 'music house' and transformed it into a Shakespearian playhouse of reputation, producing in 1849 the first critically acclaimed *Antony and Cleopatra*, which played for twenty-two nights. Phelps left most of the scenes complete and omitted a few entirely, so as to preserve the coherence of dramatic action and character development. No passage from *All for Love* was included, even though Phelps followed Dryden's stage tradition of mounting a triumph for the victorious return of Antony to Alexandria. Among his best innovations there was a new, life-like way of performing the Bacchanals at Cape Misenum by showing Antony and the revellers as completely drunk and out of control, thus convincingly pointing to the anti-heroic aspects of the leading character. As for the co-protagonist, Isabella Glyn was acclaimed as the best Cleopatra to have ever trodden the boards and was to play the role twice more during her career.

The apogee of pictorialism was reached by Lily Langtry's and Herbert Beerbohm Tree's productions. Langtry produced the play in 1890 at the Princess's Theatre; she was one of the Prince of Wales's mistresses, which fostered the audience's curiosity to see her acting in the controversial role of Cleopatra but did not save them from the boredom of four and a half hours of opulent (and extremely costly) pantomimes, with great abundance of Roman and Egyptian paraphernalia and very little Shakespeare. A few critics praised the 'pictorial effects' of the production 'for their decadent reminiscences of Delacroix, Gautier, Gérôme, and Constant'.[25] Much more critical praise was reserved for Tree's production at His Majesty's in 1906, a production that can be considered the swan song of archaeological spectacle; it was a triumph of oriental lavishness and a feast for the eye, and the audience of the opening night, including Winston Churchill, enthusiastically welcomed 'this pageant of imperial splendour', even though the actors looked to some only 'a mobile section of the scenery'.[26] This memorable production, as well as being similar to others at the high-tide of the British empire, 'reflected a profound ambiguity towards the exotic', as Michael Neill remarks, definitively turning Cleopatra into the epitome of the femme fatale, 'the supreme object of forbidden desire whose achievement constitutes its own punishment'.[27] The phantasmagorical extravagance of this kind of production was destined to wane and disappear soon, however, because theatre could not compete in terms of illusionism and visual attractiveness with the recently born cinema. Only six years after Tree's production, in 1912, Enrico Guazzoni shot *Quo Vadis*, while the following year, in 1913, Giovanni Pastrone directed *Cabiria*: the historical epic film genre was born, and theatre quickly had to find new ways of staging plays such as *Antony and Cleopatra*.

The Neo-Elizabethan Revolution

An innovative understanding of how the play could work on stage, leaving behind the spectacular pomp and ranting of nineteenth-century pictorial theatre, matured only in the twentieth century, when a genuine interest in Elizabethan and

Jacobean staging developed. William Poel had founded the Elizabethan Stage Society in 1895, soon after the discovery, in 1888, of de Witt/van Buchel's sketch of the interior of the Swan, but he had already made staging the object of serious scholarly research in 1881 while producing *Hamlet*'s First Quarto at St George's Hall.[28] His disciple, Harley Granville-Barker – actor, director, playwright and critic – took part in some of his Shakespearian productions, which could not be made in regular theatres, mainly for lack of funds, and were forced to try and make the most of halls and alternative performance spaces. Granville-Barker further developed Poel's approach and became one of the most influential personalities in the history of British theatre. Both of them brought forth the concept of 'continuous staging', and their ideas and theatrical practices, while trying to reproduce the original conditions of the early modern stage, paved the way for the most experimental productions of the twentieth century. Neither of them ever staged *Antony and Cleopatra*, but Granville-Barker, whose production of the play at the Savoy had to be cancelled because of the outbreak of the First World War, published a seminal 'Preface' in 1930 out of the materials and ideas he had stored for the project, which became the essential *vade mecum* for those who wanted to produce the play and influenced many future directors, including Jonathan Miller (1981) and Peter Hall (1987).

As a practitioner interested in the text as the most important element of the performance, Granville-Barker advised any producers tackling *Antony and Cleopatra* to 'free [it] from act and scene divisions': the five-act-and-forty-two-scene division was not in the Folio text but had been added by Rowe in his 1709 edition; conversely, in the Folio 'each scene has an effective relation to the next, which a pause between them will weaken or destroy'.[29] Granville-Barker also stated that the contemporary understanding of early modern staging had been adulterated by Rowe, who had looked at Shakespeare's plays 'in the light of his own theater', in which a 'scene' must be inevitably connected to a location, and therefore 'a change of scene meant a change of place' with its appropriate painted scenery.[30] Yet, argued Granville-Barker, this would have made no sense in an early modern playhouse; therefore, the scenery did not have to be decorative or archaeologically accurate but only serve the dramatic logic of the text, which always comes first. The key to staging *Antony and Cleopatra* had finally been found.

After the First World War, Poel's and Granville-Barker's ideas were first applied to the play by William Bridges-Adams (1921) and Robert Atkins (1922) in the two theatres that would soon become the most important venues for Shakespearian productions: respectively, the Shakespeare Memorial Theatre in Stratford-upon-Avon and the Old Vic in London. In presenting an almost uncut text and in performing the play according to the 'continuous staging' principle, with a virtually bare scenography and very simple costumes, both productions obtained a large critical and popular consent.

The period between the wars was a golden age for English theatre and saw no fewer than ten productions of *Antony and Cleopatra* between London and Stratford-upon-Avon, 'as many as the play had had during all of the nineteenth century', Lamb remarks, adding that the 'lack of funds' also helped to spread the austere approach preached by Poel and Granville-Barker.[31] Among those productions, it might be worth mentioning Harcourt Williams's; in 1930 at the Old Vic he was the first to adopt Granville-Barker's suggestion to dress the actors in costumes inspired by Paolo Veronese's painting *Alexander and the Wife and Daughter of Darius* (1565–7), with John Gielgud and Dorothy Green in the title roles.[32]

In the decade after the Second World War, roughly from 1946 to 1953, a number of productions were put on in the West End; while continuing to experiment with the new methods of presenting the play, these productions also exploited the capacity of celebrated cinema stars to attract large numbers of spectators in order to ensure box-office success. The main problem directors and designers had to solve, however, was that of the conventional proscenium stages of West End theatres; in order for them to adapt to the new continuous performances, a sort of standard scenic apparatus was arranged, that is 'a nonrepresentational two-story unit set; a revolving stage; and an arrangement of cyclorama and stairs'.[33]

Michael Benthal's production in 1951 at the St James's Theatre starred the most glamorous couple of British show business, Laurence Olivier and Vivien Leigh, who also led in George Bernard Shaw's *Caesar and Cleopatra* on alternate nights. The innovative use of the revolving stage brilliantly solved many of the problems traditionally connected to the swift changes of location, and costumes had a symbolic quality 'with Romans in cobalt blue fighting scarlet-clad Egyptians'.[34] But the definitive *Antony and Cleopatra* of the first half of the century was that by Glen Byam Shaw, who directed Peggy Ashcroft and Michael Redgrave at the Shakespeare Memorial Theatre in Stratford-upon-Avon in 1953 in a landmark production in which the two actors were universally acclaimed for their magisterial performance.

These productions marked the return of Shakespeare to the West End and the consequent marriage between commercial enterprise and classical theatre; however, the phenomenon was short-lived: a new course started with the founding of the Royal Shakespeare Company.

The RSC and *Antony and Cleopatra*: Tradition and Innovation

The 1960s saw the rise of the Royal Shakespeare Company (RSC), the repertory company founded by Peter Hall in 1960. The RSC had its base in Stratford-upon-Avon and played at the Shakespeare Memorial Theatre, which had opened in 1879 and – destroyed by fire in 1926 – rose again from its Victorian ashes in the form of a building of shameless modernity: the New Memorial was inaugurated in 1932 and changed its name into the Royal Shakespeare Theatre (RST) as soon as the company in residence was definitively chartered in 1961; it was further redeveloped between 2007 and 2010 to fit the needs of performing Shakespeare in the new millennium.

A subsidized Shakespearian theatre meant that the whole canon could be explored in the name of a legitimate and useful dissemination of culture, thus assuring creativity an unprecedented freedom from (excessive) financial worries. But when Trevor Nunn succeeded Peter Hall as director of the RSC in 1968, the youth revolution had just begun, and reconciling the cultural demand for a politically engaged art and the responsibilities of a company that was not only national and subsidized but even 'royal' became increasingly difficult. It is in this social context that Nunn conceived a Roman season: in 1972, the four Roman plays were presented in the chronological order of the historical events, opening with *Coriolanus*, followed by *Julius Caesar* and *Antony and Cleopatra*, and closing with *Titus Andronicus*. Even though the Roman plays are often considered the most overtly political in Shakespeare's canon, Nunn's Roman season 'seemed evasive of politics', focusing instead on the more general dynamics of contrasting civilizations as well as making the lovers central.[35] The polarity between Egypt and Rome in *Antony and Cleopatra* was stressed in striking visual terms in this production, which starred Janet Suzman (Cleopatra), Richard Johnson (Antony), Patrick Stewart (Enobarbus) and Corin Redgrave (Octavius Caesar). While Octavius's palace was made of black-and-white rigid forms in a space whose backdrop was a massive geographical map of the Mediterranean, Cleopatra's court displayed all sorts of bright and warm colours, soft cushions and plumed fans; costume design was strongly influenced by the extraordinarily successful exhibition of the treasures of the tomb of Tutankhamun that had just opened at the British Museum and was creating a vogue for all things Egyptian. Great importance was given to the new technological resources of the RST's stage, recently furnished with hydraulic machinery, which allowed the floor to rise and change its shape at the push of a button; however, as Michael Scott remarks, 'the transformations were geometrically dazzling but they detracted from the play'.[36]

Nunn wanted Suzman, made up as bronze-coloured and with black hair, to follow the directions in the playtext: Cleopatra has got a 'tawny front' (1.1.6) and is 'with Phoebus' amorous pinches black' (1.5.29); this was an innovative move away from the customary representation of Cleopatra as fair skinned and usually red haired. As Virginia Mason Vaughan points out, the choice reflected for the first time the changed ethnic landscape of Britain, 'as formerly colonized people of colour increasingly migrated there'.[37] The question about Cleopatra's blackness was famously raised in the same period by Janet Adelman, who speculated that 'black' for the early moderns may have been shorthand for 'other' than English.[38] Even though the issue of Cleopatra's race had finally been brought to attention, fourteen more years had to pass before a black Cleopatra, Michele Shay, actually made it to the boards; it was 1986, and it happened in an American production by Shakespeare & Company of Lenox, Massachusetts, which, as Sara Munson Deats points out, 'respond[ed] to the growing critical awareness of the African nature of Cleopatra and her court'.[39] The first British black Cleopatra, Pauline Black, was to play the role three years later in a 'radically cut version' of the play presented by the Actors Touring Company at the Lyric Studios in Hammersmith, which made clear who the protagonist was, its title being *Cleopatra and Antony*.[40] In 2001, Carol Chillington Rutter complained that 'only on the fringe, in non-mainstream companies like Talawa (Dona Croll, 1991), Northern Broadsides (Ishia Benison, 1995) and the English Stage Company (Cathy Tyson, 1998) is Cleopatra ever black'.[41] The first black Cleopatra for an RSC co-production actually appeared on stage only as late as 2013 (first-generation Angolan Joaquina Kalukango), finally followed by Josette Simon in Iqbal Kahn's 2017 production.

The consciously avant-garde *Antony and Cleopatra* of the 1970s was Peter Brook's, who directed the play in 1978, starring Glenda Jackson as a witty, androgynous and strong-willed Cleopatra. Brook bravely dismissed any form of spectacle, defying the huge size of the RST with the help of

Sally Jacobs's setting, which reproduced his concept of 'empty space' through 'four translucent, bronzed screens semi-circled across the upper centre of the stage'; it was there that the intimate world of the protagonists was displayed, while politics and war cruelly raged outside, as when the panels were splashed with the blood of soldiers fighting upstage.[42] As was his habit, Brook examined the most significant theatre criticism of the period, from Antonin Artaud's to Samuel Beckett's, including Ian Kott's, whose idea of this specific play was, however, 'reductive rather than liberating' according to Lamb, and may have inspired the experimental director to interpret *Antony and Cleopatra* mainly as a troubled, private relationship between two strong personalities.[43]

When the RSC turned again to the play, they decided to stage it at The Other Place, the company's new alternative venue created in 1974 out of a small rehearsal room. It was there that in 1982 Helen Mirren played an erotic and majestic Cleopatra under the direction of Adrian Noble, who was influenced by Brook's minimalist style. The small stage appeared as a kind of black box in which effects were realized mainly through lighting and costumes: the Romans were clothed in white togas and the Egyptians in colourful garments; Cleopatra often changed her outfit, wearing shining gold at the beginning, red at Actium, black in the monument and finally gold again for her glorious death on her throne.

In 2006, Gregory Doran directed the play at the Swan Theatre, the third venue of the RSC. Created in 1986 from the shell of the 1879 theatre, the Swan is designed as a Jacobean indoor playhouse and presents a thrust stage allowing the recreation of closeness between actors and audience; it was the perfect space for what Doran saw as 'a very intimate play, set on an international scale'.[44] Patrick Stewart and Harriet Walter played the leading roles with the confidence and ease of well-cast, experienced actors. As if quoting Nunn's staging, including a relief-map of the ancient world, the difference between Egyptians and Romans was established through the presence/absence of geometrical patterns and the use of colours related, this time, to the four elements: shades of green for water, orange for earth, gold for fire and white for air. The Battle of Actium was cunningly realized through the sound of drums, as the playtext suggests, and the projection of green and blue lights on the boards, which transformed the empty stage into a troubled sea. A brief reference should be made to the dramatic presentation of the monument scene, which has always caused much dispute among directors and producers, since 'the various theories of staging the monument reflect the changing concepts of Shakespeare's theatre and its conventions'.[45] In Doran's production, a wooden square platform was lowered from above, on which Cleopatra and her ladies stood kneeling while laboriously hoisting Antony upwards; the scene was arresting because it translated into visual performance Doran's iconic idea of the end of the great controversial hero, who dies as he lived, 'suspended between heaven and earth', but is now 'just hanging there, vulnerable as a newborn baby'.[46]

Back to the Future: *Antony and Cleopatra* at Shakespeare's Globe

A crucial turn in performing Shakespeare was brought about by the reconstruction of the playing spaces of early modern theatre – such as Shakespeare's Globe in London (1997) or the Blackfriars Theatre in Virginia (2001) – and, more generally speaking, by the recovery of the original stage and performance conditions of Shakespeare's plays. If this movement was pioneered by people like Tyrone Guthrie, the first artistic director of the Shakespearean Festival in Stratford, Ontario, ideally continuing the work of Poel and Granville-Barker, it also opened up a new understanding of the ways in which Shakespeare's plays can speak to contemporary concerns.[47] Particularly relevant in this respect has been the work on cross-gender casting, based on the fact that early modern companies assigned female roles to boy-actors.

That Shakespeare's Cleopatra, perhaps the most ineffable and enthralling representation of femaleness in Western culture, might be impersonated by a male actor would have seemed almost blasphemous a few decades ago; but when in 1999 Giles Block staged the play at the recently reconstructed Globe in London with an all-male cast, starring Mark Rylance, the then artistic director, in the female leading role, the work of feminist theorists like Judith Butler – who first drew a line between sex and gender, defining the latter as a matter of performance – seemed to come alive onstage.[48] Shakespeare's Globe, a successful example of private enterprise operating without any regular public subsidy, used its workshop to experiment with all the elements of the performance; the study of costumes, in this production, was particularly important: Jenny Tiramani created them on the basis of Inigo Jones's designs for Jacobean masques, and the queen's frequent changing of clothes was intended to emphasize her exuberant theatricality; Tiramani, however, came to the conclusion that in Shakespeare's time it would have been impossible to change costume as many times for lack of the necessary number of dressers.[49] According to James C. Bulman, the recovery of the same-sex casting was accepted by the Globe's spectators for its claimed archaeological value; however, what this original practice really did and still does was 'queering' the audience by questioning our own essentialism in terms of gender and sexual desire: 'ironically, the use of cross-dressing in contemporary productions of Shakespeare may speak with a greater force to us than it ever did to Elizabethan audiences'.[50]

In 2006, thirty-four years after Nunn's Roman season, Shakespeare's Globe inaugurated its 'Edges of Rome' season with *Coriolanus, Titus Andronicus* and *Antony and Cleopatra*; the last, directed by Dominic Dromgoole, was, according to Michael J. Collins, 'a serviceable but never, with the exception of Cleopatra [Frances Barber], a deeply engaging production', in which Antony's (Nicholas Jones) self-stabbing 'became a comic routine'.[51] Conversely, a new production directed in 2014 by Jonathan Munby received general critical acclaim and might even be considered 'a textbook example of "heritage" theatre', with Clive Wood and Eve Best starring in the title roles.[52] Best, in particular, was brilliant both in her histrionic addresses to the audience and in the more intimate moments, 'offering the audience temporary access to her inward emotional response'.[53] In addition, having played the protagonist in *Much Ado About Nothing* in 2011 on the same stage, Best brought the spirited cleverness of her Beatrice to Cleopatra, thus highlighting both the theme of the war of the sexes and the 'shrew' nature of the Egyptian queen, played to comic pitch in the scene of the beating of the messenger announcing Antony's marriage to Octavia.

Shakespeare's Globe exceptionally collaborated with the RSC in 2012 for the World Shakespeare Festival, which hosted (over seven weeks) thirty-seven productions, one for each play by Shakespeare, originated in as many different countries and languages as part of the Cultural Olympiad and a tribute to Global Shakespeare. *Antony and Cleopatra* was performed by the Oyun Atölyesi Theatre Company (Istanbul, Turkey) and directed by Kemal Aydoğan with Haluk Bilginer (Antony) and Zerry Tekindor (Cleopatra) cast as the 'mutual pair' (1.1.38). Bilginer and Tekindor are not only theatre actors of repute but also TV stars, the former a darling of British viewers for his role of seducer in *EastEnders*, the latter the protagonist of a popular Turkish TV series. The production displayed a prevailing and not always coherent comic register that may, however, have been devised to better engage a non-Turkish-speaking audience.

Made for Cinema? *Antony and Cleopatra* on Screen

Even though the play, as argued at the beginning of this chapter, does seem to foreshadow a cinematic treatment of space and time through cut-and-edit techniques, there are not as many adaptations of *Antony and Cleopatra* for the screen as one might expect and, even more significantly, there are no box-office successes or critically acclaimed masterpieces among them. If Cleopatra's myth has spawned an extraordinary number of cinematic versions – starting with Georges Méliès's two-minute reel, *Cléopâtre; or, Robbing Cleopatra's Tomb* in 1899 – films that explicitly present themselves as screen adaptations of Shakespeare's Roman play have been rare.[54]

The first *Antony and Cleopatra* for the silver screen is now lost, as most silent films sadly are. It was produced by Vitagraph, at a time when the American company decided to commit its production to '"quality films" ... based upon historical, biblical and literary subjects', so that Shakespeare was an obvious choice as an author to draw upon.[55] The movie was directed by Charles Kent as early as 1908 – the same year as *Julius Caesar*, directed by William V. Ranous – and it showed, as a reviewer reported, 'a fine picture of Roman pride and Eastern magnificence ... in less than twenty minutes! What a vast difference between the older presentation and that represented by the modernized form of amusement'.[56] Today, we can only speculate about the way in which an onscreen version of *Antony and Cleopatra* could downplay the 'unlawful' relationship between the two lovers, considering the increasing call for highly moral stories and the impending birth of the National Board of Censorship of Motion Pictures (1909).[57] It is not so surprising, after all, that no reel has survived.

In fact, when, five years later, in 1913, an Italian film was released by the Cines Film Company, *Marcantonio e Cleopatra* – starring Gianna Terribili-Gonzales and Amleto Novelli – and distributed all over Europe and the United States, the director, Enrico Guazzoni, safely shifted the focus from the transgressive love story to the overall magic of cinema as a medium capable of conjuring up not only far-away geographical locations but also events that are distant in time, thus making the spectators see, with their own eyes, history in action in its 'authentic' setting.[58] This justifies the opening sequence, which consists of documentary footage, already owned by Cines and produced during the conflict between Italy and Turkey for the possession of Libya, 1911–12, showing the Karnak Sphinxes, the Giza Pyramid complex and a flooded temple at Philae, which can all be admired in their alien and uncanny beauty. But is there any Shakespeare at all in this alleged 'adaptation'? Robert Ball had to acknowledge that Guazzoni's film was certainly advertised as related to Shakespeare's play, at least in the United States, even though there is very little Shakespeare in it.[59] Guazzoni himself claimed *Antony and Cleopatra* to be his main source, to which he added, however, Plutarch's *Life of Antony* and Pietro Cossa's dramatic poem *Cleopatra* (1879). Guazzoni's portrayal of the Egyptian queen was that of a femme fatale – played by Terribili-Gonzales in outrageously revealing clothes – opposed to the chaste Octavia – Hester Lenard dressed up to her neck – who, faithful to Marcantonio, unsuccessfully travels all the way to Alexandria to confront her rival and win her husband back (a nod to the Dryden-inspired scenes of many nineteenth-century theatre productions). There are very few intertitles in the print available at the Cineteca Nazionale, and Maria Wyke remarks that the plot is far from reproducing Shakespeare's tragic chain of events.[60] That being said, the close-up shot of Cleopatra alone in her room after Marcantonio's defeat and death, horrified by a flash-forward vision of herself brought to Rome as a captive in Octavius's triumph – long shot – surrounded by what the Folio text describes as '[m]echanic slaves / With greasy aprons, rules, and hammers' (5.2.208–10), and her consequent decision to take her own life so as to safeguard her queenly honour – back to close-up – are outstandingly in line with Shakespeare's construction of her motivations for committing suicide, which are dealt with differently in Plutarch's account.

Strangely enough, after the silent era there is only one overt adaptation for the big screen on record, namely *Antony and Cleopatra* directed by Charlton Heston in 1972.[61] It is true that Joseph Mankiewicz had already directed the most famous, expensive and financially disastrous film on Cleopatra to date

(1963); however, his work is not what Christine Geraghty would call a 'classic' adaptation of Shakespeare's play.[62]

Heston poured into his feature film on *Antony and Cleopatra* all of his enthusiasm (and money); he had cherished the project for more than twenty years, after having played Antony in both David Bradley's (1949) and Stuart Burge's screen adaptations of *Julius Caesar* (1970). Yet, even he had to acknowledge the disappointing result (not in small part due to his much criticized decision to cast the white South African actress Hildegarde Neil as Cleopatra): after the disastrous world premiere in London on 2 March 1972, virtually no commercial release followed, though the film is now widely available on video. As Samuel Crowl observes, the opening sequence is very promising, visually marking the opposition between Rome and Egypt through a difference of speed in rhythm, on the level of both contents and editing: we are first shown a galley moving fast through a scintillating Mediterranean Sea, and a messenger who, after landing, gallops tirelessly to the city of Alexandria; once there, however, the Roman messenger's pace has to slow down until it gets completely stuck in the opulent labyrinthine Egyptian palace in which Antony is almost kept prisoner by Cleopatra.[63] Viewers are bluntly shown the subjection of the man who was once a Roman military hero from his first appearance, when he is emasculated by Cleopatra, who is intent on putting lipstick on his lips while he sleeps, and later even exhibits him kept on a leash of pearls. Heston plays Antony as a stern soldier who won many battles for his country but is so enthralled by the Hollywood-like luxury of Alexandria that he forgets his military duties. Ironically, one of the sequences most appreciated by critics was that of the Battle of Actium, which was made up of leftover footage from *Ben-Hur*, bought at a bargain price from MGM.

Somehow, paradoxically for a play that is largely characterized by boundlessness, *Antony and Cleopatra* counts more adaptations on the small than the big screen. In 1963, a black-and-white miniseries of nine fifty-minute episodes, *The Spread of the Eagle*, produced and directed by Peter Dews, was broadcast by the BBC; it adapted *Coriolanus, Julius Caesar* and *Antony and Cleopatra* rearranged according to the historical order of events; the last three episodes – 'The Serpent', 'The Alliance', 'The Monument' – were adapted from *Antony and Cleopatra*, with Mary Morris and Keith Michell in the title roles. Serialization gives Antony a prominent position: as the only leading role in both *Julius Caesar* and *Antony and Cleopatra*, the tragic quality of the character, played by the same actor, appears more evidently on TV than on stage, in so far as in the TV series, as Michael Brooke writes, 'we have already been shown his glory days in earlier episodes, and can better appreciate just how far he has fallen'.[64] A sense of grandeur was given by Clifford Hatts's set design at the request of Peter Dews, who wanted 'to show great men in great places'; Cleopatra's monument was described by Brooke as 'the most eye-catching achievement' of the series.[65]

It was in 1974, however, that Nunn directed what is still considered by many critics the best screen version of the play, a film aired on ITV on 24 July, based on the 1972 RSC stage production and starring the same cast. Helped by his television co-director, Jon Scoffield, Nunn was able to make the most of the medium, as Crowl argues, by using camera devices to create a sense of intimacy, such as overhead shots in dialogues 'to break the standard eye-level perspective so common on television' or by contriving more affective visual effects, such as lens distortion at the edges to reproduce the fluidity of the Egyptian world and Antony's difficulty in holding 'either Cleopatra or himself in steady focus'.[66] According to David Fuller, however, in adapting his production for television Nunn made the love story even more central as a whole than it originally was on stage to the detriment of the political emphasis: a domestic drama fit for the chosen domestic medium.[67]

The difficulty of conveying a play of imperial breadth through a domestic mass medium like television emerged also in the adaptation for BBC Shakespeare (1981) by Jonathan Miller, who focused on the love story as well. Gone, however, was the unconventional fascination with the alternative East that had characterized Nunn's previous TV adaptation. 'Jane Lapotaire's sharp, pale, extremely ironic Cleopatra', Crowl observes, 'with a strand of pearls tight at her neck and exquisite matching earrings, might have stepped right out of a Bronzino portrait'; her composure certainly suited a conservative project (Cedric Messina's) born in an age of nascent political conservatism (Margaret Thatcher was first elected prime minister in 1979, and the BBC Shakespeare was filmed between 1978 and 1985). To be fair, Miller changed the 'house style' with his *Antony and Cleopatra*, as Bulman points out: he did not follow Messina's guidelines to keep the audience unaware of theatrical conventions and attain a straightforward cinematic realism; conversely, he 'set out to present the plays as Elizabethans would have understood them', therefore resorting to baroque painting's representation of the classical age in an attempt to reproduce early modern techniques of recreating past historical periods.[68]

Not even the 1990s, the decade that spawned the greatest number of Shakespeare films since the silent era, brought an *Antony and Cleopatra* adaptation either for the big or the small screen. Today, however, it looks as if cinema and television, as specific media, have been absorbed and integrated in the new, intermedial staging of Shakespeare that has characterized the productions of the new millennium. And to this last phase we now turn.

Intermedial Performances in the Twenty-first Century

In 1999, J. David Bolter and Richard Grusin famously stated that 'no medium today, and certainly no single media event, seems to do its cultural work in isolation from other media.' At the close of the millennium, they were drawing attention to the digital revolution: that is, to the fact that all media had begun to speak the same language, that of binary digits, and were therefore able to interface easily with each other, thus forming an interconnected circuit through which information could travel much more smoothly and quickly than in the analogic era.[69] Digitalization has since profoundly modified the way we perceive the world: if in Shakespeare's time the *imago mundi* was largely determined by a system of analogies regulating correspondences between micro- and macrocosm through hierarchical conceptual figures such as the *scala naturae*, we now make sense of the world through heterarchical and polycentric meaning-making structures, best subsumed in the metaphor of the net; we have got used to processing a huge amount of information – coming from all kinds of different platforms in dialogue with each other – that is beamed 'live' or archived in the space and time of the internet, making us participate in events that are here/not here, now/not now. Needless to say, the concept of 'live' performance itself, as Bulman remarks, has deeply changed, and 'digitalization has altered our understanding of what the term means'.[70]

The ethics and politics of the digital communication system are at the core of Ivo van Hove's highly acclaimed production of the *Roman Tragedies* for Toneelgroep Amsterdam, a six-hour show combining in the same immersive experience *Coriolanus*, *Julius Caesar* and *Antony and Cleopatra* rewritten in Dutch with surtitles in the language of the hosting country. The show, which Thomas Cartelli defines as 'the most thoroughly mediatized production of Shakespeare on record', toured Avignon, London, Montreal, Quebec City, Vienna and Zurich, and has been revived many times since its 2007 premiere.[71] Van Hove rearranged the stage space by making it resemble an international broadcast studio or, alternatively, a conference hall provided with all sorts of new technologies; the actors wore modern dress and were shown as contemporary politicians always ready to release their comments on TV talk shows or in the evening news. In order to reproduce the participatory drive of social media, smaller and larger screens were distributed all around the place to display blog pages to which members of the audience could contribute their opinions by using either onstage computers or their own mobile phones, while the same means of communication channelled the director's comments and provocative questions. The competition between old and new media to win the audience's attention that characterizes the phenomenon of remediation emerges clearly in the contention between the live bodies of actors and their images on screen, which, as Cartelli notes, 'almost always resolves in favour of their projected images for auditors who chose to leave their seats and move onstage'.[72] Particularly effective was the scene of Enobarbus's flight from the television studio, as he tried to leave behind what that studio meant but could not in any way escape mediatization and was followed by a technician holding a camera who live-broadcast his fall and death in a more or less crowded street of the 'real' world. One question arises: is there anything 'real' in the 'world as a screen' created by van Hove? As Roberta Barker points out, 'if we consider realism as an art not of plenitude but of omission and irony', then Antony and Cleopatra, who are shown drunk most of the time, can be seen as 'key realist subjects' in their unspoken, hidden moments of dismay and love for each other when their faces are obtrusively searched in close-up by the camera, in contrast with Octavius Caesar, played by a gelid blonde woman, Hadewych Minis, who dominates the camera and therefore wins the political game, but not the sympathy of her fellow human beings.[73]

Not all intermedial performances use the same high-tech devices, like computer graphics and live-feed projections on screens of variable size, or display the same disruptive and avant-garde quality as van Hove's; however, if in his production the stage overflows its perimeter to wash away the stalls and flood the audience, even the confines of theatre as a material building can be dissolved. In 2009, National Theatre Live was first launched, thus bringing a new kind of aesthetic object to the world, the theatre-cinema production, namely a production situated among different media and semiotic codes – theatre, cinema, television – in a significant and evident relation to each other, not belonging to one only but participating in each.[74] National Theatre Live was followed in 2013 by Royal Shakespeare Company Live and, in 2015, by Shakespeare's Globe On Screen: such intermedial forms of production are inevitably affecting not only the way plays are received by audiences around the world but also the way they are performed, as staging has to be carefully related to screening so that the stage director is always supported by a screen director.[75]

When the RSC launched the 'Rome MMXVII' Season (2017), under the direction of Angus Jackson, it programmed its live or quasi-live broadcast in cinemas around the globe. Jackson directed both *Coriolanus* and *Julius Caesar*; conversely, *Titus Andronicus* was directed by Blanche McIntyre, and *Antony and Cleopatra* by Iqbal Khan. While there were multiple directors, the same designer, Robert Innes Hopkins, created the set for all the plays, imagining a continuous world spreading from *Coriolanus*'s republic to *Titus*'s late empire. An interesting element of continuity was a plaster cast of a recently restored marble statue of a lion attacking a horse, which was positioned at diverse spots on the set for each production: it is a Greek work of art of the fourth century BCE, brought to Rome as booty, restored in the Renaissance by one of Michelangelo's pupils and now at the Capitoline Museum, in Rome. Powerfully representing a mortal fight between two noble animals, it can easily be interpreted as a symbol of the civil wars that characterized the segment of Roman history Shakespeare decided to adapt for the stage. However, in the case of *Antony and Cleopatra*, the work of art might also bring to mind the cover of the 'libretto di sala' by Adolfo de Carolis that was sold to cinema-goers of *Cabiria*: the xylography showed a she-wolf attacking a horse against the exotic profile of a stylized palm-tree.[76] *Cabiria* occupies a special place in the history of antiquity films in the silent era; it recovers from the past the model of a binary structure that will become a standard for films on ancient Rome. Carthage stands for a stylistically 'hybrid' other, which includes elements from many Mediterranean cultures, including the Egyptian one, whose identity is defined in opposition to the classical world of Rome and its values. The intermedial reference to *Cabiria*, if related to Khan's *Antony and Cleopatra*, would further support the contamination between screen and stage, namely one of the most captivating aesthetic features of this production.

Khan produced a staging of the play that seemed particularly apt to work both on stage and screen. The production featured a stunning music score created by vocalist, songwriter and composer Laura Mvula. Music was conceived as the emotional means through which the audience was transported back and forth between Egypt and Rome, while time was suspended between past and present, in a mix of Miles Davis's dry modernity and Prince's baroque texture, with touches of ancient musical instruments. The opening scene was impressive; Philo's lines were slightly postponed and assigned to Ventidius, who summed up a number of minor characters, thus acquiring greater importance than in the original playtext, as in Dryden's tradition; a rich, harmonious brass ensemble played the 'flourish' reported in the scene directions, then music started and, amazingly for an RSC production, the actors entered dancing and singing, all wearing Anubis-like masks making it impossible to distinguish men from women: a great sense of energy, otherness and gender fluidity was generated, and the audience was unexpectedly plunged into the alternative space of the formidable pair.

Mention should be made of the outstanding theatricalization of the battle of Actium, which was obtained through a beautifully choreographed shifting of toy ships pushed and pulled by actors on the square-patterned floor of the stage resembling a game board. The effectiveness of the scene was enhanced by impressive light and sound effects that allowed for the enactment of what is only reported or evoked through sound in the playtext, thereby making the action look at the same time as the war-game it is for the leaders who watch it from afar and a real fight for those, the brave and faithful soldiers, who die in it. The shame Antony feels for having withdrawn was played by Antony Byrne with particularly moving intensity.

Music was important in relation to Cleopatra as well: played by Josette Simon (Ira in Adrian Noble's 1982 production), born in Leicester and of Caribbean heritage, Cleopatra 'danced' her role with every single part of her body, occupying the entire stage with her tall, slender, energetic figure, always in perfect command of the 'infinite variety' of her movement and voice. At the end of the play nothing remains of that fascinating mobility, and the audience is instead left to witness the metamorphosis of Octavius (Ben Allen) into Augustus, when, after delivering the closing lines that secure a high-state funeral for the couple, in place of the 'exeunt omnes' (5.2.365SD) of the original stage directions, Octavius literally rises – standing on a platform – over the dead body of Cleopatra, who has died seated on her throne. The white armour he is wearing and the bright light that pours on him from above transform his body into a marble statue in the posture of the Augustus of *Prima Porta*, the masterpiece held in the Vatican Museums showing him as a divinity. Music is brought to a final epic pitch while Augustus casts his shadow on the colourful Cleopatra.

A strong inclination towards the use of a cinematic style was evident in the production of the play directed by Simon Godwin for the National Theatre at the end of 2018. Ralph Fiennes' and Sophie Okonedo's outstanding performances were received by critics with such acclaim as had been reserved only to the superb acting of Judi Dench and Anthony Hopkins when they were directed by Peter Hall in 1986 on the same boards; no wonder they won, as their legendary predecessors, the Evening Standard Award for best actor and best actress respectively. The modern-dress production consciously winked at celebrity culture, thus emphasizing the sophisticated glamour of a couple with the lifestyle of the rich and famous; Cleopatra's haute-couture clothes, in particular, were so dazzling they would have had a high impact on the catwalk in Cannes or Venice, while the visual approach to the battles seemed to recall Fiennes' 2011 own adaptation of *Coriolanus* to the war-film genre. Despite these eye-catching features, however, at the core of the production stood the director's vision of a play that is 'about regime change and ... has urgent connotations. You could talk about Libya or you could talk about Syria. When and why do you intervene and what happens when the person you send to intervene takes up the opposing cause?'[77] It is a refreshing perspective, much in line with contemporary debates on intercultural relations and international military actions in a globalized and mediatized world, and it will certainly foster new, exciting critical paths on a play that 'age cannot wither' (2.2.245).

3

The State of the Art

Domenico Lovascio

As stale as the quotation is liable to sound, it is hard to abstain from remarking that the years 2000–16 have unsurprisingly witnessed the publication of an 'infinite variety' of scholarly takes on *Antony and Cleopatra*. Although many of these contributions seem to rely rather heavily upon seminal twentieth-century interpretations by Janet Adelman, Robert S. Miola, Linda Charnes and Coppélia Kahn, the past sixteen years have nonetheless succeeded in providing an exciting range of original and thought-provoking insights into the play.[1]

I have purposely refrained from considering editions and adaptations in the following survey, since they would deserve a separate chapter each. In addition, as they are likely to prove to be the most influential and the ones circulating most widely, I resolved to limit myself to contributions written in English, which I have then organized into the ensuing categories on the basis of their primary focus:

- Sources
- Death
- Passions
- *Antony and Cleopatra* and its predecessors

- Race, empire and commerce
- Politics
- Ethics, gender, hermeneutics and genre
- Messengers
- Food
- Apocalypse

A simple cursory look at this list should make one immediately aware of how early twenty-first-century scholarship on *Antony and Cleopatra* differs from how it used to be before 2000. Discussions of characterization and of the range of locations employed by Shakespeare have become rarer, together with the early twentieth-century emphasis on the play's challenge to conventional notions of morality.

Yet scholars have kept on considering sources (even though 'affectively rather than genetically', in Adelman's phrasing), thereby yielding revealing insights into the broader cultural context in which the play was first performed and received.[2] Continuity is also apparent in discussions of race and gender (especially as regards Antony's masculinity or lack thereof) – which also seem to have been preponderant as opposed to other critical concerns – as well as the play's familiar generic confusion, with a restricted number of riveting analyses also tackling a few aspects of the play's structure. Topical readings have notably continued to thrive, especially in connection with early Jacobean concerns regarding early English attempts at colonization, James's unpopular irenicism, Scottishness, licentiousness and neglect of statecraft, as well as the increasing importance of diplomatic relations on the early modern political stage.

Fresh insights have also been provided by considering Shakespeare's play side by side with other contemporary dramatizations of the couple's tragic love story, a perspective that has been adopted by a significant number of studies in the time span considered. Death and suicide have been repeatedly explored as crucial elements, both in relation to the early modern English reception of Stoicism and in terms of the spectacularization of politics that lies at the heart of the play. The current interest in early modern conceptions of food and emotions has decisively affected a large number of recent readings of the play, and scholars have also intriguingly taken into account the play's topical Christian and apocalyptic overtones, as well as its depiction of the intricate relationship between politics and historiography.

Sources

As they focus on *Antony and Cleopatra* in relation to its sources, the contributions by John H. Astington, Catherine Belsey and Robert A. Logan appear as an appropriate starting point. Astington suggests that Enobarbus's description of Cleopatra sailing down the Cydnus as 'O'er-picturing that Venus where we see / The fancy outwork nature' (2.2.210–11), besides drawing upon Plutarch, may have also been influenced by *The Triumph of Venus*, a pictorial tapestry that was part of 'a linked series of triumphs of the gods' held at Whitehall.[3] This is lost, but 'a later weaving from the same cartoons, completed in the 1560s' is extant and largely tallies with Enobarbus's description.[4] As 'the Triumph of Venus must have formed part of the decorative programme of the Elizabethan' and 'Stuart courts', Shakespeare is likely to have 'had some knowledge of this tapestry', whose 'general spirit ... may have contributed to the sensual intensity Shakespeare adds to North's description'.[5] Moreover, by dint of being 'the most remarkable image of the goddess made in the sixteenth century, and the only one showing her at the centre of a triumphal journey by water', *The Triumph of Venus* may have influenced the reception of the play 'among those reasonably familiar with the court'.[6]

The protagonists' first encounter as narrated by Enobarbus is also explored by Belsey, who contends that by mocking Antony's unmanly, teenage-like behaviour before and during the feast, Enobarbus 'integrates a sceptical point of view into the record of a legendary love affair', so that, 'if the account of the spectacle inflates the queen's enchantment, the tale of Antony's capitulation diminishes the general'.[7] However, since 'the detraction is ascribed to a fictional figure, it cannot be attributed to Shakespeare as authoritative', which leads Belsey as far as to contend that Shakespeare 'invented the unreliable narrator, usually associated with the nineteenth-century novel', using it in *Antony and Cleopatra* to 'keep us guessing ... on the nature of drama, which makes space for more than one narrative voice'.[8]

The play's relation with Christopher Marlowe's *Dido, Queen of Carthage* lies at the core of Logan's discussion. Superficially, Marlowe's 'strongest influence' lies in Shakespeare's deployment of 'the Marlovian style of epic grandeur, majestic amplitude, hyperbole, and sharp emphasis'.[9] Yet, at a deeper level, *Antony and Cleopatra* seems to indicate 'that Shakespeare consciously moved in a direction contrary to that of Marlowe' concerning 'the relationship between personal happiness and sociopolitical responsibility'.[10] Hence, it appears inadequate simply to characterize Marlowe 'as an overreacher and iconoclast and Shakespeare as a conservative and traditionalist'.[11] In fact, whereas Marlowe's play supports 'a moral and political status quo which reflects a commonly held, patriarchal perspective', Shakespeare's 'refuses to side with society against the individual'.[12]

Death

The link between Marlowe's and Shakespeare's tragedies is also remarked upon by Lisa S. Starks, who argues that *Antony and Cleopatra* 'continues the challenge begun ... in Dido' to reverse 'the gender hierarchy of masculine duty over feminine passion', thereby extending 'Marlowe's move to encompass a radical displacement of the epic tradition and its masculine values of heroism through the figure of Antony as masochistic hero', in so far as Antony's sacrificing himself for love is decisive in making him a martyr.[13] As a result, the 'staged tableau of the goddess/Virgin Cleopatra holding the bleeding body of Antony/Christ in her arms ... resonates as a powerfully erotic *pietà*', drawing 'its erotic charge from medieval to early modern representations of the male hero-martyr'.[14]

Enobarbus's death, possibly the only Shakespearian instance of a character dying on stage for shame, functions for David Read 'not as a tragic catastrophe' but 'as a means of ... withdrawal in advance from the consequences of the actions that lead to a tragic outcome'.[15] Seen in this light, Enobarbus's demise provides insights 'into a somewhat mysterious feature of Shakespeare's later career', namely the notion 'that characters concerned in the same action might experience dissimilar outcomes rather than a single overarching one', an idea that, despite not 'fit[ting] comfortably with a traditional notion of tragedy', effectively 'approximate[s] the messiness of ordinary experience'.[16]

Eric Langley, who examines the deaths of Enobarbus, Antony and Cleopatra under the lens of Stoicism, holds quite a different view of Enobarbus's fate. According to Langley, in leaving Egypt because he construes Antony's excesses as merely denoting lack and emptiness, Enobarbus renounces 'largesse and mutuality in favour of a Roman form of willed individualism'; however, by endorsing this form of 'autarkeia' he ends up isolated, so that his death comes to look like 'a kind of worthless semi-Stoic suicide where self-assertion is a poor substitute for mutual love'.[17] Before committing suicide, Antony too 'aspires to an act of self-will, self-assertion, and annihilation'; yet 'Shakespeare sets up an alternative suicidal model in Cleopatra's feigned suicide', which is framed as 'an act of hand-in-hand loving reciprocation'.[18] As for Cleopatra's actual suicide, it emerges as an action that is both 'emphatically private' and 'an act of ... political potency'.[19] The political valence of suicide in the play is also highlighted by Barbara L. Parker, who states that suicide functions 'as the ultimate weapon in the battle for control of the world', as evidenced by the fact that both Antony and Cleopatra ultimately 'commit suicide to defeat Caesar, and the last thoughts of both are of having vanquished Caesar'.[20]

That Cleopatra sees death as an opportunity to force Octavius to 'come to terms with her as a political agent' is a conviction similarly shared by Jacqueline Vanhoutte, whose main focus is, however, Antony's suicide, which 'originates ... in private despair but ... ends in public display' and seems to be consistent with Antony's 'desire for agency over his own body inform[ing] ... his behaviour throughout the play'.[21] In Vanhoutte's reading, 'Antony perceives his body as shaped by others' thoughts', so that it ends up bearing 'an excess of signification', which 'Antony experiences ... as a somatic disintegration'.[22] Suicide is thus for Antony 'an attempt to reassert control over his "visible shape" by removing himself from the determining cultural pressures that he thinks are destroying him'.[23] Yet the 'misreadings of Antony's suicide that proliferate after his death' indicate 'the ultimate failure of [his] enterprise', which ultimately 'feeds the ideological forces that he had attempted to defeat'.[24]

Passions

A more circumscribed attention to the role of feelings, passions and emotions is shared by a few other scholars. In a fascinating psychoanalytical discussion, David Bevington speculates that Shakespeare's writing of *Antony and Cleopatra* was driven by personal issues: as he was 'forty-three or thereabouts' at the time, Shakespeare was 'stirred by the phenomenon of anxiety about the loss of male potency and a sense of everything closing in on one's only chance at living a full human life'.[25] Aware that it might be 'anachronistic to use modern terminology' in dealing with early modern texts, Bevington contends that Antony's behaviour reveals a typical pattern of what is commonly known today as midlife crisis, namely 'the erratic swinging from an extreme of irresponsibility to one of self-condemnation, as [Antony] alternates between moments of drunkenness and sobriety, and the determination on the morning after his excesses to give up his dissipation'.[26] Yet Antony is unable to stick to his resolution and 'lacks the will to deny himself pleasure forever'.[27]

According to David Schalkwyk, the opening scenes of the play exemplify the notions that love is not an emotion, that it does not reside 'in the material conditions of the humoral body' (as one would assume with reference to Renaissance conceptions) and that it cannot 'be isolated as a particular kind of set chemical components in the blood or synapses in the brain', as cognitive theory would have it.[28] The opening exchange between Antony and Cleopatra exposes 'love as a disposition that unfolds over time' and that is 'intrinsically bound up with a performative and dialogical navigation of effects, affects, and meanings'.[29] Hence, the play makes love emerge as 'a complex dynamic' involving 'a variety of emotions, some of which are usually considered antithetical to love: exasperation, anger, impatience, shame, regret, sorrow, and helplessness'.[30]

From a different standpoint, Gail Kern Paster argues that the play exposes 'how the early modern idea of humans and animals as linked by their shared subjection to the passions works to produce a form of bodily self-experience epistemically ... other than our own'.[31] Early moderns regarded 'emotions as especially visible and knowable in animals', since the former were thought to be produced in the latter 'physiologically by the same means but without the inhibiting filters and self-appraisals imposed' by civilization.[32] When Octavius 'remembers the young Antony's stoical triumph over disgust as the sign of his strong difference from beasts and ordinary men', he is identifying 'a superior form of manliness' paradoxically marked 'by Antony's imitation of animal eating'; in other words, 'Antony is manlier than other men ... by willing himself to be more animal-like than the animals.'[33] Not dissimilarly, in her 'equine imaginings' Cleopatra 'uses the passions attributed to all animal life to gesture toward a horizon' in which her 'restless desires [may] override the paltry containment of species'.[34]

Antony and Cleopatra and its Predecessors

Examination of *Antony and Cleopatra* in the light of how sixteenth-century French and English neo-Senecan drama treated the same subject has yielded some richly suggestive insights into different aspects of the play. Daniel Cadman maintains that Shakespeare's tragedy 'exhibits a significant degree of continuity with' – rather than being antagonistic towards, as often mistakenly assumed – Mary Sidney's *Antonius* (1592) and Samuel Daniel's *Cleopatra* (first edition 1594), particularly as regards 'the plays' representation of the politicization of the *theatrum mundi* tradition and their resistance to the appropriation of theatricality in the construction and promulgation of sovereign power'.[35] Shakespeare's play therefore seems to reflect on Elizabeth I's and James I's conscious deployment of the *theatrum mundi* tradition as well as registering anxieties about 'the dependency of the sovereigns upon the mediation and representation of their political authority'.[36] Among the 'numerous metatheatrical moments' in which the different plays engage, Cadman singles out Cleopatra's retreat to the monument, invariably portrayed as 'a space where Cleopatra is able to reassert her agency over how she is represented in a way that is untrammelled by the influence of Rome or the constricting values upheld by Octavius'.[37]

A comparison of Shakespeare's tragedy with Sidney's and Daniel's is set up by Mimi Still Dixon in order to discuss Cleopatra's treatment as a female tragic hero in *Antony and Cleopatra*. While in the late Elizabethan plays 'Cleopatra speaks in lengthy, self-revealing monologues', Shakespeare's queen is denied any soliloquy.[38] It is paradoxically 'through her silences', claims Dixon, that 'Shakespeare achieves Cleopatra's tragic subjectivity', inasmuch as he makes 'her silent bodily presence on stage the object of our attention and speculation', so that by being 'forced to ... imagine a Cleopatra in the gaps and between the words, we ourselves construct that interior, a truer and more authentic self, precisely because it is not offered up for display'.[39]

In Warren Chernaik's view, 'Earlier Cleopatra plays ... place relatively little emphasis on the struggle for dominance in Rome', which is central to Shakespeare's tragedy.[40] This clash is especially exemplified by Cleopatra's 'tendency ... to turn the play into comedy', which should be understood as 'a deliberate challenge to Roman values and to Roman hegemony, asserting a rival set of values contesting imperial Rome's domination over Egypt'.[41] Shakespeare's play also differs from previous dramatic takes on Antony and Cleopatra's liaison in devoting 'more attention ... to Antony's varying fortunes and fluctuating moods between Actium and his suicide'; in 'maintain[ing] suspense as to whether the changeable, worldly Cleopatra will be able to maintain her resolve to ... embrac[e] the finality of death' in the final act; and in bringing out an eroticism in death that is 'far removed from the cloying sentimentality of Garnier's or Daniel's concerned mother and loyal, obedient spouse'.[42]

With a view to demonstrating that the idea of 'luxury' was undergoing conceptual disruption and reformulation as early as the seventeenth century (rather than not until the eighteenth, as usually assumed), Alison V. Scott discusses the reception of Cleopatra in early modern drama as a figure that 'conjured a nexus of meanings and associations encompassed in the shifting idea of luxury', thereby also illuminating Shakespeare's play.[43] Here, Cleopatra embodies an idea of luxury that 'sometimes stands in contradiction to the idea's standard vocabulary in both Christian and classical traditions' as carnal lust, in so far as Cleopatra 'conforms to the Greco-Roman persona of emasculating Luxuria ... at the same time as she re-embodies a Hellenistic aesthetic of luxury as beneficial excess (bounty), pleasure and beauty'.[44] Luxury is therefore not defined in the play in merely moral-religious terms but appears to have already started taking on an aesthetic and political dimension as a 'proto-liberal notion of negative liberty' and 'a sign of commitment to and fulfilment of personal desire'.[45]

Cleopatra's 'racial make-up' as 'a crucial ingredient in the characterization of the queen as a body natural and a body politic' in Shakespeare's play as compared to Etienne Jodelle's *Cléopâtre captive* (1553), Robert Garnier's *Marc Antoine* (1578), its translation by Sidney and Daniel's *Cleopatra* is at the heart of Pascale Aebischer's analysis.[46] Although the 'racial markers of whiteness' typical of the French dramatic representations of Cleopatra tend to be downplayed in the late Elizabethan plays, they reappear in Shakespeare, 'regain[ing] the performative character they had possessed in the French text', while also 'set[ting] aside signifiers of blackness in such a way as to undermine any essentialist understanding of race'.[47] For Shakespeare's Cleopatra, 'racial attributes are ... theatrical properties to be deployed and discarded at will': she harnesses whiteness whenever she 'wishes to present herself as a Petrarchan mistress who demands the submission of her Roman lover, or when, as with the cutting of her lace, she appeals to the audience to identify with her actions and distress'.[48] Consequently, her 'politically and sexually motivated performances of race dismantle the binaries of Rome vs. Egypt, self vs. other which Romans and critical tradition alike have used as a means of fixing her identity'.[49]

Race, Empire and Commerce

Aebischer addresses the crucial questions of race and empire, and discussions of the play's engagement with these issues have continued to abound, offering many intriguing interpretative possibilities and proving to be the dominant mode of critical discourse. Ania Loomba examines how the gender reversal inherent in Antony's relationship with the dark-skinned

Cleopatra 'speaks to contemporary English fears about the erosion of racial identity and masculinity', especially by offering 'no reassuring scenario of a foreign queen's assimilation' and questioning 'the pattern of representing the colonized land as a sexually available female'.[50] The construction of Cleopatra's Egyptian self is essential in 'the political struggle between the imperial power and its would-be colony'.[51] Interestingly, 'Cleopatra plays the Egyptian flamboyantly ... flaunting the difference that Rome assigns to her' until she has political power; then, aware that 'she will no longer be able to control the terms of the performance, she stages her suicide', a trademark of Roman culture.[52] The play therefore seems to capture 'the contradiction that lies at the heart of race' by implying that racial roles are 'fluid and yet not ... easy to manipulate'.[53]

Looking at the differences between Rome and Egypt in the play from an entirely different viewpoint, Mary Thomas Crane contends that they are largely 'cognitive' and 'perceptual', and 'have different epistemological underpinnings' and 'political implications'.[54] Whereas the Egyptian understanding of the 'porous interrelationships' between humankind and nature still depends on the intuitive 'Aristotelian system of elements and humors', the Romans seem to have espoused a new system that 'look[s] forward to a Cartesian mind–body split' in which 'subjectivity [is] separated from ... the natural world and imagining itself as able to control it'.[55] As a result, the two civilizations perceive empire very differently: the Romans 'name their environment the "world"' and divide it into cities and nations they attempt to control and colonize by naming; the Egyptians 'inhabit the "earth", in which they imagine themselves to be immersed and which' emerges as a space 'resistant to human division and mastery'.[56]

In a thought-provoking two-chapter analysis of *Antony and Cleopatra*, which ends up filling nearly half his monograph, Arthur L. Little Jr tackles the play's complex engagement with issues of race, gender and empire. The book's most valuable insights seem to arise from Little's claim that it is not enough to interpret Antony as 'an effeminate or feminine man', since

Antony is turned 'iconographically into a woman' through 'a discursive interplay between blemish, blushing ... shame' and 'leaking'.[57] Antony becomes the female sacrificial victim needed by Octavius's male, white narrative of empire, not unlike the abandoned Dido, the raped Lucrece and the penetrated Julius Caesar. According to Little, Antony's lost *romanitas* resonates with early modern English preoccupations about Ireland. Just as Antony needs to be cast off from Rome's imperial narrative, so did England feel that the 'wild Irish' had to be abjected, so that 'the symbolic and tangible act of cutting the primitive out of a newfound national and imperial civility' could be performed.[58] It is Octavius who embodies this new civility by chastising his own body in order to provide 'the definitive and evidentiary proof of a formidable and stable Roman imperium'.[59] Yet Antony's death 'at the feet of his black queen ... as a violated woman and a penetrated man' ends up betraying 'the inauthenticity of Roman nostalgia', which is exposed as 'very much mired in the political present'.[60]

Twenty-first-century concerns impinge upon Paul A. Cantor's suggestion that the play explores 'the connection between empire and what we now call globalization'.[61] *Antony and Cleopatra* develops the imperial 'urge to demolish existing borders and create one world', a desire for universality and infinite horizons that marks the empire's difference from the 'self-contained' world of the republic.[62] Even more interestingly, the play foregrounds that 'military power does not simply translate into cultural power', in that even though 'Roman religion has ... begun to permeate Egyptian society', the Romans actually seem to be more deeply affected by the encounter, in that their firmly masculine 'Roman identity is shaken as they become open to foreign influences'.[63]

The clash between the two cultures is also analysed by Richmond Barbour, who believes that the play's representation of 'the East as a place of debilitating excess speaks ... to the concerns of London's investors' in the Asiatic markets, in so far as in Antony's 'neglect of Roman designs, shareholders could have seen a pattern for the indifference of remote employees to

London's will'.[64] In addition, Shakespeare seems to impute to Cleopatra 'the vivid, changeful marginality of the Globe', so that the dangers embodied by Egypt look akin to 'those that Puritans find in theatre: it volatilizes gender, destabilizes personal and social identities, and confuses patriarchal agendas'.[65] Anxieties about commerce with the East are also crucial to the essay by Arthur Lindley, who identifies in the play 'A process of ironic marginalization of embarrassingly monetary val[u]es'.[66] In contrast to usual readings of the difference between Rome and Egypt as one between 'business and pleasure', Lindley argues that said difference is actually predicated on a contrast 'between two different kinds of business', as 'One society trades in honor and hoarded treasure, the other "trade[s] in love"'.[67] More specifically, 'Cleopatra embodies the vitality of the open market, Octavius the principle of monopoly.'[68] This conflict is reflected in the two societies' antithetical approach to change: while 'Egypt is immersed in mutability', Octavius aspires to defeat time 'by imposing the illusion of changeless stability'.[69]

Andrew Hiscock joins Lindley in remarking that Octavius 'wishes to triumph over time', even though, in Hiscock's view, Octavius does so 'through the manipulation of the textual remains of the past' also in order 'to re-create history and to delimit its meaning'.[70] Through staging 'captivity-as-performance for Cleopatra', Octavius would like 'not only to repress, conceal and censure' opposition but also 'to re-present the Egyptian queen ceremonially as mistress of politically and erotically deviant space'.[71] Yet the play highlights 'the protagonists' ability to affirm alternative and unexpected value-systems which may coexist and contradict prevailing ideological assumptions', as is the case with Cleopatra, who 'is not only able to disrupt narratives of historical progress and male heroism so reassuring to Rome, but also to question and to reconfigure ... fragments of the imperial past'.[72]

Octavius's urge to possess time and 'to control the history of events as much as the events themselves' is also discussed by William Junker, who argues that *Antony and Cleopatra* 'posits a conceptual and temporal fissure between the successful exercise of military power and the actualization of political imperium' by showing that the former is insufficient for the perfect attainment of the latter.[73] This fissure 'is bridged by the triumph', which displays the 'past within the present time of its performance', thereby generating 'the paradigm of imperium's own temporality', i.e. 'an ongoing present that is performed as the meaning of the past'.[74] Yet through her suicide Cleopatra deprives Caesar's imperium of the 'means of actualizing what as yet remains only its potentially eternal present', which suggests the possibility of a different future.[75]

Politics

The importance of triumphs is also stressed by Anthony Miller, whose reading is one among a number of critical takes focusing on various political and topical issues raised by the play. Miller argues that in *Antony and Cleopatra* 'the classical military triumph has receded into naive dream', as demonstrated by how 'Cleopatra succeeds, imaginatively if not actually, in outdoing or thwarting Rome's own triumphs' through both 'her manifestation on the river Cydnus' – nothing short of 'a *naualis triumphus*, like the ones imagined for Elizabeth by the Armada poets' – and her suicide, which 're-enact[s] the splendid display of Cydnus' and makes Caesar's triumph appear hollow.[76] In 'reintroduc[ing] the transgressive figure of the female *triumphator*, and admiringly recall[ing] the audacious heroism of Elizabeth and her victories', the play seems to convey scepticism about using 'the *pax augustana* [as] the model for James's pacific triumphalism'.[77]

That the play carries some message for the king – in this case concerning 'the protocols and psychological cost of the political merger between England and Scotland' – is also apparent to Lisa Hopkins, who fascinatingly argues that *Antony and Cleopatra* 'sneakily incriminates Scotland' while 'covertly and subtly embarrassing' James by foregrounding the idea of gypsies, who 'were both disreputable and ... associated with Scotland'.[78] In order to disparage the Scots, 'Shakespeare also draws on images of Irishness and of freemasonry, both of which were associated with Scotland and the lower classes and, like gypsies, thought to have their origins in Egypt.'[79] At the same time, however, Shakespeare seeks 'to recuperate a suitably inspiring form of Englishness' by drawing upon the 'well-established tradition of associating Cleopatra with Elizabeth I, particularly in terms of opposing the biblical mode of allusion, which was frequently used to characterize Elizabeth I, against the classical mode [commonly] identified with Scotland'.[80]

Barbara L. Parker shows that when considered in historical order Shakespeare's Roman works can be seen to chronicle the constitutional decline of a state from monarchy to tyranny as illustrated in Plato's *Republic*: *Lucrece* (abolition of monarchy), *Coriolanus* (oligarchy), *Julius Caesar* (transition to tyranny), *Antony and Cleopatra* (final stage of tyranny). Admittedly, Michael Platt had advanced a similar reading of Shakespeare's Roman plays as mapping out the rise and fall of the republic in 1976.[81] However, Parker's contribution is notable in her claim that a concept of tyranny 'closely adhere[nt] to that articulated by Plato' informs the play, which does not celebrate 'the ennobling power of love', instead portraying 'the perverse love, rooted in vitiated reason, that dooms the state': if Antony is 'Plato's quintessential tyrannic man', Cleopatra is 'the personification of Eros'.[82] Sadly, not even Caesar is 'fit to govern' because he too pursues 'power for self-gratification and ... personal gain', while ignoring 'the legitimate concerns of rulership'.[83] Thus, the play 'hints strongly at topical concerns', as all three rulers, and not just Caesar, figure James, with Antony and Cleopatra embodying the king's 'infamous licentiousness', 'decadence' and 'neglect of statecraft'.[84]

The exchange between Pompey and Menas on the boat raises in Andrew Hadfield's view 'the familiar dilemma of the assassination of the tyrant central to resistance theory as well as republicanism'.⁸⁵ The dialogue is especially noteworthy in showing that rather than having qualms about the rightfulness of the action Pompey is simply worried about being publicly associated with the proposed murder. Rooted as it is 'in a comprehension of public appearance [and] not ethical behaviour', the code of 'honour' Pompey refers to would have 'reminded the audience of the dying cult of honour of their own aristocracy'.⁸⁶ Pompey's 'stated ideals' suggest that, even if he had had the triumvirs killed, 'he would undoubtedly have been no better than' them; the play accordingly seems to indicate that 'the ideals of the republic have ... become more perverted than they had in *Julius Caesar*, when there was at least some form of commitment to the restoration of liberty'.⁸⁷

Ethics, Gender, Hermeneutics and Genre

In a broader discussion of Shakespeare's development of 'his sense of the limitation of the moral perspective' as his career proceeded, Richard Strier observes that whereas Antony's passion is viewed as insanity because of its excessiveness, it is precisely this overflowing of the measure – as celebrated in his hyperbolic statement 'Then thou must needs find out new heaven, new earth' (1.1.17) – that seems to suggest that paradoxically 'a morally debased character like Antony has access to spiritual wisdom'.⁸⁸ The motif of how 'seemingly negative phenomena, especially passions' suit 'special individuals, and [are] part of what makes them special, is repeated and emphatic' in the play, suggesting both that 'through personal charisma' defect becomes perfection and that 'aesthetics trumps, transcends, and confounds the moral'.⁸⁹ Such a reading is also borne out by Antony and Cleopatra's being, with Falstaff, 'the only characters in Shakespeare for whom a happy postmortem existence is evoked', whereby the

Octavius's writings, which should impose his narrative of what has happened over the losers', 'is superseded by the call to see the queen', so that 'the play ends not ... with the viewing of his letters, but ... inside Cleopatra's monument'.[103] Antony is 'torn between these two cultures', and his 'decline from Roman etiquette' is displayed in his decision to send on an embassy to Octavius the Schoolmaster, who turns out to be 'shockingly incompetent, presenting a verbal petition and then immediately ... assuming it will not be granted'.[104]

Such a reading is at loggerheads with Carol Chillington Rutter's view that the Schoolmaster's speech 'is a perfect textbook display of ambassadorial competence', as he is 'properly impassive' and 'makes no answer to Caesar's diplomatic blanking of his master ... nor to the treacherous bargain he conditionally proposes as Cleopatra's ransom'.[105] Rutter reads the Schoolmaster's and Thidias's embassies against early modern theorizations of diplomacy as spelled out in Alberico Gentili's *De legationibus libri tres* (1585) and Jean Hotman's *The Ambassador* (1603). Ambassadors could be seen as 'angels' when lawfully performing as mouthpieces for their sovereign, or as 'pimps' when sent undercover as spies. While the 'Schoolmaster-turned-ambassador has acted the angel', something 'different happens in the reciprocal mission' of Thidias, whom Caesar instructs to corrupt Cleopatra and spy on Antony, i.e. 'to play the pimp'.[106] Hence, when Antony attacks Thidias, although he 'is violating the law of nations', his behaviour might in fact find justification in contemporary texts because Thidias is violating the public faith.[107]

A final angle on messengers is offered by Lloyd Davis, Peter J. Smith and Greg Walker, for whom the fabrication of the plot intrigue used in *Antony and Cleopatra* derives 'from the circulation of news and gossip via a series of more or less reliable messengers'.[108] The protagonists' contrasting deployment of messengers and ambassadors opens a window on 'their own differing political priorities', in that whereas 'Caesar shrewdly uses messengers to gather intelligence', Cleopatra 'uses them as public gestures' and as 'another mode of extravagant display'.[109]

Food

Another question a few recent critics of the play have taken up is that of food. Peter A. Parolin investigates Shakespeare's exploitation of early modern attitudes towards food and its creative potential as a way 'to define characters', 'to structure the play's political conflict and to suggest competing ideas about what constitutes value'.[110] Although for the Romans 'Antony and Cleopatra's sumptuous feasting [i]s a decadent pursuit that demonstrates their unfitness to rule', they do manage to create 'a desirable alternative to Caesar's grim vision of political gain through self-denial' and his 'monolithic imperial narrative'.[111] They do so by consistently deploying food 'as a means of conspicuous consumption meant' to 'construct images of themselves as powerful, generous, larger-than-life figures' in order 'to ensure the loyalty of their followers'.[112] In suggesting 'that pleasure, consumption, and the exchange of food and drink' are 'legitimate tools for the construction' and not just the demolition of personal identities and relationships as well as 'of political and social meaning', the play seems to echo 'the rhetoric of [early modern] cookbook authors, who claimed an artistic power to refashion the world through their culinary skills'.[113]

Concentrating on the use of the verbs 'discandy' and 'discandying' – exclusive to *Antony and Cleopatra* in the history of the English language – Jennifer Park argues that Shakespeare engages with an ancient tradition interested in food preservation that was 'embodied by the figure of Cleopatra as a medical, gynaecological, and alchemical authority' emerging from the so-called *Book of Cleopatra*, which early moderns believed had been written by the Egyptian queen herself.[114] For Park, 'Cleopatra provides a model and an embodiment of preservation that withstands or subverts Roman ideas of permanence' by dint of its being 'both dynamic and organic'.[115] Cleopatra's preservative process, which paradoxically embodies 'longevity and eternal freshness' at the same time, enables her to resist the Romans' attempts at incorporation.[116]

Apocalypse

Apocalyptic allusions are the focus of a couple of provocative accounts of the play. Grounding Antony's 'new heaven, new earth' reference to the Book of Revelation in the early seventeenth-century cosmological revolution, Gilberto Sacerdoti sees the play as influenced by Giordano Bruno, in particular one of his *Dialogues* (1584), *De l'infinito universo*, which describes a new infinite universe that has the same characteristics as the one referred to by Antony and must have been created by a god who is 'inside nature, and not outside or above it'.[117] The recurrence of the idea of overflowing the measure would therefore seem to draw upon Bruno, inasmuch as 'at the centre of the new, infinite universe' of the play there exists 'a core of infinite heat and lustful creative energy that goes on flowing and overflowing, endlessly regenerating itself and producing from within all the infinite variety of the universal life'.[118]

Within an ampler discussion of the 'rise of Presentism as ... achieved by glossing over' the notion that 'the historical contexts of an early modern text are paradoxically "inconceivable"', Adrian Streete considers how the deployment of apocalyptic imagery throughout *Antony and Cleopatra* exemplifies 'the potential for the past to radically disrupt the ethical focus of the present', thereby demonstrating that early modern texts 'are much less fixed in their historicity than Presentism often suspects' and that 'the present and the future are no less ideologically and politically determined than the past'.[119] This is apparent in how Cleopatra's 'quot[ing] from the book of Revelation which she could never have known' proves her to be 'an ideological product of an early modern culture that sees apocalypse as imminent', since 'For many men and women in

1607, antichrist was present and identifiable as was the belief that soon enough, Christ would come again to judge the quick and the dead.'[120]

Conclusion

As this overview should have made evident, although early twenty-first-century criticism of *Antony and Cleopatra* may not have contributed to finding either new heaven or new earth, as it were, it has nonetheless undoubtedly managed to challenge conventional wisdom about quite a wide range of central issues informing the play. The most innovative attempts at unravelling the complexities of *Antony and Cleopatra* can be identified in a fresh interest in analysing the depiction and role of emotions in the play through the critical tools provided by recent contributions in the subfields of the history of emotions and animal studies side by side with more traditional psychoanalytical instruments; in the attention to the deployment of food as a central element in the structuring of the political conflicts informing the play; and in the widespread critical concern with Octavius's desire to control space and subjugate time not only in the present but especially as regards the past and the future through his calculated use of the triumph and his tendentious shaping of the historical record.

Many of the most insightful discussions have focused on race, empire and commerce, thereby further exposing to what extent the play effectively spoke to contemporary English concerns with the disturbing fluidity of masculinity and racial identity, and the resulting dangers of manipulating these. Early modern English philosophical and commercial anxieties have also been substantially illuminated, while a simple opposition between Antony and Octavius based on a straightforward loser/winner dichotomy has been interestingly called into question.

A sustained effort to look at the play in comparison with how sixteenth-century French and English neo-Senecan drama treated the story of Antony and Cleopatra ranks among the most frequently trodden critical paths, shedding light on a dazzling array of such diverse issues as the appropriation of theatricality in the construction, mediation and representation of sovereign power; Shakespeare's Cleopatra's unique lack of soliloquies among other dramatic depictions of her; the more pronounced eroticism of Shakespeare's rendition; the innovative portrayal of luxury as inhabiting an aesthetic-political rather than a more traditionally moral-religious dimension; and the depiction of race as serving in the capacity of some sort of disposable theatrical property for Cleopatra.

Finally, a further critical avenue that looks particularly noteworthy is the apparently ever-increasing attention to the play's grappling with the mechanisms of gender hierarchy and their ethical and socio-political implications, especially as concerns the tension between the private and the public spheres, as well as the conflict between individual aspirations and the requirements of society. Such an invigorating abundance of engrossing, exciting and thought-provoking readings cannot but make the critical future of the play look as promising as ever.

4

New Directions After Decorum: Self-Performance and Political Liminality in *Antony and Cleopatra*

Curtis Perry

Antony and Cleopatra explores the problem of consistent self-performance in a time of political transition. The play's Antony, of course, is torn between competing versions of what it means to act 'like himself' (2.2.4).[1] And even when characters carry themselves with more certainty, the play tends to foreground the gap between self-performance and the way public personas are mediated and shaped by report or propaganda. As Janet Adelman put it, audiences and readers of the play are 'forced to notice the world's view' of the main characters 'more often than their view of the world'.[2] The final contest between Caesar (the future Augustus) and Cleopatra over the meaning of the heroes' exemplary lives renders overt a set of concerns that in one way or another have been at the heart of the play all along: what does it mean to act like oneself? How does the meaning of an exemplary life become fixed? How does political power shape the process? What is the relationship between the performance of self and its always-mediated consumption by readers or spectators?

Such questions might seem in some ways to be quintessentially Roman ones, at least for an early Jacobean writer. Roman literature and history provided an essential repertoire of exemplary figures and stories for Shakespeare and his contemporaries, and the culture's thinking about exemplarity included a set of destabilizing questions about self-performance, imitation and the mediation of meaning via historical report.[3] And yet *Antony and Cleopatra* also seems disconcertingly more experimental in its treatment of exemplarity than Shakespeare's earlier staging of larger-than-life Roman figures in *Julius Caesar*. One is left to wonder if it is still even a Roman play in the way the earlier play was: Sarah Hatchuel has suggested that *Antony and Cleopatra* might be thought of as a 'postmodern sequel' to *Julius Caesar*, in the sense that while the historical story it tells follows relatively closely upon the events dramatized in the earlier play, *Antony and Cleopatra* seems to double back upon and to problematize or complicate ideas associated with Rome in the earlier play.[4]

I like this formulation because it clarifies for me an ambivalence characteristic of the critical tradition that *Antony and Cleopatra* has engendered – between those who treat it first and foremost as a Roman play and those who focus upon its postmodern-seeming treatment of the story it happens to take up. To be sure, the play has received considerable attention from scholars interested in Shakespeare's investment in the cultural legacy and exemplarity of Rome. This has been true at least since Paul A. Cantor's 1976 study of *Shakespeare's Rome: Republic and Empire*, which found in *Antony and Cleopatra* Shakespeare's evocation of an imperial Rome much changed from its prior republican essence.[5] But *Antony and Cleopatra* – with its sceptical take on political propaganda, its utter demolition of anything resembling unities, its interest in race, alterity and empire, its obsession with the perspectival ironies of self-performance and its pervasive sense of belated nostalgia vis-à-vis an older idea of heroic masculine virtue – has often seemed to critics to be using its Roman material in such a highly idiosyncratic manner as to be more centrally about Shakespeare's formal experimentalism and his early modern scepticism about heroism and empire than about Rome per se. Following in the tradition of path-breaking critics such as Adelman and Linda Charnes, it has been possible to think of the play's metadramatic, postmodern-seeming interest in ironies associated with self-performance as representing Shakespeare's characteristically sophisticated take on Roman exemplarity, written from a self-consciously belated and specifically early modern point of view.[6]

Here, I want to argue for a tighter and more integral connection between the play's overtly experimental depiction of its exemplary heroes and the Roman history that it takes up. That is to say: I want to suggest that the play's experimental qualities are designed to capture Shakespeare's understanding of triumviral Rome as a specifically liminal period in between the fall of the republic and the establishment of the principate under Augustus, one in which the nature of Rome, and thus of Roman identity and self-performance, is up for grabs and uncertain. Shakespearians tend to think of the triumviral period as depicted in the play either as a continuation of the death throes of the republic (in which case *Antony and Cleopatra* is a sequel to *Julius Caesar*) or (with Cantor) as already representative of empire. But the period depicted in the play might be better understood as characterized by an utter uncertainty about the nature of the polity and thus about what Rome or *romanitas* might be: it is a period of deep institutional instability, in which all that was clear was that 'history and politics had changed and were changing still'.[7] *Antony and Cleopatra*, in so far as it is about Rome, is about this specific period's real uncertainty concerning the nature of Romanness, and the play's experiments in staging and characterization, I will suggest, are conducted to dramatize this unique, transitional moment of Roman history. In the triumviral period, one might say, Rome is something like a postmodern sequel unto itself.

As will become clear, however, I am not proposing that Shakespeare was an especially dedicated Roman historian or that he knew more about the ins and outs of Roman political life than he could have intuited from familiarity with well-known authors such as Plutarch and Cicero. I am proposing, though, that Shakespeare thought of *romanitas* in its different historical eras as being bound up with Ciceronian questions concerning the theatricality of decorous self-presentation.[8] And also that *Antony and Cleopatra* stages a post-republican crisis that resolves itself, in Act 5, into a new style of self-performance associated with the power relations of the principate. Part of what is at stake for me here is a desire to rethink aspects of the play that seem sophisticated and modern in terms of robust engagement with the historical and literary material that Shakespeare read rather than just as the product of his own special genius. If we think about *Antony and Cleopatra* only as Shakespeare's modern critique of Roman exemplarity, then we run the risk of treating the Roman material that the play takes up as inert and neutral, something dead that Shakespeare seizes upon and turns inside out for his own purposes. To do so, I believe, is to mischaracterize the nature of Shakespeare's complex and vibrant engagement with the exemplarity of Rome.[9]

The contrast between *Julius Caesar* and *Antony and Cleopatra* can be illuminating for thinking about the dramatic affordances of Roman history. Take, for example, the famous moment, near the beginning of the earlier play, in which Cassius recruits Brutus to his cause by offering to serve as his mirror:

CASSIUS
    Tell me, good Brutus, can you see your face?
BRUTUS
    No, Cassius; for the eye sees not itself
    But by reflection, by some other things.

CASSIUS   'Tis just,
    And it is very much lamented, Brutus,
    That you have no such mirrors as will turn
    Your hidden worthiness into your eye,
    That you might see your shadow: I have heard
    Where many of the best respect in Rome
    (Except immortal Caesar) speaking of Brutus,
    And groaning underneath this age's yoke,
    Have wished that noble Brutus had his eyes.
BRUTUS
    Into what dangers would you lead me, Cassius,
    That you would have me seek into myself
    For that which is not in me?
CASSIUS
    Therefore, good Brutus, be prepared to hear.
    And since you know you cannot see yourself
    So well as by reflection, I your glass
    Will modestly discover to yourself
    That of yourself which you yet know not of.
                                    (*JC*, 1.2.51–70)[10]

This episode might be taken to intimate that Roman honour is a hall of mirrors, and in that way it might be seen to anticipate *Antony and Cleopatra*, where report and representation are so often prioritized over authenticity. But I think it is closer to the truth to say that Cassius, in this exchange, speaks from a conventional, late-republican attitude towards public self-performance and decorum associated (for Shakespeare and his contemporaries) with Cicero. I'm thinking here of *De officiis*, which has been described as being 'second only to the Bible as a source of moral wisdom' for Elizabethans, and also of Shadi Bartsch's description of late-republican specular politics from her wonderful 2006 book *The Mirror of the Self*.[11] Bartsch treats Roman elite identity in the era of Cicero as being anchored in a culture of reciprocal public viewing such that theatrical language of public self-performance specifically does not imply inauthenticity or that some other, truer inner self is being covered up.[12] This is implicit in *De officiis*, where (in Nicholas Grimald's Elizabethan translation) the inner quality of 'honesty' cannot be separated from the legible external signs of 'comeliness', and where others' lives can and should be treated as 'our glass'.[13] In *De re publica*, Cicero has Scipio describe the ideal statesman as a man whose duties comprise 'improving and examining himself, urging others to imitate him, and furnishing in himself, as it were, a mirror to his fellow-citizens by reason of the supreme excellence of his life and character'.[14] Cassius here says to Brutus, in effect, that he has a public duty that should rightly be thought of as part of his authentic persona, and that in order to adhere to this duty he should take cues for self-performance from the elite community that serves as his glass and witness.

The irony of the exchange between Cassius and Brutus, in *Julius Caesar*, is that they are conspirators and have to act in secret (hence the frame of 'hidden worthiness' in Cassius's conceit). Republican Roman decorum as conceived of in Cicero is predicated upon a coherent elite collectivity of values, and that is precisely what falls apart in the first half of Shakespeare's play. Cassius, by offering to be Brutus's mirror, is offering to recreate for him the specular conditions of elite republican Roman identity in an environment where that is no longer really possible. This is precisely why Cassius's approach is appealing, why it works on Brutus as a mode of recruitment. Brutus, as a highly visible and conspicuously honourable Roman, yearns for the kind of public mirroring that constitutes the milieu of republican decorum; Cassius offers to play the role of stand-in for this milieu, thereby creating a simulacrum of the public approbation that men like Brutus are conditioned to pursue.

Mirroring gazes in *Antony and Cleopatra* work differently, particularly where they occur between the Roman Antony and the Egyptian Cleopatra. Situated outside of any masculine, Roman community of mutual regard they instead demarcate the lovers' potentially solipsistic isolation from the rest of the world. This is what happens, for instance, when Cleopatra reminisces about being face to face with Antony at a time when 'eternity' was in their 'lips and eyes' (1.3.36). Right from the play's famous opening tableau, it is made clear that *Antony and Cleopatra* will operate according to a resolutely post-republican or post-Ciceronian specular logic of self-presentation. As the play opens, Philo and Demetrius are present to 'behold and see' (1.1.13) Antony's very different kind of looking:

> Those his goodly eyes,
> That o'er the files and musters of the war
> Have glowed like plated Mars, now bend, now turn
> The office and devotion of their view
> Upon a tawny front.
>
> (1.1.2–6)

The old idea that Roman identity might rest upon reciprocal mirroring among peers is completely done away with. Antony and Cleopatra (as so often in the play) are now treated as a spectacle set apart to be gazed upon. And, of course, Antony's gaze now refuses to confine itself to the Roman; instead of reinforcing Romanness, Antony, looking upon Cleopatra's tawny front, practises a kind of specular miscegenation. To the Roman viewers, this renders him pliable, distracts him from noble Roman rectitude. But even the rather weird image of Antony's 'goodly eyes' as having previously 'glowed' over his army seems to treat godlike inhumanity as the definitive quality of the noble Roman rather than imagining stature in terms of mirrored reciprocity among peers.[15] The internal logic of Philo's account would seem to suggest that older, republican ideas about decorum had already given way to something more isolating or autocratic before Antony turned his wandering eyes upon Cleopatra. So perhaps we can already intuit, in the play's inaugural moments, that Antony's bending away from Roman virtue is a symptom rather than a cause of the play's Roman identity crisis?

Antony and Cleopatra is obsessed with spectacle, of course: the wonderful spectacle of Cleopatra on the barge at Cydnus; the scandalous spectacle of Antony enthroned with Cleopatra in 'the public eye' (3.6.11); the promised spectacle of Caesar's eventual triumphs, which both Antony and Cleopatra are so keen to avoid, and so on.[16] But spectacles in the play – as they are reported, gossiped about, interpreted, used for propaganda and so on – are often elusive, hard to get a fix on, open to interpretation. This is because the social circulation in which their meaning is discussed happens perforce outside of the kind of stable interpretative community upon which a Ciceronian idea of decorum is based. Containment within a stable and reciprocally validating interpretative community is a precondition for Ciceronian decorum – for the successful performance of elite republican identity – and so the demolition of the republic creates a crisis of Roman elite identity as well. Hence the play's emphasis upon the conflict that takes place (as Charnes put it) across 'the terrain of Antony's identity'; hence too Antony's own experience of this conflict as an inability to 'hold' any one 'visible shape' (4.14.14).[17] Geoffrey Miles, who reads *Julius Caesar* and *Antony and Cleopatra* as contrasting explorations of the paradigmatic Roman virtue of constancy, argues that the heroes of the latter play 'redefine decorum by emptying it of its Ciceronian and Roman associations with constancy'.[18] I would reframe this point by suggesting that they have no choice: when we look at the matter from the vantage point of *Antony and Cleopatra*, we can see that Ciceronian decorum is a republican ideology, one that loses coherence after the republic has come undone. The question *Antony and Cleopatra* takes up is this: what can a heroic or larger-than-life identity mean in a Roman play after the social conditions enabling Ciceronian decorum have fallen away?

Miles also points out that Grimald, in his translation of *De officiis*, translates decorousness as 'becoming', which is an oft-repeated keyword in *Antony and Cleopatra*. Grimald's Cicero opines, for instance, that 'both what becommeth, is honest, and also what is honest, becommeth'.[19] In *Antony and Cleopatra*, to give just two of several instances, Enobarbus tells us that 'the vilest things / Become themselves' in Cleopatra (2.2.248–9), and Caesar asks Thidias to 'observe how Antony becomes his flaw' (3.12.34). At such moments, Shakespeare exploits the keyword's semantic slipperiness in order to underscore the difference between the world of *Antony and Cleopatra* and the Roman world that *De officiis* presumes to inhabit. The point is not just that anything might be becoming in this new world but that anyone might become anything. In such a world, what can self-performance as Roman mean? In Act 1, Cleopatra excuses herself to the departing Antony as follows: 'But, sir, forgive me, / Since my becomings kill me when they do not / Eye well to you. Your honour calls you hence' (1.3.97–9). I hear this as an instance of Cleopatra's teasing mimicry of Roman honour: she is using the language of decorum as a specular correlative to virtuous action in a parodic manner in order to excuse her own efforts to seduce Antony away from becoming a becoming Roman again.

Compared to that of *Julius Caesar*, the Rome of *Antony and Cleopatra* seems more like an idea than a place. As Robert S. Miola puts it, the latter play's Rome is no longer 'a city of definite dimensions and familiar landscapes, but an Empire that spans vast spaces'.[20] It has proven tempting, therefore, to think of *Antony and Cleopatra* as being about a distinctly imperial version of Rome rather than about the collapsing republic of *Julius Caesar*. And certainly this is accurate, at least in so far as the term 'imperial' names the condition of ruling far-flung territories, rather than the other sense, that of being ruled by an emperor. It is a truism of the critical tradition around *Antony and Cleopatra* – one that is spun in different ways by many of the readings that I most admire – that the play both establishes a binary between Rome and Egypt and then deconstructs that binary.[21] Like the play's Antony, the play's Rome is in danger of becoming enthralled with the outlandish.[22] In this regard, the play might be said to instantiate a very familiar colonialist anxiety about contamination by contact with the conquered Other.[23] This is a common enough idea in classical literatures, though it is not an especially prominent feature in Plutarch's *Life of Antony*.[24] Plutarch's Antony is generous; lacking in self-discipline; and overly susceptible to the allure of women, revelry and feasting long before his fateful meeting with Cleopatra, and there is no sense that his fundamental character undergoes significant changes as a result of living in Egypt or going native.[25] In other words, the Egyptian setting is inherent in Shakespeare's Plutarchan source material but not the play's deconstructive attitude towards global Romanness, which I would imagine Shakespeare derived from a range of influences including his own attitudes and experiences as a denizen of an increasingly global early modern London. As Ania Loomba puts it, 'Antony's fatal attraction to Cleopatra speaks to contemporary English fears about the erosion of racial identity and masculinity.'[26]

But of course Rome was an empire – again, in the sense of having far-flung networks of military conquest and colonial dependencies – long before the events depicted in *Julius Caesar*. In *De officiis*, Cicero relates the decline of the republic to a change for the worse (2.26–7) in the quality of Rome's caretaking of its conquered dependencies, and in his *Verrine Orations* he accuses the corrupt Roman governor of Sicily of a series of crimes that might be said to prefigure Antony's. Cicero's Verres – a corrupt governor of Sicily, one who represents for Cicero the malign potential of late republican empire – wastes his time and money on 'dinner parties and women' (2.5.32). Instead of attending to his duties as a Roman governor, he simultaneously goes native and is rendered effeminate: Cicero depicts him 'in slippers, wearing a purple Greek cloak and long-skirted tunic, and leaning on one of his women' (2.5.33).[27]

But there is little sense in Cicero that Rome's entanglement with a world of foreigners changed the essential character of Romanness in any way. John Richardson notes how insular Cicero's notions of Us and Them remain, despite the expansion of Rome's political and military influence. And C. E. W. Steel – who mines Cicero's oratory to understand late republican attitudes towards empire – likewise emphasizes Cicero's unwillingness to think of corruption in Rome's administration of its far-flung dependencies in structural terms or as implying any transformation in what Rome is.[28] Verres's corruption, Steel argues, is given as being symptomatic of one man's bad character, not of any larger existential threat that Rome might face via imperial contact. Temptations associated with empire, in Cicero, explain why Romans might fail to maintain the ideals of Romanness, but there is no sense that the fundamental ideals themselves are thought of as being compromised or altered by contact with foreign dependants. Cicero's thinking is inhospitable to the idea (so central to *Antony and Cleopatra*) that running a global empire entails a threat to the essential character of Roman identity, or that the story of imperial expansion might become the story of dissolution or of the contamination of the centre.

The key point here is to notice how closely Ciceronian ideas about decorum are tied up with insular and reciprocally self-reinforcing notions of Romanness. Though Cicero in *De officiis* enjoins his readers not to do anything that violates norms associated with common humanity, civic duty is the highest priority, and decorous self-performance is anchored to the ability to adhere to a civically sanctioned role. Decorum – an ideal tied closely to membership in a specific community in a specific place – acts as a container for Roman identity. What *Antony and Cleopatra* does, with its sprawling geography, its complicated specular logics and its deconstructive playfulness about Roman virtue, is show what happens after that containment has been compromised.

Decorum, as Cicero thinks of it, involves the authentic performance of one's public role, which in turn entails the suppression or management of such impulses as are motivated by bodily pleasure. Men who are somewhat 'uprightlye minded' but still inclined to pleasure, Cicero writes, will tend to hide and dissemble their desires 'for verie shamefastnesse'. This proves that the pleasure of the body 'ought to be despised, and rejected'.[29] Cicero's point is not to recommend the kind of extreme or heroic abstemiousness that Caesar associates with his memory of Antony after the defeat at Modena (1.5.56–72) but rather to say that all men may have an inclination to pleasure and that Roman peer pressure helps discourage this inclination. It is therefore becoming for a man to be cautious and measured in the enjoyment of bodily pleasures.

The Rome of *Antony and Cleopatra*, by contrast, is shown to be structured by a pervasive economy of lack and desire:

> It hath been taught us from the primal state
> That he which is was wished until he were,
> And the ebbed man, ne'er loved till ne'er worth love,
> Comes deared by being lacked. This common body,
> Like to a vagabond flag upon the stream,
> Goes to and back, lackeying the varying tide,
> To rot itself with motion.
>
> (1.4.41–7)

Caesar here treats the pursuit of what is lacked as a permanent feature of the political life of the Roman state, but he also assumes that such undisciplined desire is inherent only to commoners, as though the Roman elite, chastened by 'shamefastnesse' and so acculturated to decorum, might be able to approach politics in a more rational manner. But Antony, meditating on the irony of his feelings about Fulvia, shows that the structure of desire Caesar decries is not only characteristic of the undisciplined Roman mob:

> There's a great spirit gone! Thus did I desire it.
> What our contempts doth often hurl from us
> We wish it ours again. The present pleasure,
> By revolution lowering, does become
> The opposite of itself. She's good, being gone.
> The hand could pluck her back that shoved her on.
> I must from this enchanting queen break off.
>
> (1.2.129–35)

What is at stake for Antony here has everything to do with the question of decorous self-performance since his changing evaluation of Fulvia is the catalyst for a renewed effort at the performance of Roman duty. And of course the nature of such desire is given as fundamentally unstable since everyone in the play knows that Antony will return to Cleopatra.

This structure of desire may be treated dismissively by Caesar – as merely that which has always made mobs fickle – but it is also in some sense imperial, at least when experienced by elite Romans who are empowered to seek out whatever they do not already possess. Cicero laments the glory of the lost republic as a time when Rome was 'the protection more truelie, than the empire of the world', a magnanimity enabled by the fact that 'our magistrates, and capteins' desired above all 'to gette greate praise' for their treatment of dependants and provinces.[30] Cicero does not emphasize this, but the loss of the republic, as an interpretative community determining what is decorous or praiseworthy, makes it less feasible to imagine governance of empire as the pursuit of peer approbation. What we see in *Antony and Cleopatra* is the restlessness of Roman desires after they have been cut adrift from republican ideas about what is becoming, desires that must tend instead to be easily bored and endlessly acquisitive. Since Cleopatra both performs variety for Romans and functions as a screen onto which Romans project infinite variety, one might say that she is given in Shakespeare's play as the perfect object of imperial desire: one who is never sufficiently pinned down to become the object of what Antony calls 'contempt'.

One of the most striking features of *Antony and Cleopatra* is the apparent disjunction, in terms of dramatic form and characterization, between the body of the play and its finale. In one sense, Shakespeare follows Plutarch's *Life of Antony*, which is unusual among Plutarch's lives for the degree to which it sticks with Cleopatra's story even after the death of its ostensible subject.[31] But in Shakespeare's play, the last episodes with Cleopatra also seem to represent a shift in dramatic style. The global sprawl characteristic of most of the play is compressed and focused into the space of Cleopatra's monument, and the play's tendency to treat its main characters as objects of observation and speculation is replaced in the end by the scene of Cleopatra's highly deliberate self-performance. Cleopatra's scene-stealing conclusion has been understood in a range of different ways: as part of 'the sleight of hand by which Shakespeare transforms our sympathies towards the lovers', for example; as the apotheosis of Cleopatra as a representative figure for theatrical practice as such; as a reclamation of political agency through theatrical self-performance; or as an instance of colonial mimicry whereby Cleopatra wilfully and subversively misappropriates the self-determining rhetoric of a 'marble-constant' Roman (5.2.239).[32] Part of what is suggestive to me, though, is the fact that this shift in the play's treatment of Cleopatra's self-presentation corresponds to the moment at which the liminal, triumviral period of Roman history comes to an end after Caesar's victory at Actium and its immediate aftermath. Shakespeare is of course aware of this as a watershed moment in world history – the beginning of the reign of Augustus, the dawning of the *pax romana*, the 'time of universal peace' (4.6.5) – and it is as if this epoch-making shift in the power structure of Rome corresponds to a change in the representational conventions governing the play.

Within the play's political narrative, Caesar's elaborate promises of clemency towards Cleopatra encode the new power relations, and Cleopatra's final performance likewise emblematizes a new political reality. Clemency, of course, is the paradigmatic imperial virtue, celebrated as such in Seneca's influential essay *De clementia*, which was written for Nero in 55–56 CE.[33] Though acts of clemency towards conquered peoples had been seen as praiseworthy long before the time of Julius Caesar or Augustus, Leah Whittington has described a culture of suspicion concerning supplication and clemency within Roman society in the late republican period. Clemency was seen as a 'monarchical virtue' and thus as potentially humiliating to Romans and as incompatible with republican elite egalitarianism.[34] When Proculeius visits Cleopatra on Caesar's behalf, his purpose is specifically to ensure that Cleopatra understands the new political dispensation, and to remind her that she is 'fallen into a princely hand' (5.2.22). Caesar is eager to 'let the world see / His nobleness well acted' (5.2.43–4) because to do so enacts and bodies forth a new, top-down model of power and authority in which he is the sole, quasi-divine source of beneficence. 'Make your full reference freely to my lord', Proculeius advises Cleopatra,

> Who is so full of grace that it flows over
> On all that need. Let me report to him
> Your sweet dependency, and you shall find
> A conqueror that will pray in aid for kindness
> Where he for grace is kneeled to.
>
> (5.2.23–8)

Cleopatra understands both that Caesar's promises are self-serving and that his gestures of magnificent clemency are part-and-parcel of the fact that he is now 'sole sir o'th' world' (5.2.119).

Cleopatra's self-performance in the play's finale is likewise shaped by – and so emblematic of – this new political reality. This is why the play's final scene begins with her articulation of a Roman Stoic's stern indifference to the contingency of the political world:

> My desolation does begin to make
> A better life. 'Tis paltry to be Caesar.
> Not being Fortune, he's but Fortune's knave,
> A minister of her will. And it is great
> To do that thing which ends all other deeds,
> Which shackles accidents and bolts up change,
> Which sleeps and never palates more the dung,
> The beggar's nurse and Caesar's.
>
> (5.2.1–8)

With Caesar monopolizing political agency, neo-Stoic self-possession as a response to abjection is the only heroic role left to play. This shift in Cleopatra's style of self-performance mimics an inward turn in the rhetoric of Roman virtue under the principate, one that responds to the redefinition of the public sphere as a space structured by the perspective of the 'sole sir o'th' world'.[35] As Bartsch has shown, imperial monopoly over the meaning of public display resulted – over time – in a 'new dynamic of the gaze' in which

> Some members of the Roman elite reacted by creating new standards for *virtus* and by seeking to dispense with the community at large as a locus of approval or shaming. The change goes so far as to recast the public persona as a form of self-presentation that is now sullied with the taint of performance, rather than being the normative self on view of the Roman citizen in the public eye.[36]

The form of Stoicism that Cleopatra evokes in Act 5 – as a self-protective alternative to public identity – is reminiscent of the more inward-looking standards for *virtus* produced in response to imperial power.[37] In her mimicry of Roman Stoic virtue, the Cleopatra of Act 5 might even be said to embody (or perhaps even to allegorize?) what Bartsch identifies as the new 'taint of performance' associated with public life under the emperors: the way public self-performance, stripped of its republican habitus and located in a more abject relation to imperial absolutism, comes to be redefined as showy and inauthentic rather than being part of a becoming Roman identity.

To play her new role, we might say, Cleopatra requires a shift in the genre of the play she inhabits. Michael Shapiro has argued that the Cleopatra of the play's final act is based in part on dramatic conventions drawn from the 'pathetic heroine plays of the neo-classical tradition': that is, from neo-classical plays that emphasize the suffering of tragic female protagonists, including those by writers such as Robert Garnier and Samuel

Daniel in which Cleopatra herself is a major character.[38] Indeed, with its narrowing of focus to a specific locale, and its emphasis on Cleopatra's self-dramatization *in extremis*, it makes sense to read the finale as something of a pastiche of a play like Daniel's, which likewise focuses on Cleopatra's experiences after the death of Antony. Cleopatra's declaration that even Caesar is 'but Fortune's knave' would not be out of place in such a play: Daniel's *Tragedie of Cleopatra*, for instance, ends with Cleopatra scorning 'Death and Caesar' and declaring that 'to the mind that's great, nothing seems great'.[39] Such sentiments are utterly commonplace in neo-Senecan tragedy.

But my point here is not to argue that Shakespeare is alluding to specific literary antecedents so much as to suggest that the configuration that prevails at the end of *Antony and Cleopatra* – the bravura performance of self-determination as a response to abjection under imperial absolutism – is itself familiar from Senecan and neo-Senecan tragedy. Senecan tragedy, in so far as it lies in the background of *Antony and Cleopatra*'s finale, is an imperial form of drama. I mean by this two interrelated things: first, that plays in the Senecan tradition often feature characters who seek to impose their will upon others and/or characters experiencing extraordinary abjection; and, second, that Seneca's own plays, which were written in Neronian Rome, were often associated in England with fears about imperial-style absolutism.[40] English neo-Senecan tragedy, as Daniel Cadman has demonstrated, tends to focus on political powerlessness, exploring subjects' recourse to Stoicism as a compensation for the experience of tyranny and the loss of liberty.[41] The last act of *Antony and Cleopatra* evokes the core scenario of such neo-Senecan plays, and this is perhaps why distinctively Stoic rhetoric offers itself to Cleopatra at times, as in the speech quoted above or the moment at which she imagines death as 'liberty' (5.2.236) and declares herself to be 'marble-constant' in her suicidal resolution.

But perhaps we get closer to the essence of the thing by setting aside the comparison with neo-Senecan tragedy in particular and recalling instead T. S. Eliot's notorious formulation concerning what Shakespeare derived from Seneca more generally, namely 'the attitude of self-dramatization assumed by some of Shakespeare's heroes at moments of tragic intensity'.[42] Eliot is grudging and dismissive in his attitude towards Seneca, but he does put his finger on something essential about the Senecan tragedy's imperial valence: an attitude of self-dramatization represents a form of self-assertion that remains available within Senecan play-worlds even if political agency has been monopolized elsewhere. That, I would argue, is also part of what the ending of *Antony and Cleopatra* stages.

For Arthur L. Little Jr, Cleopatra's final self-dramatization opens up a space 'to both mimic and interrogate' Roman ideas of virtue, exposing in the process the inherent 'performativity' of Roman exemplarity itself.[43] This strikes me as true to the way the play feels at the end. But part of the story must also be that the conditions of Roman performativity are themselves transformed once Caesar has conquered Alexandria and the rest of the Roman world. With Caesar's epoch-making victory, Shakespeare seems to be implying, a new set of conditions and constraints for self-performance snap into place, reorienting once again what it means to act in a becoming or decorous manner. The only remaining question is whether or not one will accede to one's role in the spectacle of Caesar's triumph. From this perspective, Cleopatra's interrogatory mimicry – her self-awareness with regard to the performativity of exemplary suicide – is in effect a Senecan 'attitude of self-dramatization' that has been relocated by Shakespeare to its point of origin at the inception of imperial Rome.

This way of understanding the play's final movement discloses a connection between the ostensible thematic content of the end of the play – Caesar's victory and his attempts to control the images of the vanquished – and the formal innovation represented by its sudden shift of focus to Cleopatra's confinement and self-staging. The first four acts of *Antony and Cleopatra*, we might say, explore the consequences – for Rome and *romanitas* – of the loss of a republican worldview predicated upon decorum, one in which self-performance is authenticated by the reciprocal gaze of peers. The end of the play feels different because it registers – in form as well as in content – the beginning of a new regime with its own top-down specular logic. The power relations of Act 5 are imperial and absolutist; they follow the logic implied by Caesar's own performance of clemency, a logic in which subjects must first be beholden in order to earn their place in the story. Cleopatra's suicide is at once a powerful gesture of self-assertion and a sacrificial acknowledgement of abjection. It is a bravura performance, but it is also an acknowledgement that Senecan self-dramatization is the only form of resistance available as an alternative to Caesar's triumph.

5

New Directions

Determined Things: The Historical Reconstruction of Character in *Antony and Cleopatra*

John E. Curran Jr

When Caesar tries to allay Octavia's shock at the news that her husband, Mark Antony, 'hath given his empire / Up to a whore, who are now levying / The kings o'th'earth for war', he chooses telling words: 'Be you not troubled with the time, which drives / O'er your content these strong necessities, / But let determined things to destiny / Hold unbewailed their way' (3.6.67–9, 84–7).[1] It is difficult to see how this could be comforting; world-altering forces are at work imposing strong

---

This is dedicated, gratefully, to Sarah Stefanko.

necessity – so, 'Cheer your heart' (83)! Of course, the talk of destiny might simply nod, like Caesar's later remark that 'The time of universal peace is near' (4.6.5), to the audience's cognisance of the time's significance to world history. Christian historiography had made much of the coincidence of Augustus's monarchy with the birth of Jesus; Caesar's nearing victory is predetermined by Divine Providence itself, 'some secrete determination for the natiuitie of [God's] only sonne'.[2] And yet, unlike with the unsubtle *pax romana* reference, here we are made aware of his interlocutor – 'Nothing more dear to me' (88) – and his speech's conversational context. As naturalistic dialogue, Caesar's words do provide comfort, for they suggest a supreme confidence on his part. This troublesome time should not trouble Octavia, it's implied, for it does not trouble him; the way things are determined to go will be bewailed by Antony's side, not theirs. He does not know as we do, but he seems to sense who will win. And if so, it may well also seem that this quasi-prescience about his destiny will do much to bring that destiny about.

Thus this moment clues us in to the circular pattern of internal and external compulsion, and agency and non-agency, by which things are determined in this play: things are determined by a character's own mode of responsiveness to the determining circumstances of the time, otherwise known as Fortune. Here, Caesar bends himself to the demands of circumstances – he must react decisively to having slipped into a time of 'negligent danger' (83) – and so determines things even by his submission to their determining him. Meanwhile, his seeming assurance that things are to be determined in his favour contrasts with his adversaries' attitude; rather than engage the particular time, as Caesar does, Cleopatra wishes, much against fact, that Antony 'and Caesar might / Determine this great war in single fight', for Antony looks 'gallantly' in his fighting outfit (4.4.36–7). Antony would surely determine the outcomes of things merely by an assertion of decorous Antonyness – if only the things were completely different from what they are. In their determination to be Antony and Cleopatra, Antony and Cleopatra determine the strong necessities of their tragedy.

This discussion explores the twist Shakespeare's play puts on the paradox that 'character is fate': specifically, the complex manner in which *Antony and Cleopatra* ties up character with performativity and with Fortune, and links this nexus with the causality of historical events. Commentators have long observed how theatricality is key to the play,[3] and some have contended the seriousness of Shakespeare's historical portraiture.[4] Combining these strands, I argue that the kind and degree of commitment to the performing of the self differentiate Antony, Caesar and Cleopatra, and, lying at the heart of each one's character, determine what each invariably does in the face of Fortune and so, in turn, lock what happens determinately into place. Who they are forces them to play who they are in the way they do. The play's deployment of the life-as-theatre metaphor boils performance down to two basic kinds: acting and reacting. In the first there is stubborn adherence to the decorum of the persona one is bound to play; in the second, negotiation and improvisation take precedence over a core idea of identity or 'conceit', as Hamlet terms it. Cleopatra and Caesar represent the extreme degrees of these opposing kinds: she's a pure actor, he a pure reactor. Antony, then, determines his destruction by Fortune by rejecting the chance Cleopatra offers him to be purely an actor. He guarantees – determines – his loss by fixing on a 'conceit' of himself as a reactor, when he is not one. His character consigns him to perform against his character. Only self-determining heroes can rise above the actor/reactor dialectic, heroes like Antony's mythical and actual models, Hercules and Julius Caesar. Having shared this transcendence with Julius Caesar, Cleopatra reacts to degraded circumstances by abjuring reaction and embracing the actor's part to near fullness. Thus it is she who comes much closer to a staging of heroism than anyone else in a play Michael Goldman has aptly described as uniquely about greatness.[5]

Mark Antony's Daemon

This discussion builds on my thesis regarding Antony's psychology, that he is chilled with the deep feeling of his inferiority to Julius Caesar.[6] As Shakespeare reconstructs him, his dilemma goes beyond a pat opposition between Rome and Egypt, duty and pleasure, and even beyond a triangulation between Egypt and two Romes, old (heroic) and new (*Realpolitik*).[7] His dilemma is that his character determines him to a self-fulfilling prophecy of loss, in that it unnerves him for being in any sort of dilemma at all. Dilemmas are for ordinary mortals. Allusions to Julius Caesar punctuate the play, including the very name of Antony's antagonist, and they recall the conqueror who made both the world and its most awesome woman his own. My interpretation centres on the Soothsayer passage affirming Antony's fate always to lose to the heir and namesake of Julius Caesar:

ANTONY
  Whose fortunes shall rise higher, Caesar's or mine?
SOOTHSAYER
  Caesar's.
  Therefore, O Antony, stay not by his side.
  Thy daemon – that thy spirit which keeps thee – is
  Noble, courageous, high unmatchable,
  Where Caesar's is not. But near him, thy angel
  Becomes afeard, as being o'erpowered; therefore
  Make space enough between you.
ANTONY   Speak this no more.
SOOTHSAYER
  To none but thee; no more but when to thee.
  If thou dost play with him at any game,
  Thou art sure to lose; and of that natural luck
  He beats thee 'gainst the odds. Thy lustre thickens
  When he shines by. I say again, thy spirit

Is all afraid to govern thee near him;
But, he away, 'tis noble.

(2.3.15–29)

Though the ancient concept of 'daemon' is obscure – Shakespeare and North both use the vague 'angel' as a synonym – it clearly conveys the circularity of the Soothsayer's diagnosis.[8] His words make little apparent sense: how can Antony be inherently noble if to maintain this nobility he must avoid confrontation with the one person in the world he must confront? And yet, the insight feels true, as Antony himself perceives (31–9). In fact, we can unravel it if we observe the weirdly powerful way in which the 'daemon' idea intertwines what belongs to Fortune with what belongs to spirit, or character.

For the idea of 'natural luck', though tautological, is not oxymoronic.[9] By 'daemon' is figured both one's individual life force and one's luck, and therefore it is useful for getting at their chicken-and-egg causality. Invisible powers furnishing you with good luck will tend to edify in you the kind of self-possession, courage and drive that are commonly rewarded with good luck – so much so that the original allotment of good luck may well have been bestowed out of those powers' responsiveness to those qualities in you. Conversely, Antony's luck will leave him as a response to the loser's qualities he has when he tries his luck with Caesar. Something in him knows viscerally that Caesar must always beat him, and this feeling, intrinsic to his interior spirit or soul, is mutually reinforcing with an exterior spirit or guardian angel that implants that dreadful anticipation and then confirms it in the world of events. And yet, with Antony, this feeling, however intrinsic, might, hypothetically at least, not be activated – if Antony stays in Egypt and makes space between himself and Caesar, his interior spirit will be all it should be. Away from Caesar is where he can possess 'that great property / Which still should go with Antony' (1.1.59–60). But this means Antony can fully inhabit the role of Antony, and satisfy the directives of his daemon, only by putting on Antonyness to the exclusion of action in the world.

He can play Antony, and do so nobly, but only by absenting himself from playing the games of politics and war that confer nobility substantively; Fortune will smile on him only if he makes himself irrelevant to her. This dilemma – between being a nugatory, histrionic winner and being a loser in the world of Fortune – adumbrates Julius Caesar, I argue, because, as references to him in this play and the rendition of him in John Fletcher and Philip Massinger's prequel, *The False One*, prove, it is an opposition Julius conspicuously never had to face.[10] Julius Caesar was always a winner, but he was also Cleopatra's lover, and he remained a winner, 'great Caesar', even when she made him 'lay his sword to bed' (2.2.237). Returning to Egypt, Antony heeds the Soothsayer's advice but not – though he agrees that all the luck is Caesar's: 'The very dice obey him' (2.3.32) – the Soothsayer's warning. It is a warning the gist of which might be translated as 'Go to Cleopatra, and forget Fortune. Julius could have both; but you are not he, and you can't.'

Acting, Reacting and Fortune

The histrionic dimension of this warning marks the step forward I am taking here in my analysis of the play's historical reconstruction of character.[11] Indeed, the Melanchthon passage I cite to exemplify the view of Antony as psychically crippled by his inferiority to Julius suggests this connection: 'Antonium fefellit imitatio Caesaris, et saepe fit, ut ingenia infirma extra suam vocationem, et supra vires, non recte appetant similitudinem magnorum virorum' [imitation of Caesar beguiled Antony, and often it happens that pusillanimous natures wrongly, beyond their proper calling and above their capacities, aspire to the likeness of great men].[12] For Melanchthon, the exceeding rareness in history of 'heroica fortitudo', and its mysterious derivation from divine empowerment, made it no less real; Achilles, Alexander, Scipio, and of course Julius Caesar had all actually been endowed with exceptional, unique minds, minds rising to heights of virtue 'supra communem captum hominum' [beyond the common possession of men]. Such heroic virtue did not come trouble-free, since a mind functioning so far above common capacities might often drive the hero 'extra regulam' – a point Melanchthon makes by citing an old saw about Hercules rowing the Argo so vehemently that he broke the oars. The 'conceit' of himself as a hero like Julius Caesar causes Antony to strive to imitate him, but, unlike Julius's own efforts to imitate Alexander, which led to a self-actualization so complete he could imitate no one but himself, for Antony imitation is mere pretending, 'similitudo'.[13] For the few true heroes of history, the relation between being and doing, between authenticity in selfhood and success in interaction with the world, fades into inconsequence. But for Antony, as the Soothsayer makes plain, only the former, and a lesser version of it, is possible.[14]

That there are different kinds of roles, and that all people but a few select heroes are consigned to play them, had been elucidated by Cicero in a famous passage of his famous work, the 'Four Personae' section of the *De officiis*.[15] Though Cicero divides the metaphor comparing life to theatre into four categories, the dichotomy between acting and reacting comes across. In summing up the section, he stipulates that Nature is the most powerful influence, with Fortune coming second: in a successful life, one has asserted one's fundamental nature with consistency – 'constantia' – to the highest extent allowed for by circumstances. That is, for Cicero the well-played life consists mostly of playing one's proper role unswervingly. The best life-performers act themselves rather than reacting to vagaries of Fortune or to desirable roles not their own: if circumstances – 'necessitas' – force an uncongenial role, the best response is not adaptation but careful mitigation, so that if 'decorum' could not be maintained, still the ugly and base could be averted; and instead of imitating the virtues of impressive persons, one should always keep 'decorum', which can be lost in such imitation. Moreover, for this imperative to stay true to one's *natura* and act the true self consistently, theatricality is explicitly illustrative: actors choose not the best but the best-suited roles for themselves, and actors should not be wiser than we are. And yet, too, Cicero also lets fall that this challenge to act one's Nature and if possible avoid reaction to one's Fortune does not pertain to heroes. Beset with limitations of Nature and Fortune, we cannot simply choose self-actualization, as Hercules did when he deliberated on Pleasure versus Virtue.

We get a consonant medieval treatment of the theatre metaphor in John of Salisbury's *Policraticus*.[16] Helpfully, John's example for the workings of Fortune's world-comedy, a tragedy from the perspective of the worldlings enmeshed in it, is Cleopatra herself. John cites Petronius on the theatre metaphor – all the world's a stage – but his Christian application reduces nearly all this-world action to farce. Better than skilful role-playing is holily to abjure Fortune's theatre and turn from player to spectator looking down on its vanities. Cleopatra's tragedy was one such spectacle, especially conducive to showing how pitifully dependent those stuck in the world-comedy are on each other. Cleopatra's ambition drove her from Julius to Antony, and then to despair when Augustus was uninterested in her charms. For John, she proved the dire – and degrading – consequences of playing life as a reaction to Fortune's determinations. The decree of Fortune (*decretum fortunae*) might easily separate 'personas' cast together and defining themselves off each other, leaving each part displaced and useless.

Reacting: Caesar and Octavia

For Cicero, and emphatically for John, it was debasing to approach the theatre of life reactively, with improvisatory responses to Fortune; in this light, it is significant how *Antony and Cleopatra*'s Caesar is envisioned as the consummate histrionic reactor, yet without a hard judgment on him. Rather than squaring him to moral or political categorizing, his reactiveness emerges as a way for us to imagine, historically, who he was: a life-performer essentially unconcerned with essence. In the article on Fortune in *The French Academie*, Pierre de La Primaudaye, referencing the Soothsayer episode, remarks on Augustus's singular bent for 'attributing to Fortune, as a principall worke, the honour of making him so great as he was'.[17] Moreover, the dying Augustus himself was reported by Suetonius to have looked retrospectively on his life, a life of nearly always winning at worldly games, by comparing it to theatre (*mimum vitae*): 'Since well I've played my part, all clap your hands / And from the stage dismiss me with applause.'[18]

Accordingly, the Caesar of *Antony and Cleopatra* is a calculating expert at political showmanship, but his skill is never exercised as an expression of selfhood. He does not seem to me to betray much frustration at being deprived of a triumph with Cleopatra as the main attraction, calmly ordering that his army 'In solemn show attend this funeral' (5.2.362–3); perhaps this is because that triumphal show for which the funeral substitutes was never going to be about him. He wanted it, but did not need it for self-validation. Its loss can be taken as simply another thing-that-happens.

Historical details help Shakespeare weave this pattern. Suetonius had noted Augustus's constitutional abstemiousness towards wine, and in *Antony and Cleopatra* this appears, though not because of any need to stay in character.[19] Rather, the 'wild disguise' of drunkenness, which has nearly 'Anticked' everyone at the meeting with Pompey, is bad mostly in that 'Our graver business / Frowns at this levity' (2.7.119–25). Decorum matters not because of how Caesar should act to play Caesar but because of the 'business' at hand, which has all his attention when it has no one else's. Drink has turned the other Romans into antic players, silly ones with depleted ability to react to the moment. Similarly, his reactions to Antony's gallant but fatuous challenges to single combat are devoid of any preoccupation with heroism. To Enobarbus it is a joke to suppose that Caesar will 'Unstate his happiness, and be staged to th' show' (3.13.30); he rightly perceives that for Caesar, style-points are meaningless. Depicting this reactiveness leads Shakespeare to a revealing misreading of North's translation: Caesar says, 'Let the old ruffian know / I have many other ways to die; meantime / Laugh at his challenge' (4.1.4–6).[20] Shakespeare's Caesar refers to his own prospective death, not Antony's, which drives home his non-interest in the aesthetics of dying. Of course Caesar would lose a physical fight, and neither this fact nor the general recognition of it bothers him a bit. Antony's bravado is simply another happening, and how to react to it is so swiftly determined that any inkling of doing otherwise is laughable.

Caesar's disposition towards, and Antony's inadequacy for, this improvisatory mode of performance, wherein Fortune is played to rather than identity played at, are figured in many ways but most resoundingly by Octavia; it is no coincidence that the envisaged future victory-celebration of 'full-fortuned Caesar' (4.15.25) is repeatedly associated with her (4.12.38, 4.15.28, 5.2.54). Here I venture disagreement with the brilliant iconological study by the late Peggy Muñoz Simonds, which would align Fortune with Cleopatra and hypothesize that 'Octavia ... might well have saved Antony if he had remained with her.'[21] But I submit that it is Octavia who represents the seduction of Antony to his ruin, and her siren song that calls to him against his better nature. Promising her that, despite his past history, 'that to come / Shall be done by th' rule' (2.3.6–7), Antony is setting himself in compliance with her rule, in admitted denial of his own impulse, and tasking himself with reacting reliably in accordance with this rule into the future. When he is drawn back towards Rome, where, unknown to him, marriage to Octavia awaits, Antony, fittingly, tells Cleopatra that 'The strong necessity of time commands' (1.3.43). While implicitly aligning freedom of self-determination with the Egyptian queen, Antony also, anticipating Caesar's 'determined things' passage, couches alertness to the time as an obedience to strong necessity. But unlike Caesar Antony is not addressing the time – he only mistakenly thinks he is. And by this mistaken belief in his reactiveness he imposes strong necessity on himself: he throws himself on the mercy of the merciless world-of-affairs, where, as the Soothsayer says, his daemon cannot protect him.

Octavia symbolizes this causality, for marrying her marks a point-of-no-return instantiation of it. The marriage to Octavia is an occasion, a thing-that-happens that presents an opportunity for those ready to meet their cue and seize it. Enobarbus's suspicion about the union's stability cements this connection: Antony 'married but his occasion here' (2.6.133). To marry Octavia is to subject himself to luck and to commit himself to the seizing of opportunities and the taking of occasions. He is singularly bad at such extempore cue-meeting, and so, as Enobarbus predicts here, Octavia 'shall prove the immediate author of their variance' (131–2). Because married to her, and thus dropped into a contest he does not even know he is in before Caesar has made any number of opening moves (3.4.1–9), Antony must strive to react to Caesar's machinations and make 'preparation' for a showdown (26–7), but since, for him, what is at stake is self-verification – 'If I lose mine honour, / I lose myself' (22–3) – he is not preparing for the game he is actually playing. Octavia is thought a 'blessed lottery' to Antony (2.2.252–3), but this is to neglect that he always loses to Caesar at such games: 'If we draw lots, he [Caesar] speeds' (2.3.34). He fancies that marrying Caesar's sister is a self-advancing choice integrating him with a Roman immersion in affairs of state: hastening to contend with Pompey, he asks, 'ere we put ourselves in arms, dispatch we / The business we have talked of' (2.2.175–6), the business of binding himself to Octavia. But his business is not business – 'graver business' is Caesar's purview alone. Such is first evident in his effort to go with 'Roman thought' – as Cleopatra calls it (1.2.88) – and react to the news of Fulvia's death: to Rome he must return, for 'The business [Fulvia] hath broached in the state / Cannot endure my absence' (1.2.178–9); to which Enobarbus, corroborating the Soothsayer as usual, answers that 'the business you have broached here cannot be without you, especially that of Cleopatra's' (180–1). Though Enobarbus reduces the Egyptian business to Cleopatra's histrionic and sexual extravagancies (148–52), he also unironically argues the purity of her love (153–4); for him, what Antony suddenly construes as debilitating 'idleness' (137) is where he belongs, and for departing there is no 'compelling occasion' (144). It is with Octavia, whom he unknowingly embraces here, that occasion compels him; with Cleopatra he can exist in stasis, free of it.

Non-reacting: Antony

The decision to fight at sea is a crucial emanation of the tendency of Antony's to displace attention to situational business with attention to self-portrayal, while envisioning his combining of the two. Here, as we are aware of the need for the most intense reactiveness to the time – 'With news the time's in labour, and throws forth / Each minute some' (3.7.80–1) – we see Antony not only run all options through the filter of what becomes his personal decorum but also exhibit an inability to consider them in any other way. Since aesthetic appropriateness can be secured with neither a man-to-man duel with Caesar nor a relocation of the battlefield to Pharsalia (30–2), there must be a sea fight: indeed, Antony appears wholly of Cleopatra's mind, when she asks rhetorically, 'what else?' (28). And yet, Antony never seems to feel much of a sense that he is failing to engage the time or that what expresses his honour conduces to what merely gives him up to chance and hazard (47). He does not choose self-expression over practicality so much as refuse to acknowledge that he must choose. Inviting Cleopatra to join him in marvelling at Caesar's swift progress, to her wry criticism – 'Celerity is never more admired / Than by the negligent' (24–5) – Antony answers as if his true military competency were being affirmed: 'A good rebuke, / Which might have well becomed the best of men, / To taunt at slackness' (25–7). Even heroes like me need to guard against complacency! Similarly, to the fatal sea-fight resolution, Antony appends a contingency plan – 'if we fail, / We then can do't at land' (52–3) – as if fate were not hanging on this battle, and as if he were the gamesman thinking several steps ahead. Caesar knows that 'Our fortune lies / Upon this jump' (3.8.5–6); Antony constitutionally cannot do this, cannot face and deal with fast-flowing serendipity – in large part because he cannot conceive he is not doing it.

For Antony, that is, it is impossible to maintain the 'conceit' of himself as Antony without Fortune's favour as a great property going with it; he conflates role-playing with game-playing, and this conflation works as a cause both of his decisions and of his manner of suffering. Unlike Plutarch's Romans, we can well believe Antony's in-the-moment discomposure at Actium.[22] We have seen a series of non- and even anti-reactive determinations – returning to Rome after Fulvia's death, marrying Octavia, ignoring the Soothsayer's warning, rousing himself to counter Caesar's initial power-plays, fighting at sea – which he framed for himself as reactions but which served what becomes Antony; it makes sense that with Fortune's contingencies at their slipperiest, he cannot react at all. Simultaneously, it makes sense that in Actium's aftermath, whatever his past battlefield luck has been, Antony cannot treat luck as a thing extrinsic to himself.[23] He does not look back on the event as a failure of in-the-moment nerve but as a failure of self: 'I have fled myself' (3.11.7); 'I have offended reputation, / A most unnoble swerving' (49–50). What has been fled and swerved from is not a mere facility with crises but an idea of who Antony is; hence, he repeatedly articulates alienation from Fortune as dissolution of self: Caesar is infuriating for 'harping on what I am, / Not what he knew I was' (3.13.147–8); that 'Fortune and Antony part here' equates to 'the very heart of loss', a striking phrase conveying the most integral bond of life-event and life-force (4.12.19, 29); to the 'pageants' of the shape-shifting clouds he compares himself, for, 'Here I am Antony, / Yet cannot hold this visible shape' (4.14.8, 13–14).

This peculiar pain, wherein his life's pageant refuses to hold Antonyness, to register or solidify it, with anything shaped or visible, and hence seems to him to invalidate it, is acutely emblematized by the Hercules topos – and so too is a possible alternative to the pain. Central to the idea of Hercules, as we saw with Cicero and with Melanchthon, is that in him, as in some precious few others, the highest pitch of thought and will not only coincided with victorious events in the world but created them. Both Seneca's Hercules plays capture this vividly: in *Hercules Furens*, Juno's only recourse is artificially to madden the hero, for his aspirational is as soaring as his physical power, such that his only possible enemy is himself; in *Hercules Oetaeus*, which revolves around the hero's abundantly justified case for deification, he understands that his deeds have elevated him singularly above the human and super-human and that they proceed not from reacting to adversity but from acting as himself.[24] In the *Oetaeus*, furthermore, this total uniqueness is expressed in first bearing the unbearable throes of the shirt of Nessus, and then wilfully becoming apathetic to both them and his funeral flames.[25] Whereas Antony's genealogical and analogical tie to Hercules was sometimes taken earnestly, such as in the Countess of Pembroke's *Antonius*,[26] Shakespeare's Antony never relates to Hercules except in pitiful contradistinction.[27] It is Hercules, not Bacchus as in Plutarch, that is the deity fleeing with his defeat imminent (4.3), shifting the implied condemnation of Antony from one of excess to one of deficiency – instead of by too much Pleasure, he's brought low by too little Virtue.[28] Moreover, when Antony invokes Hercules, it is to cry out, with abject futility, his irrevocable parting from Fortune, and he calls down not Hercules' valour, patience or self-awareness but his fury: 'The shirt of Nessus is upon me. Teach me / Alcides, thou mine ancestor, thy rage' (4.12.43–4). Bereft finally of any prospect of Fortune bolstering it, Antony experiences a searing melting away of identity, but with no compensatory reasserting of Herculean amplitude; instead, we have distinctly un-Herculean impotence, all the more withering for its venting at Cleopatra.

Playing Hercules

And yet, perhaps this impotent rage at Cleopatra sounds so unseemly, so un-Herculean, precisely because it is she who has all along furnished him with the way to act like Hercules. His surprisingly successful sally shows his reflex to seek Cleopatra's approbation of his heroism (4.8.2) but also his utter dependency for that search on what happens to happen in the world. For Cleopatra, however, this link is easily severed. Indeed, she would just as soon have had him tarry in bed with her as take the field (4.4.1); it is his concern that their troops 'thrive' (9), not hers. That she offers him a severance between formal and material heroism is clear in an early Hercules reference of her own: after decrying how 'the greatest soldier of the world, / Art turned the greatest liar', she mockingly asks Charmian to observe 'How this Herculean Roman does become / The carriage of his chafe' (1.3.39–40, 84–6). He's got the 'hot-tempered hero' routine down pat – such is her attack, aligning 'Roman thought' with sheer imposture. The insincerity of his professions of adoration is mutually exclusive with his soldiership, even though he has been exercising no soldiership; and just so, Antony's threatening to grow angry at her anger is tantamount to his merely striking a Roman pose, even though he is now actually heading for Rome. For her, his attempt to leave gracefully is the taking on of a sham rather than an authentic performance, and thus it is also, implicitly, the giving away of what had been authentically Herculean in his 'carriage'. Heading for Rome to reclaim his heroic ethos, he disclaims heroism, exchanging it for an imitation of it.

We cannot discount Cleopatra's argument; perhaps Antony is truly heroic, able to play to a noble 'conceit' of Antony, only apart from true heroism, active participation. As she very much does here, Cleopatra forces our recognition that there is pretence on either side.[29] Even if we accept the world of Rome and Fortune as the real one, Antony's functioning in and with it remains a form of pretending, wherein he imitates the reactiveness of a victorious Hercules. Meanwhile, the alternative form of pretence, wherein he styles himself in a Herculean vein safely away from Fortune, can be held up as the more 'real', in that it is friendlier to his *natura*. Pretending to be a hero is in a way not pretending, for the persona is coherent with his inmost self – just as the Soothsayer tells him.

His consistency in portraying himself, his *constantia*, is exactly what Cleopatra argues he is relinquishing by moving into Roman business, and what she argues her company allows for. She needles him that, with any latent interest in Roman goings-on, 'Antony / Will be himself' (1.1.43–4) – will, that is, fall into his accustomed insincerity; she is prompting him to repudiate such an Antony-idea and to believe in and live up to the Antony ringing out in his boast that, for him, their world is the world:

> Let Rome in Tiber melt, and the wide arch
> Of the ranged empire fall! Here is my space!
> Kingdoms are clay! Our dungy earth alike
> Feeds beast as man. The nobleness of life
> Is to do thus, when such a mutual pair
> And such a twain can do't, in which I bind,
> On pain of punishment, the world to weet
> We stand up peerless.
>
> (1.1.34–41)

If this looks 'gallantly', we must also note how extreme is its disavowal of Rome and Fortune, to the point where the spatial plane itself is levelled with beasts. We may note, too, how this attitude plays on that opposition of solidity versus melting which will scorch Antony later, with the shirt of Nessus: whereas he will feel adverse Fortune dissolve his Antony persona – the accoutrements of it, his supporters' awe of him, 'discandy' (4.12.22) – here with the queen, he stands up peerless, forceful and built-up as against the melting world-of-affairs. His rejoinder to her dig that he 'Will be himself' in insincerity is that he indeed will be himself, his authentic and inspiring self, because he's inspired, 'stirred by Cleopatra'

(44). After Actium in 3.13, Cleopatra opens negotiations with Caesar, only to insist to Antony that if she ever did so – 'Not know me yet?' (162) – she and Egypt should be washed away in a 'discandying' storm (170), and this partition of liquefied, liquefying world from solid persona transfers to Antony; breaking off from his abysmal rant, marred by self-annihilating misogyny and despondency – 'Authority melts from me' (95) – he gallantly exclaims, with the real situation hopeless, that 'There's hope in't yet' (181). For this he is rewarded with Cleopatra's approval of this resumption of proper roles: 'since my lord / Is Antony again, I will be Cleopatra' (191–2).

Redefining the terms of what great property should go with the part, Cleopatra gives Antony the stage and the script for acting free from reacting, a noble, courageous, high unmatchable rendition of himself, predicated on its removal from what is happening; this redefinition brings up distinctive possibilities for assessing how Antony's Egyptian indulgences cause his fall. Is Antony debilitated by play-acting, or by the diluting of it? Before heeding Cleopatra and becoming 'Antony again', he proclaims 'I am / Antony yet' as he childishly orders Thidias's whipping (97–8); he lowers himself not by clinging to the Antony persona but by hinging it on doing something. Here and throughout, we must question the notion of Egyptian theatricality visiting a change upon Antony, one contrary to his *natura*.[30] For the moralist Thomas Rogers, Antony exemplified 'Docility': all Roman in Rome, in Egypt who 'coulde playe his parte in wickednesse more kindly then he?'[31] While Shakespeare's Romans mostly share Rogers's outlook, Enobarbus reports that Antony was more than apt to immerse himself in Cleopatra's fantasy-pageant, for he's 'Our courteous Antony, / Whom ne'er the word of "No" woman heard speak' (2.2.232–3). For Enobarbus, this is our Antony; given our familiarity with him, his over-eager primping for the meeting seems hardly to violate character. Rather, it seems to fulfil it. Finally typecast, he enters a waited-for role with gusto. With Cleopatra, the catching of fish is false, for they have been artificially placed on his hook, but the 'fervency' he feels is true;

and all the while, as she recounts, circumstances disappear: 'That time? O times!' (2.5.15–18). One viable interpretation of cause, then, is that Cleopatra sets up conditions by which Antony can be Antony, and he undoes himself not from losing track of innate *romanitas* but from failing to lose track of it, from failing to overcome the compulsion to buckle identity to Fortune.

Acting: Cleopatra

We must also reassess our esteem for Cleopatra, for in this light not only is she in a symbiotic relationship to Antony, endowing a non-great man with a feeling of greatness, a feeling he requires in order to act as himself; she is also a consistent opponent of Fortune.[32] Fletcher and Massinger pick up on this current in *The False One*: their Cleopatra can 'deride / Fortunes worst malice' and declare, 'I am still my selfe'; exuding not merely fortitude but constancy, she drives Julius Caesar to act like himself and shake off that 'common-strumpet love of hated lucre' which threatens to dissolve his greatness.[33] Shakespeare's queen similarly overturns what 'falsity' means. For his love-and-sex-addled state, Shakespeare's Romans call Antony 'a strumpet's fool' (1.1.13), which immediately ties Cleopatra to various well-known negative associations: she is a whore, she is Fortune and she makes a jester as well as a lecher of Antony.[34] The play's subsequent interrogation of this cluster of negativity is consolidated as its last scene opens: Cleopatra remarks, ''Tis paltry to be Caesar. / Not being Fortune, he's but Fortune's knave, / A minister of her will' (5.2.2–4). Being under Fortune's control is self-disintegrating, but hers is the opposite path, the path of constancy to that which is essential, 'Which shackles accidents and bolts up change' (6). To carry herself with a loftiness becoming Cleopatra – 'I will be Cleopatra' – is an exercise in essence and substance as against accident and change.

Cleopatra resists Fortune's dominance and acts herself even when she has functioned as Fortune's minister. In fact, her complicity in Fortune makes her defiance of it, in favour of her own persona's decorum, all the more insistent, and impressive. Contrasting with that of the Countess of Pembroke's queen, Cleopatra's complaint at Fortune is unleavened with remorse: instead of punishing pride, Fortune is an upstart, a 'false huswife' (4.15.45–7), whose sluttishness, common rather than menacing, is an affront, an 'offence', obstructing the deserved flourishing of Cleopatraness – such complaint bespeaks a rarefied sense of self, but the context makes it more rarefied still, for she has done much to cause the circumstances and has certainly caused their awkwardness.[35] Antony's twice-botched glorious, Roman-worthy suicide has led him here, hoisted up to her with grimly comic clumsiness as he sputters his life away, and she interrupts his noble death-speech (he: 'let me speak a little –'; she: 'No, let me speak'); his final, pathetic effort to line up ideal life-role with real life-event is drowned out, by her, and so not even in his dying will any what-happens hold Antony's visible shape. But Cleopatra acknowledges none of this. Instead, she corrects him on the difference between real-life and role-life – safety and honour 'do not go together' (49) – and launches into her noble lamentation over the 'Noblest of men', at whose gaping absence 'The crown o'th'earth doth melt' (61–5). Once more, firmness of spirit opposes sublunary melting, as the grandeur of Antony and Cleopatra and their love is held to be substantial, as against the insubstantial realm beneath the moon, in which there is naught 'remarkable' but they (69–70). With his ignominious death, as with 3.13 and her turn from entertaining Thidias to refashioning an 'Antony again', the unremarkableness that Cleopatra's own reactions have repeatedly facilitated has no bearing on her performance of self. The phallic farce of the asp interlude is dangerously at odds with the majesty of her own death-preparation, both in mood and in symbolism, with the hint that her luxurious hours with Antony were ridiculous as well as poisoned (see 2.2.96) – and yet, no disruption occurs. The bawdy tenor of her dialogue with the clown – 'Will it eat me?' (5.2.270) – does nothing to blunt her 'Immortal longings' (280), her assumption of a regal, even goddess-like state, and the equally elevated state of wife, conferred through the sheer conviction of her performance: 'Husband, I come! / Now to that name my courage prove my title!' (286–7).

Though this blocking out of circumstances can seem like infantile make-believe, we are not allowed to rest on this impression, because of the time-honoured superiority of acting over reacting and the irrepressible charisma of Cleopatra's act, but also because her persistent, insistent and consistent acting is performed, we are made aware, by a person who formerly did not need it. Much of 3.13's poignancy stems from this disparity, as the defeat she's embroiled in now is set off against former triumphs beside Julius: she invites Thidias to kiss the hand Julius used to kiss, as he 'mused of taking kingdoms in' (87–90); Antony, at his nadir, calls Cleopatra a 'cold' leftover of Julius (121–2), recalling the vacuum in the conqueror's wake and his successors' smallness; to certify her loyalty, she invokes Caesarion, as though her most sanctified role is as the mother of Julius's child (167–8). *The False One*'s young Cleopatra enjoys a relationship much more power-balanced, with no dichotomy between acting and reacting; for Julius Caesar, Cleopatra and victory are on the same side, and with her, Fortune and falsity, in all their forms, can be subdued: she captures this when she apprizes him, 'I love with as much ambition as a Conquerour / And where I love, will triumph.'[36] For Shakespeare's older Cleopatra, the dichotomy rules the world, and it is only by relentless imaginative work that she can remove Antony from its consequences. Antony's arm, his power to affect the what-happens, is mighty solely because her thinking makes it so: she styles him 'the arm / And burgonet of men' even as he is really speeding helplessly towards his fatal marriage to Octavia (1.5.24–5); 'his reared arm / Crested the world' when he is really not only dead but thoroughly humiliated (5.2.81–2). In each place, Cleopatra gives the lie to those, first Charmian and then Dolabella, who would nullify her image of Antony; in each place, to uphold it takes mental gymnastics: with Charmian she must remake her own emotional history – 'Did I ... Ever love [Julius] Caesar so?' (1.5.69–70) – in spite of having just reminisced about 'Broad-fronted [Julius] Caesar' (30); with Dolabella she must go so far as to posit her own metaphysics, arguing that the hugeness of the imaginary exaggeration disqualifies itself as imaginary exaggeration, since 't'imagine / An Antony were nature's piece 'gainst fancy' (5.2.94–9) – but perhaps the crowns and crownets, realms and islands dominated by this fancied Antony echo the 'kingdoms' Julius actually mused of and then, simply, made his own. To play out her role as Cleopatra means continually to transform an unbalanced love affair into a balanced one, and to do so when she has known much more even, and satisfying, dynamics.

Conjuring an idea of heroism when heroism is of a bygone time, Cleopatra can take on heroic proportions herself, as she must imaginatively create an alternative world, a 'new heaven, new earth', of sufficient scope to contain an exalted Antony and Cleopatra, and indeed her exertions win Caesar's concession to endorse, for posterity, something very like her 'conceit': 'No grave upon the earth shall clip in it / A pair so famous' (5.2.358–9). Gratifyingly, Antony will be recalled as 'her Antony' (357), implying that he belongs both with her and to her; her inferior in life, he'll be envisioned as her partner in death, and thus the Antony-idea she fashioned – her Antony – is what will live on. And yet, we are not able to rest on this sense of Cleopatra's expansiveness, either. The hours in a way truly are poisonous, unhealthily asynchronous with the rhythm of time determining all people, into the strong necessities of which even the most extraordinary actors, even Hercules and even Julius Caesar, must eventually melt. Cleopatra herself signals comprehension of this. Stretching her imagination to form an Antony looking gallantly and thinking of her, Cleopatra breaks for a moment: 'Now I feed myself / With most delicious poison' (1.5.27–8). The laborious upkeep of her and Antony's pageant, and the shielding of it from impinging externalities, has its own toxicity, and it is knowingly self-administered. Comprehension also lies in her extreme aversion to being displayed in Caesar's triumph. For why can she, proud to immunize herself against accident and change, not abide this happening? But Cleopatra understands Caesar's show as devoid of any means to play herself – and as such, it would reveal that persona as not substantial. The foreseen spectacle at Rome actually bodes little beyond embarrassment, but for her, it is categorically death, which makes the poison of the asp perversely life-bringing: not only desirable, in pursuit of immortal longings, but imperative. For her, the 'absurd intents' (5.2.224) of the triumph-staging Romans must absolutely be thwarted, qua their absurdity. Fittingly, she clinches the irreconcilability of the integrity of Antony-and-Cleopatra-ness with the absurdities of life's flow, by imaging them as low-brow reactive theatre: 'The quick comedians / Extemporally will stage us and present / Our Alexandrian revels' (215–17). That poison enshrines the graceful performance, and prevents graceless parody, with its mundane extemporaneous mockery, from overtaking it – Caesar perceives that the asp leaves Cleopatra unblemished and looking as though 'she would catch another Antony / In her strong toil of grace' (346–7) – seems a steep price to purchase what is, finally, merely an aesthetic grace.

Then again, if Cleopatra garbles, rather than heroically redefines, what is real and what is not real, and what is life and what is not life, she has made this determination herself; more so than either Antony or Caesar, her character determines her fate in accordance with her own choice.[37] It is determined for Caesar to react, and for Antony to act while mistakenly thinking himself both acting and reacting; but it is determined for Cleopatra purely to act, and to act determinedly. Such is the principal distinction in Shakespeare's reconstructive analysis of historical cause.

6

New Directions
Creative Misreadings and Memorial Constructions: The North Face of Alexandria

Julia Griffin

You may prove yourselves, that there is no prophane studye better than Plutarke. All other learning is private, fitter for Universities than cities, fuller of contemplacion than experience, more commendable in the students themselves, than profitable unto others. Whereas stories are fit for every place, reach to all persons, serve for all tymes, teach the living, revive the dead ... [1]

Introduction

In the later sixteenth century, Plutarch, historian and moralist, reached all persons eager to read him without benefit of

Greek. The first complete translations appeared between 1559 and 1572: the most significant of these, both for scholarship and influence, were the work of Jacques Amyot, the learned bishop who published his translation of Plutarch's biographies, *Les Vies illustres*, in 1559.[2] Sir Thomas North probably encountered his work when visiting France on diplomatic business in 1574: he translated Amyot's French, rather than Plutarch's Greek, to produce his own *Lives of the Noble Grecians and Romanes*, first published in 1579.[3] The book was large and handsome, finely printed and expensive; whether or not Shakespeare owned it, he must have had it in his hands for some time. In it, he found, as we all know, not only a rich source of material but an inspiration for his own dramatic language. Plutarch gave him details and hints for plays at both ends of his career; in the middle of it, Plutarch became a primary source. And Plutarch, for the *Lives*, meant Plutarch through North – complete with its distinctive verbal vividness and occasional confusion. Never is this truer than in *Antony and Cleopatra*, one of the two plays for which Plutarch – North's Plutarch – was by far the most important benefactor.[4]

Consider, by way of a reminder and an introduction, the grand scene in which Cleopatra enters the *Life of Antony* – a scene that, in the play, becomes a public reminiscence by Enobarbus: 'The barge she sat in …'. Plutarch's own literary artistry is here on dazzling display. He offers a feast of sensual experience: the golden stern, the silver oars, the purple sails; the mingled sound of flutes and strings. As we shall see, Shakespeare makes intense, selective use of it all; the first, and most familiar, part of that is his adoption of North's phrasing.[5] It still seems surprising when we find the 'pavilion of cloth-of-gold of tissue' and the 'pretty boys' already there in the prose.

Shakespeare found in that prose, in fact, more than Plutarch himself had provided. Continuing his reminiscence, Enobarbus describes the other women on the barge: 'Her gentlewomen, like the Nereides, / So many mermaids, tended her i'th' eyes' (2.2.216–17).[6] 'So many' elegantly veils the fact that this is a gloss: would the audience know about Nereids? North clearly thought not, because the gloss actually comes from his translation: 'the fairest of them were apparelled like the nymphes Nereides (which are the mermaides of the waters)' (274).[7] But then North himself was following the gloss in his direct source: not Plutarch himself, but Amyot, who first explained what those Greek mythological 'Nereides' were.[8] In recent years, we have been made much more aware of the role of the mediating translator. Critics such as John Denton have drawn attention, for example, to North's words for items of Roman clothing and their likely impact on Shakespeare's imagination – Caesar in a 'doublet'; Coriolanus in a 'gown'.[9] Add to them Cleopatra's mermaids.

In fact, some particularly inspirational details of North's Plutarch, details used with powerful effect by Shakespeare, were either misleading translations from Amyot or actual inventions by North himself; and even when he appears to be departing radically from his source, we can find the seeds of change in North's wording. In this chapter, I shall not tackle Shakespeare's debt to Plutarch head on (there is a great deal of criticism out there already, both excellent and recent) but approach it selectively and obliquely by way of four passages from *Antony and Cleopatra*: Cleopatra's remark about her birthday (3.13), Caesar's reaction to Antony's challenge to single combat (4.1), the departure of the 'god Hercules' (4.3), and finally the conversation between the dying Charmian and the anonymous Roman soldier after Cleopatra's death (5.2). In each case, I shall try to show how Shakespeare draws on North's language in ways not fully recognized to create dramatic moments that epitomize something important about his characters and about the structure of the play itself. Finally, we will return to Cleopatra's barge for a glimpse of its last Shakespearian, Northian send-off.

'It is my birthday'

Our first scene involves both the famous lovers, in one of their bitterest lovers' quarrels. As Plutarch narrates, in chapter 73 of the *Life of Antony*, Octavian Caesar, triumphant at Actium, sends one of his freedmen, Thyrsus, to Cleopatra to woo her away from Antony: he has a long interview with her, in which her behaviour is, at least, disturbing. The man's name is lightly corrupted in transmission, and Amyot calls him 'Thyreus'; he is followed in this by North, who describes the scene thus:

> He was longer in talke with her then any man else was, and the Queen herself also did him great honor; insomuch as he made Antonius gealous of him. Whereupon Antonius caused him to be taken and well favoredly whipped, and so sent him unto Caesar: and bad him tell him that he made him angrie with him, bicause he shewed himself prowd and disdainfull towards him, and now specially when he was easie to be angered, by reason of his present miserie. (306)

This second sentence is a fair example of the sort with which North, for all his literary gifts, made most work for his reader: 'bad him tell him that he made him angrie with him, bicause he shewed himself prowd and disdainfull towards him'. It is intelligible, of course, but the four consecutive 'him's, all referring, presumably, to different people (Thyreus, Caesar, Antony, Thyreus again), require quite a high degree of concentration, not required by a reader of the French or the Greek.[10] Even in those languages, however, there remains a possible ambiguity, to which I alluded with that 'presumably', above: is it Thyrsus/Thyreus or is it Caesar himself who has offended Antony (and thus is 'him' no. 4)? Modern translators of Plutarch plump for the former but only by adding his name: 'a written message stating that Thyrsus ... had irritated him'.[11] Possibly the ambiguity was intended: Caesar might choose to take it more diplomatically; or not.

The result of the tantrum, at any rate, is to increase Cleopatra's solicitousness towards her offended lover; and here is North again:

> From thenceforth, Cleopatra to cleere her selfe of the suspicion he had of her, she made more of him then ever she did. For first of all, where she did solemnise the day of her birth very meanely and sparingly, fit for her present misfortune: she now in contrary manner did keepe it with such solemnitie, that she exceeded all measure of sumptuousnes and magnificence: so that the ghests that were bidden to the feasts, and came poore, went away rich. (306–7)

So paradoxical is Cleopatra, in Plutarch and all his followers, that the oddity of this proceeding, so presented, has rarely been remarked by North's readers. Where she 'did solemnise the day of her birth very meanely and sparingly', she 'now ... did keep it with such solemnitie'. How often, we might wonder, would she expect to celebrate it, in one year? Or was she being mean and sparing the year before Actium, when it would surely have appeared rather defeatist? However, if we look back past North to his sources, the situation resolves itself. What he found in Amyot was this:

> Car tout premier, *là où elle solennisoit le iour de sa nativité petitement & escharsement comme il convenoit à sa fortune presente, au contraire elle celebroit le iour de la siene* de tel maniere que plusieurs conviez au festin, lesquels y estoyent venus povres, s'en retournoyent tous riches. (1143, emphasis mine)

Literally translated, the crucial part of that runs: 'whereas she celebrated the day of her birth modestly and cheaply, as befitted her present fortunes, on the other hand she celebrated the day of his'. 'Sa nativité'; 'la siene' – she makes a contrast between her own birthday and his, in order, by that contrast, to make much of him and calm his fears about her loyalty. But North read this sentence carelessly and represented Amyot's careful 'la siene' with his own favourite device of a pronoun: 'she now in contrary manner did keepe it'.

Not such an interesting mistake, one might think; but, thanks to North, Shakespeare made it too; and here it becomes interesting. In 3.13, Thyreus – whose name, in the Folio, has slid away further from the Greek into 'Thidias' – learns the hard way how 'easie to be angered' is Antony in his defeat:

> Get thee back to Caesar;
> Tell him thy entertainment. Look thou say
> He makes me angry with him. For he seems
> Proud and disdainful, harping on what I am,
> Not what he knew I was. He makes me angry,
> And at this time most easy 'tis to do't.
>
> (3.13.144–9)

'He makes me angry with him': so much for that ambiguity, impossible once the narrative had been transferred into a second-person address, and here resolved into aggression. Shakespeare's Antony, as we will see again later, is not one to avoid a confrontation. What about his Cleopatra? She has a much harder time than Plutarch's, as Antony turns on her in his fury:

> You were half blasted ere I knew you ...
> I found you as a morsel, cold upon
> Dead Caesar's trencher – nay, you were a fragment
> Of Gnaeus Pompey's.
>
> (3.13.110, 121–3)

But an impassioned speech from her seems to bring him round again; and soon he is proposing – half-hysterically, it seems – 'one other gaudy night' (3.13.188). Whereupon she makes an impromptu announcement: 'It is my birthday. / I had thought t'have held it poor, but since my lord / Is Antony again, I will be Cleopatra' (3.13.190–2). It is North's mistake; and, as a consequence, it has passed almost unnoticed by Shakespearians. Michael Neill, echoing David Bevington, comments: 'Where Plutarch's Cleopatra chooses to celebrate her birthday with exceptional "sumptuousness and magnificence" in order to "clear herself of the suspicion he had of her", Shakespeare's is simply responding to Anthony's [sic] gesture of defiance.'[12]

On the classical side, scholars have assumed that Shakespeare made the change himself: so Christopher Pelling, in his great edition of Plutarch's *Antony*: 'Two birthdays would be clodhopping on the stage, and Shakespeare makes Cleopatra respond to Antony's spirit by a simple change of plan.'[13] It is not Plutarch's story; but it is not Shakespeare's either. The only scholar, to my knowledge, who has noticed what has happened is David Green, who uses it to confirm his own picture of Shakespeare's Cleopatra:

> Shakespeare obviously did not know [Plutarch's account of the birthdays] and had somehow to make sense out of North, which he does ... The birthday has nothing to do with Thidias and Antony's suspicions. She will celebrate her birthday to suit her lord, not according to base fears as in Plutarch.[14]

Green's Cleopatra – Green's Shakespeare's Cleopatra – is a heroine of integrity, not a manipulator, but we are not compelled to read her speech quite so straightforwardly. Certainly she is 'suit[ing] her lord', but Shakespeare has played up to the maximum her suggestive behaviour with Thidias, which Antony has just seen. Coming so soon afterwards, her apparent single-mindedness about Antony here may or may not convince, but the speech is breathtaking without that, for another reason. Antony, in his rage, has accused her of faithlessness; that is painful, no doubt, but surely not as painful as his other insult, which cannot be denied: 'You were half blasted ere I knew you', i.e. you are no longer young, you, who think you are so seductive: you were stale and used up before ever I came to Egypt. We know already that Cleopatra thinks about her age: 'Think on me / That am with Phoebus' amorous pinches black / And wrinkled deep in time?' (1.5.28–30). Then she was a 'morsel' for Caesar, she remembered, perhaps with a certain reminiscent satisfaction; Antony here curdles that image, and in public: 'a morsel cold upon / Dead Caesar's trencher'. How splendid, then, how brave, to respond with a big celebration of her own birthday, thus embracing the passing of time just when it has been so cruelly cast up to her. 'Suit her lord' she may, or perhaps that is something of an act; but her own superb courage is beyond dispute.

'Many other ways to die'

Just before the Thidias encounter, the defeated Antony was planning a grand gesture of defiance towards Caesar:

> His coin, ships, legions,
> May be a coward's, whose ministers would prevail
> Under the service of a child as soon
> As i'th' command of Caesar. I dare him therefore
> To lay his gay caparisons apart
> And answer me declined, sword against sword,
> Ourselves alone. I'll write it.
>
> (3.13.22–8)

Just after Thidias, the scene shifts to Caesar's camp, where Caesar receives this challenge. He answers it: 'Let the old ruffian know / I have many other ways to die; meantime / Laugh at his challenge' (4.1.4–6). Here we have another example of a creative misreading – and a much better-known one than the last. This time, the misreading is not North's of Amyot, but Shakespeare's of North, who had written this: 'Antonius sent againe to chalenge Caesar, to fight with him hande to hande. Caesar aunswered him, that he had many other wayes to dye then so' (307). North is here faithfully following Amyot; but that pronoun 'he' ('il') is in fact a fatally misleading translation:

the Greek spells out that it is Antony, not Caesar, who has these 'many ways'.

This aberration from Plutarch, unlike the birthday one, has been duly noted by commentators, but not, I think, its full implications. Let us follow this idea of a challenge as it develops through Plutarch's account and Shakespeare's play. According to Plutarch, the first time Antony made the suggestion was before Actium. Here the two generals are taunting each other:

> So Octavius Caesar sent unto Antonius, to will him to delay no more time, but to come on with his army into Italy: and that for his owne parte he would give him safe harber, to lande without any trouble, and that he would withdraw his armie from the sea, as farre as one horse could runne, until he had put his army a shore, and had lodged his men. Antonius on the other side bravely sent him word againe, and chalenged the combate of him man to man, though he were the elder. (297)

'On the other side' more or less makes clear what the Greek makes explicit: Antony is *antikompazōn* – boasting in return, matching Caesar's own boastful style. Nothing comes of either invitation: Caesar makes no response, or none that Plutarch records, and Antony, for his part, briefly outwits Caesar by approaching from an unexpected angle. Shakespeare has no equivalent to this scene; instead, he finds a very different way to use the idea of a pre-Actium challenge. Here Antony is insisting on fighting at sea, a choice his subordinates know is disastrous. They protest:

CANIDIUS
    Why will my lord do so?
ANTONY   For that he dares us to't.
ENOBARBUS
    So hath my lord dared him to single fight.
CANIDIUS
    Ay ... But these offers,

> Which serve not for his vantage, he shakes off,
> And so should you.
>
> (3.7.29–31, 32–4)

Plutarch is insistent that the reason Antony fought by sea, against everyone's advice, was that Cleopatra (for her own dark reasons) egged him on; Shakespeare has another explanation. The meaning of this little exchange is clear: Caesar has sent Antony a challenge, knowing that Antony will not be able to resist it; Caesar, for his part, is quite prepared to ignore a challenge from Antony. Caesar, in other words, is not playing by the same rules. So, when, in defeat, Antony tries the same thing again – 'I dare him therefore / ... sword against sword, / Ourselves alone –', we are not surprised by Enobarbus's private reaction:

> Yes, like enough high-battled Caesar will
> Unstate his happiness, and be staged to th' show
> Against a sworder! ...
> Caesar, thou hast subdued
> His judgement too.
>
> (3.13.29–31, 36–7)

'Like enough', indeed: Shakespeare's Caesar will not even pretend to consider it. Plutarch's Caesar declined the challenge while implying that he, Caesar, would certainly win it: by doing so, he accepted, however insincerely, the standard of personal *virtus*, manly courage, to which Antony was appealing. In the play, by contrast, Caesar implies no such thing – indeed makes it clear that he is sure Antony would win, were Caesar fool enough to join in his 'old ruffian', 'sworder' games. But he is not, and Antony's implied charge of cowardice is simply shrugged away. Shakespeare found the germ of this idea in North's misleading translation – that 'he'; from that passage, the idea radiates back and forward through the play, producing a new and far more radical distinction between the two opponents.

It is a distinction that feels deeply satisfying, which may be due, in part, to the historical accuracy it paradoxically conveys.

Stephen Oakley, in his study of single combat in Rome, concludes that the practice, once quite popular among Roman grandees, was in decline by the time of Actium and had disappeared completely by the end of Augustus Caesar's reign; Shakespeare shows us that decline in action – thanks to North.[15]

The God Abandons Antony

So far, we have been looking at places in which Shakespeare followed North, and thus deviated from Plutarch. Sometimes his use of North's vocabulary was bolder and more eclectic; in one case, it seems, it led him to alter North's own scene into something different, inspired by a rogue word from another passage. I have in mind the strange little scene at 4.3, in which a group of Antony's soldiers, keeping watch, hear a sound from beneath the earth:

> 2 SOLDIER   Peace! What noise?
> 1 SOLDIER   List, list!
> 2 SOLDIER   Hark! ...
> 1 SOLDIER   Peace, I say!
>
> (4.3.13–15, 20)

This is based on a sequence in Plutarch that runs like this:

> within litle of midnight, when all the citie was quiet, full of fere and sorrowe, thinking what would be the issue and ende of this warre: it is said that sodainly they [presumably 'his frends and men', from the sentence before] heard a marvelous sweete harmonie of sundrie sortes of instrumentes of musicke, with the crie of a multitude of people, as they had bene dauncing, and had song as they use in Bacchus feastes, with movinges and turninges after the maner of the Satyres: and it seemed that this daunce went through the city unto the gate that opened to the

enemies, and that all the troupe that made this noise they heard, went out of the city at that gate. [*Marginal note*: Straunge noises heard, and nothing seene.] Now, such as in reason sought the depth of the interpretacion of this wonder, thought that it was the god unto whom Antonius bare singular devotion to counterfeate and resemble him, that did forsake them. (308)

The differences between these two are many and very attractive to study. Susanne Wofford, in a superb essay, compares the two and points out, first, that the timing is different: in Plutarch, the sounds are heard rather later: 'on what will turn out to have been Antony's last night alive, and immediately before his humiliating defeat. Shakespeare moves these scenes forward to a moment in which Antony is about to demonstrate heroism' – just before a brief moment of success before Actium: a moment that Shakespeare builds up considerably from a few lines in Plutarch.[16] The next, and most salient, point is the identity of the departing deity. Plutarch does not name him, but it is clear, from the Greek and from North's translation, that it is Bacchus, god of wild parties, departing with his train of revellers. Shakespeare makes a different decision:

> 1 SOLDIER Peace I say! What should this mean?
> 2 SOLDIER 'Tis the god Hercules, whom Antony loved
> Now leaves him.
>
> (4.3.20–2)

Wofford discusses the difference between these two figures, both associated by Plutarch with Antony; she concludes that 'To turn to Hercules ... is not only to avoid some of the more disturbing features of Dionysus, but is also to emphasize the mortality of Antony.'[17] But, she notes, he also 'draws on the full resonance of the Bacchic scenes in the Plutarch, so that he creates an Antony who embodies both Hercules and Dionysus'.[18] Here I want to explore some different answers to the question: why 'turn to Hercules'?

It is possible, of course, that Shakespeare, a busy working playwright, read the paragraph quickly and simply failed to recognize the pointers to – and the mention of – Bacchus.[19] Apart from being the least interesting answer, this is also the least convincing: Shakespeare clearly read the *Life of Antony* with astonishing attention and intelligence. By switching deliberately, then, to Hercules (who was, incidentally, also connected to the Globe Theatre), he made a radical change; and I suggest that Plutarch, through North, prompted him to do so. Consider the music playing here: 'a marvelous sweete harmonie of sundrie sortes of instrumentes'. This is much fuller than what North found in Amyot, which was much closer to the original Greek: *emmeleis phonas* – 'tuneful sounds'. It sounds, in fact, rather more like an earlier passage in Plutarch, where Antony entered the city of Ephesus:

> in the citie of Ephesus, women attyred as they goe in the feastes and sacrifice of Bacchus, came out to meete him with such solemnities and ceremonies, as are then used: with men and children disguised like Fawnes and Satyres. Moreover, the citie was full of Ivey, and darts wreathed about with Ivey, psalterions, flutes and howboyes, and in their songes they called him Bacchus, father of mirth, curteous, and gentle: and so was he unto some, but to the most parte of men, cruell, and extreame. (272)

Shakespeare does not include this scene, which the farewell scene so clearly echoes; the instruments from it, however, seem to have made their way into the one he includes. The stage direction tells us: 'Music of the hautboys is heard under the stage.'

What exactly did a hautboy sound like on, or under, the wooden Renaissance stage?[20] Here is Bruce Smith, in his study of Shakespeare's sound-world:

> What hautboys could provide that early modern trumpets could not was melody... It must have been the example of shawms in town bands that cast hautboys as aural

components of 'the processional scene'. The ceremonial movement of bodies in space helps to explain the conventional use of hautboys as accompaniments to dumb shows in entertainments at the universities, the inns of court, and the court of the realm, not to mention 'The Murder of Gonzago' in the folio text of *Hamlet* [...]. In *Antony and Cleopatra*, acted at the Globe in 1609, the direction 'Musicke of Hoboyes is under the Stage' underscores the pageant-like scene in which Hercules abandons Antony. Within that highly reverberant space the sound of the instruments must have been very loud indeed – and its totalizing sweep complete.[21]

Clearly they had the power to be loud – a stage direction in *Timon* calls for 'Hautboys playing loud music' (1.2SD); they also, however, had the power to be musical.[22] As Smith says, they could provide melody.[23] It may be that the sound of them under the stage was very loud; the comments of the soldiers who hear it, however, suggest that it is not: 'Peace!', 'List, list!', 'Hark!' would be odd – worse, laughable – in response to a deafening blast from below. Before and after this, hard-drinking characters in the play have called for noise: 'Make battery to our ears with the loud music', cries Enobarbus (2.7.109); 'Trumpeters, / With brazen din blast you the city's ear', charges Antony (4.8.35–6). But meanwhile, Hercules has departed, with very few to hear him.

What – a second, rather different question – did North, not a man of the theatre, imagine when he faithfully followed Amyot and wrote 'howboyes' for Plutarch's 'salpinges' – a word translated by modern scholars as 'trumpets'? He found them not only here but in a still more famous scene – the description of Cleopatra's barge. In his version, as a result, howboyes had their place along with the purple oars and all the rest. Shakespeare removed them: the only instrumental sound he includes is the sweetly onomatopoeic 'tune of flutes'. The argument I am approaching here is a tricky one – that is, that North thought of hautboys as not only loud, like trumpets, but tuneful, like flutes, and that Shakespeare had a similar feeling about them, which led him to use them rather differently. Their omission from the rather crowded barge is of a piece with the other changes he made to North/Plutarch there: his scene is more erotic, more intimate, and hautboys were louder, more public, and thus less seductive than flutes.[24] But I suggest that he borrowed the hautboys from North's Ephesus scene for his own, altered version of the farewell scene, in which Antony is left not by the sociable god, dancing away unscathed by Antony's misfortunes, but by the tragic, solitary figure of Hercules – whose similarity to Antony, as Wofford observes, 'Soon ... seems to be a matter of suffering'.[25]

There is one more piece, or rather combination of pieces, which I think influenced Shakespeare here. The most famous example of a solitary divinity leaving a fated mortal comes almost at the end of another classical work: not Plutarch, or North, but Virgil's *Aeneid*. The hero Turnus is about to face his last defeat, and his sister, the river nymph Juturna, mournfully departs. In the lumbering words of Thomas Twyne, whose translation Shakespeare will certainly have known: 'This much she said, and straight her head in mantle blewe she hid, / Sore sighing, and anon she threw herselfe the streame amid.'[26] This moment echoes another, two books earlier, when young Pallas, an ally of Aeneas, is about to die: and this time the grieving immortal is Hercules himself: 'Alcides heard the youth, and from his heart within doth yeeld / A woful grievous grone, and frustrate teares let fall amaine.'[27] It was this, I think, that clinched it for Shakespeare: it should be the god Hercules, whom Antony loved, who now leaves him. From this combination of elements – Plutarch, two Virgilian laments and North's hautboys – he created his dark, reticent scene.[28]

'Ah, Soldier'

I began this discussion with Plutarch and Shakespeare on Cleopatra's grand entry to Antony's life: the burnished, burning barge. The queen's exit, as described by Plutarch, is correspondingly grand. Antony is dead; Dolabella has revealed Caesar's plans for her; now Cleopatra provides herself, and her attendants, with a way out. An old countryman enters, with a basket of figs and asps. Here is the end, as reported by North:

> Her death was very sodaine. For those whom Caesar sent unto her ran thither in all hast possible, and found the souldiers standing at the gate, mistrusting nothing, nor understanding of her death. But when they had opened the dores, they founde Cleopatra starke dead, layed upon a bed of gold, attired and araied in her royall robes, and one of her two women, which was called Iras, dead at her feete: and her other woman called Charmion halfe dead, and trembling, trimming the Diademe which Cleopatra ware upon her head. *One of the souldiers* seeing her, angrily sayd unto her: Is that well done, Charmion? Verie well sayd she againe, and meete for a Princes discended from the race of so many noble kings. She sayd no more, but fell downe dead hard by the bed. (316, emphasis mine)

It is a powerful scene – the dying Charmion's determination to finish fixing the crown is especially poignant – and it clearly excited North's imagination, for he added something of his own, not anticipated by Amyot. This 'souldier' is new: Plutarch says only *eipontos de tinos orgei*, 'when someone angrily spoke', faithfully rendered in French 'quelqu'un qui luy dit en courroux' (1149). It might seem a natural enough expansion, but not everyone interpreted the 'someone' this way. Before Shakespeare, the young French playwright Étienne Jodelle had written a play on the subject: he had given the question to Proculeius, the Roman envoy who had previously tricked his way into Cleopatra's monument. After Shakespeare, John Dryden would give the line to an Egyptian priest. Dryden's version is, in fact, very fine – well worth quoting:

SERAPION 'Twas what I feared. –
Charmion, is this well done?
CHARMION
Yes, 'tis well done, and like a queen, the last
Of her great race: I follow her.   [*Sinks down: dies.*²⁹

But Shakespeare followed North – to truly extraordinary effect:

1 GUARD
What work is here, Charmian? Is this well done?
CHARMIAN
It is well done, and fitting for a princess
Descended of so many royal kings.
Ah, soldier!   *Charmian dies.*
(5.2.324–7)

This addition to Plutarch has been often noted and praised – most famously by T. S. Eliot, who found that the last two words introduce a difference that 'only Shakespeare' could have made; it is always noted, however, as an addition to North.³⁰ But, as we have just seen, the addition is not to him but by him. It was North who directly inspired Shakespeare to that enigmatic little ending, which complicates so richly the grandeur and pride so strongly conveyed by Plutarch. Rather than declaiming, this Charmian is speaking to an individual: a man, who (we here become vividly aware) somehow knows her name. 'Ah, soldier!' sounds not so much lofty as mocking; teasing – whatever the precise tone we hear in it, it sounds personal. And at that moment the bedazzled Roman soldier and the elusive, intransigent Egyptian enact a private epitome of the whole tragedy: *The Tragedy of Antony and Cleopatra*.

North's scene includes another odd little addition, or twist, this one concerning neither Antony nor Cleopatra nor even Caesar, but that other adversary, the killer asp. In Plutarch's Greek, this is referred to as feminine, simply because asps are: this is their grammatical gender, rather than their biological sex. (In Amyot's French, they are masculine, in the same sense.) North, by contrast and in accordance with English idiom, makes the asp, or 'aspic', an 'it' – except in one curious sentence:

> Some report that this Aspicke was brought unto her in the basket with figs, and that she had commaunded them to hide it under the figge leaves, that when she shoulde thinke to take out the figges, the Aspicke shoulde bite her before she should see her. (316)[31]

'Before she should see her': North's pronouns are at their tricky work again; but whether the snake is looking at the queen or the other way round, they seem, at this moment, to be two of one slippery kind. 'Where's my serpent of old Nile?' (1.5.26). Here, perhaps, in this one wayward pronoun, she/her, looping Cleopatra with her final nemesis.

Conclusion: 'Well Worth Watching'

There is more to be said (and more has been said by others before) of the echoes North left in Shakespeare's mind: the 'marvelous sweete harmonie' we have observed in his account of Antony deserted found no place in *Antony and Cleopatra*'s altered scene but re-emerged some five years later, when the shipwrecked Gonzalo describes his new, haunted surroundings (*The Tempest*, 3.3). But let us say farewell to Plutarch's Cleopatra as Shakespeare also said it: in a memory of a memory of her most famous scene.

> First, her bedchamber –
> Where I confess I slept not, but profess
> Had that was well worth watching – it was hanged
> With tapestry of silk and silver, the story
> Proud Cleopatra when she met her Roman,
> And Cydnus swelled above the banks, or for
> The press of boats or pride: a piece of work

So bravely done, so rich, that it did strive
In worksmanship and value, which I wondered
Could be so rarely and exactly wrought,
Since the true life on't was –

(*Cym*, 2.4.66–76)[32]

Here Iachimo, the last and greatest of Shakespeare's voyeurs, conjures up his vision of the virtuous Innogen's bed chamber. 'Watching' has the primary sense of 'staying awake'; but here it is irresistibly ambiguous, as Iachimo draws his listener into visualizing after him.[33] The scene has always had a voyeuristic element – it was intended, after all, to make a certain effect. Enobarbus presented it to a titillated audience, acting as a sort of tempter, luring them into seeing Cleopatra as a prospect to be desired (rather than the modest, unsexy Octavia). Plutarch himself, Shakespearians seldom remember, had attributed the whole idea of the barge scene to one Quintus Dellius, a Roman who predicted, quite accurately, the effect it was likely to have on Antony:

> when he had throughly considered her beawtie, the excellent grace and sweetenesse of her tongue, he ... assured him selfe, that within few dayes she should be in great favor with him. Thereupon he ... perswaded her to come into Cilicia, as honorably furnished as she could possible. (273)

Iachimo's whole speech is an act of multiple remembering; it is woven thick with allusions. The silk and silver set up a directly reminiscent gleam; the pride of Cleopatra meeting 'her Roman' harkens back to her declaration, as she prepares herself for death: 'I am again for Cydnus / To meet Mark Antony' (5.2.227–8). The swelling and the pressing, with their air of displaced eroticism, recall the swollen tackle and the beating oars. And the 'piece of work', here literally that, brings back to mind the queen herself, as Enobarbus brought her back to Antony's:

ANTONY Would I had never seen her!
ENOBARBUS O sir, you had then left unseen a wonderful piece of work, which not to have been blest withal would have discredited your travel.

(1.2.159–62)[34]

'Now Antony must leave her utterly' (2.2.243) is the wholly unconvincing response of Maecenas to Enobarbus's marvellous evocation of their meeting. 'Never!', responds Enobarbus, 'He will not.' How is the playwright himself to say farewell to Cleopatra? Shakespeare presents Cleopatra's entrance into Antony's life, as we have seen, at second hand, as a report; in Plutarch, the last details of her death are presented in a similar way. The asp is brought in; Cleopatra shuts the doors; and the narrator pulls back. 'Her death was very sodaine', he says; but he does not commit himself to its exact means. 'Some report' the story about the figs.

> Other say againe, she kept it in a boxe, and that she did pricke and thrust it with a spindell of golde... Howbeit fewe can tell the troth. For they report also, that she had hidden poyson in a hollow raser when she caried in the heare of her head: and yet was there no marke seene of her bodie, or any signe discerned that she was poysoned, neither also did they finde this serpent in her tombe. But it was reported onely, that there were seene certeine fresh steppes or trackes where it had gone, on the tombe side toward the sea, and specially by the dores side. Some say also, that they found two litle pretie bytings in her arme, scante to be discerned... And thus goeth the report of her death. (316)

The word 'report', in one form or another, occurs here four times: after the spectacular tableau of Cleopatra's death, the snake's disappearance comes as a strange, elusive contrast.[35] Shakespeare draws on this scene, or lack of scene: the 'trackes' of the snake are seen and identified on Cleopatra's body by

Dolabella and the guard. (It is likely that Shakespeare was inspired particularly by the idea that they were seen when they were 'fresh' – North's word, the result of a misunderstanding of Amyot.[36]) The wonderful 'litle pretie bytings' (nothing like this in Plutarch or in Amyot) are transferred in the play to the asp itself, the 'pretty worm'. And the mysteriousness of the whole passage informs the last words he gives to Cleopatra herself – one of only two Shakespearian characters to die mid-sentence:[37]

> As sweet as balm, as soft as air, as gentle –
> O Antony! – Nay, I will take thee too.
> *[Applies another asp to her arm.]*
> What should I stay –   *Dies.*
> (5.2.310–12)

Charmian guesses what she meant to say: 'In this vile world?' (5.2.313). Iachimo, immediately after evoking Cleopatra's first appearance, breaks off too, presumably interrupted by his keenly listening auditor, Innogen's anguished husband. What was he about to say? Something, we might assume, about the true life of the represented scene – but what it was we cannot be sure. Since the true life was lost in the past, so it could not be surely imitated? Since (or perhaps 'ever since') the true life was dead and not to be revived?

What he saw, or said he saw, in the tapestries was something 'rare'. North, describing the scene immediately after that – Antony's dinner with Cleopatra – uses the superlative form, as he enters a room hung with lights: 'so artificially set and ordered by devises, some round, some square: that it was the rarest thing to behold that eye could discerne, or that ever books could mencion' (274–5).

The books are added by Amyot: 'few sights were so beautiful or so worthy to be seen as this', is Bernadotte Perrin's much closer translation. The rareness is North's addition.[38] Shakespeare, following him, associates the word 'rare' strongly with Cleopatra through the Romans' response to Enobarbus's story – 'Rare Egyptian!' (2.2.228), 'rare for Antony!' (2.2.215). Iachimo, the incongruously modern Italian in an ancient setting, clearly responds to the ecphrastic vision much as his ancestors had done.[39]

It was the rarest thing that ever books could mention. We have Plutarch's word for it – or rather the word of Sir Thomas North: teacher of the living; reviver of the dead.

7

New Directions

The Passion of Cleopatra: Her Sexuality, Suffering and Resurrections in *The Mummy* and *Ramses the Damned*

Sarah Olive

I will argue that the novels *Ramses the Damned: The Passion of Cleopatra* and *The Mummy* (confusingly subtitled *Ramses the Damned*) are 'passion' texts, in two senses of the word; first, in describing Cleopatra's passionate sexuality in a way that

---

I gratefully acknowledge the help of three opera-loving colleagues, some of whom are also trained musicians, in trying to decipher the influence of particular productions of *Aida* on the authors. My sincere thanks to José Alberto Pérez Díez (Leeds University), Samantha Landau (University of Tokyo, Komaba) and Clémentine Beauvais (University of York) for their advice in the preparation of this chapter. Also thanks to my Facebook friends for citations about the impact on and importance of Anne Rice to modern American literature.

is demonstrably indebted to Shakespeare's characterization of her in his play (something I show is a hypotext for and elaborated on in various popular culture representations of Cleopatra); second, in giving an account of her death and suffering (as in the Gospels' recollection of the Passion of Christ). *Ramses the Damned* (2017) is a co-authored sequel by Anne Rice and her son Christopher, coming almost thirty years after Anne's *The Mummy* (1989). Anne Rice is the author of over thirty novels: 'Rice's books have sold nearly 100 million copies, placing her among the most popular authors in recent American history.'[1] Christopher Rice had published four *New York Times* best-selling novels by the age of thirty. He writes thrillers, 'dark supernatural suspense' and erotic fiction.[2]

Ramses the Damned and *The Mummy* are set in 1914, in Africa and Britain. I have chosen them as the focus for this chapter on the influence of Shakespeare's *Antony and Cleopatra* on popular culture partly because of Anne Rice's best-selling author status and partly because of the sheer newness of *Ramses the Damned*. Yet, while the sequel is new, its premise (from the Latin for that which is 'set before': here, the texts which are set before) is old. Thus, the Rices' novels contain a plurality of resurrections, a fitting topic to dwell on in this chapter because it is only through the medium of various restorations (theatrical, filmic, televisual, musical, fictional and so on) that Shakespeare can even be considered popular culture in the early twenty-first century.

In these novels, Cleopatra's suffering occurs after – and directly stems from the physical and mental anguishes brought on by – her resurrection rather than as a precursor to it. Another facet of her suffering is represented as stemming from confronting her own pre- and early twentieth-century artistic and critical representations. The representation of her sexual allure, and resultant sexual power (particularly in its workings on Mark Antony), in popular texts, from Shakespeare to the Rices' novels, is almost ubiquitous. I demonstrate this with texts drawn from diverse genres (historical romance, parody, soft porn, adventure, science fiction), forms (such as graphic novels and animation) and intended audiences (from primary-school-aged readers to 'adults only'). Portraying the bulk of her suffering as that of a woman whose reputation has been slandered allows the characters of both novels to explore critically a range of Cleopatra narratives, including, but not confined to, Shakespeare. It invites readers to do the same by extending their consideration of her representation beyond the Cleopatra narratives available at the time and in the places in which the novels are set to those they are familiar with from their later twentieth- (and early twenty-first-) century schooling, reading and viewing. The examples I will draw on to demonstrate this hail from the UK, United States and Japan. They include anime and film. The Rices' popular fiction can be read as akin to fictocritical writing (a practice of writing that blurs traditional divisions among fiction, theory and literary criticism within a single text), as they perform feminist and post-colonial reading, critique methods for interpreting Plutarch, and scrutinize ways of determining 'authenticity' in scholarly research. This chapter concludes with a consideration of the metafictional aspects of the Rices' Cleopatra texts.

The plots of the novels, which combine elements of the adventure, horror, supernatural thriller, historical romance and erotica genres, are deliciously convoluted, so a brief synopsis of both is necessary. Anne Rice published *The Mummy* in 1989. Fictional Egyptologist Lawrence Stratford (Rice chooses her names carefully, so this may well be a deliberate Shakespearian echo) has discovered the tomb of Ramses the Great, when he is murdered by his dissolute and avaricious nephew, Henry. His daughter, Julie, aspiring to follow her father into an archaeological career, is about to be murdered by her cousin when Ramses awakes and saves her, scaring off Henry. Ramses explains to Julie that during his reign as pharaoh, he discovered the formula for an elixir of eternal life and became immortal. He served as a counsellor to the kings and queens of Egypt, including Cleopatra. He became her lover, encouraged her relationship with Julius Caesar to secure Egypt's safety from Roman domination but despised her relationship with Mark Antony. He refused to give Antony the elixir as he lay dying, suspecting Antony would then demand the elixir be used to create an immortal Roman army. After Antony's death, Cleopatra killed herself in despair, refusing Ramses' offer of the elixir for herself. The distraught Ramses had himself sealed up in a tomb.

In Julie, and her beauty, especially her brown eyes, the reawakened Ramses finds echoes of his lost love, Cleopatra.[3] Julie and Ramses begin a sexual relationship, with Ramses adopting the persona of 'Reginald Ramsey', also an Egyptologist, to pass among London society. On a visit to Cairo, Ramses recognizes an unidentified mummy as Cleopatra and revives her with the elixir. However, he is too sparing with the elixir, and the resurrection is incomplete – parts of her body remain rotted away; her brain has not been fully restored. She is sometimes incoherent as well as experiencing the compulsion to have sex with, then kill, a number of men, and to murder women of whom she is jealous, or who otherwise obstruct her. Indeed, she plots to murder Julie to exact revenge on Ramses for resurrecting her against her wishes and refusing Antony the elixir. This is not the imagined immortality leading to reunion of Shakespeare's *Antony and Cleopatra*, or Burton and Taylor.[4] As the book reaches a climax, Cleopatra falls passionately in love with the fiancé Julie has discarded for Ramses, Alex Savarell, and he returns her feelings. However, she appears to be killed in a collision between her car and a train, attempting to outrun Ramses in a chase through the desert. In fact, she awakens in a British-run hospital in Sudan, seduces her doctor, Teddy, and convinces him to elope with her, intending to resume her vengeful pursuit of Ramses. In the meantime, Julie has accepted Ramses' offer of the elixir so that they can remain together for eternity.

Ramses the Damned is the first collaborative novel from this mother and son, already independently established authors in their own right. The novel opens as the American 'Egyptian novelist' Sybil Parker ventures on a tour of England. It is no coincidence that the Rices choose for this character the name of the mouthpieces of the ancient oracles and seers: the material for Sybil's historical romances comes to her in vivid dreams about the lives of the Egyptian rulers. This inspiration is added to through research – including, in her mother's opinion, 'too much Plutarch!'[5] On arrival in the UK, Sybil visits the stately home of Alex, who is hosting an engagement party for Julie and Ramsey. Also on the move, this time from Africa to England, Cleopatra has decided to attend the event to rekindle her relationship with Alex and to confront Ramses and Julie. One of the realizations brought about by this collision of characters is that Cleopatra's soul has been repatriated in Sybil's body; that is to say, the 'dreams' that have inspired Sybil's novels are actually flashbacks. Additionally, they are sometimes intense forebodings or current experiences of Cleopatra's. They include, for example, occasions when Cleopatra is endangered (as much as an immortal can be) and when Cleopatra unites with Alex for passionate sex.[6] Cleopatra's memories, her 'true spirit', are housed in the 'vessel' or 'tabernacle' of Sybil.[7] This is supposed to explain the changes Sybil discovers in herself at the novel's outset, having developed a 'new authoritative voice' and 'assertiveness'.[8] To a limited extent, Sybil and Cleopatra are able to converse virtually. Cleopatra, on first learning of the psychic connection, suspects Sybil of trying to usurp her identity and stealing her memories. Though her body is now totally healed, the restoration of her mind remains imperfect. She particularly grieves the loss of her memories of her son Caesarion, and recalls relentlessly the death of Antony and her desire to avenge it.[9] To pacify and befriend Cleopatra, Sybil presents her with copies of all her Egyptian novels.[10] The hope is that Cleopatra will be able to fill the gaps in her mind and find peace through reading about her past experiences and emotions as recorded by Sybil.

Sexual Passion: Shakespeare's Model for a Creative Consensus on Cleopatra

The Rices' description of Cleopatra's attractiveness and passionate sexuality is part of a popular creative consensus inherited from Shakespeare, among others. In the novels, Cleopatra is robustly beautiful.[11] The Rices demonstrate a Shakespeare-like 'enjoy[ment in] the staging of Cleopatra's allure'.[12] Where Shakespeare's text establishes that Cleopatra is sexually enchanting and gratifying ('sensuous') to the point of seeming a magical being, through descriptions of her by Antony as 'this great fairy' (4.8.12) and his detailed accounts of being aroused by her, they follow and extend, making her literally magical through her resurrection.[13] Where Shakespeare has her enemy, Octavius, declare that the dead Cleopatra looks 'as she would catch another Antony / In her strong toil of grace' (5.2.346–7), Anne Rice has Ramses describe the partially unwrapped mummy in the Cairo museum, which he identifies as Cleopatra, in similarly captivating terms: 'that beautiful face ... her thick rippling hair ... the whole form had almost glistened in the dim light'.[14]

Following the Shakespearian precursor, the Rices' Cleopatra is not just beautiful but sexually passionate, skilful, indefatigable and able to use her sexual magnetism to render men subservient to her wishes: she is the 'fabled seductress of a thousand talents'.[15] Her strength and agency are manifest in her looks rather than a surprise that lies beneath more fragile features: 'the fine dark eyebrows gave her a distinct look of will and determination'.[16] Sometimes, she uses brute force in the bedroom, throwing Ramses across the bed and straddling him.[17] This is a useful reminder that in the Rices' novels some of her unique sexual force is attributed to her immortal strength and stamina. Perhaps evidence of the Rices' engagement with critical and cultural movements such as feminism, her sexuality in their novels is no longer monstrous because it is female but because it is the product of an only partially successful, supernatural resurrection. That Cleopatra is not just beautiful but also physically passionate is rooted in Shakespeare, including Antony's lines inviting her to embrace him: 'O thou day o' th'world, / Chain mine armed neck! Leap thou, attire and all, / Through proof of harness to my heart, and there / Ride on the pants triumphing!' (4.8.13–16). Her sexual agency is reiterated by several Roman characters, although in language that suggests it is excessive, even false. Shakespeare's Romans such as Scarus, as well as Antony himself, connect her sensuousness with sexual power over the leaders with whom she has united and its political consequences. The Rices' novels show flashes of this destructive sexuality in the deaths of several of the resurrected Cleopatra's six successive conquests.

Other hugely popular versions of Cleopatra's story, originated between Shakespeare's play and the Rices' novel of 2017, focus extensively on the source of her sexual allure in her physical beauty. She is termed the 'Queen of Beauty' in Rider Haggard's novel *Cleopatra* (1889).[18] Joseph Mankiewicz's 1963 film conveys Cleopatra's beauty (and sexual availability) through long, languorous shots of Elizabeth Taylor, lounging on Egyptian daybeds, her petite hourglass figure enhanced by a range of 'revealing gowns' that have become a hallmark of stage and screen productions.[19] The 1970 Japanese animation *Kureopatora* by Osamu Tezuka builds on and pornographically exaggerates live-action films in its portrayal of Cleopatra as ivory-skinned and long-legged, with voluptuous, oversized hips and thighs; almost-unfeasibly pert breasts studded with erect, pink nipples; and a black shoulder-length bob. While her beauty is ubiquitous in these Cleopatra narratives, there is rather more variation in terms of whether it translates into agency and political power. Haggard's Cleopatra is the subject of an assassination plot. Her suicide is not a powerful choice to maintain autonomy over her body but a course of action suggested to her by the duplicitous Charmion (as it is spelt in Haggard's novel), saving her faction the effort of murdering Cleopatra and overcoming the hurdle that they have struggled with to find a willing and capable assassin. Befitting the soft-porn genre it is intended to make a contribution to, her agency in *Kureopatora* is much reduced: she seduces on command from a faction within Egypt, she is subjected to the humps of a lecherous leopard when bound as a parcel for Caesar, and she is so dejected at her rejection by the homosexual Octavius that she commits suicide in despair. On top of this, her great beauty is explained away as supernatural: at the start of the film, she is an average, freckled girl given a magical makeover by an Egyptian wizard who slathers and sculpts her body with a potion. The notion of Cleopatra's feminine sexual wiles married with masculine sexual agency is at the core of Mankiewicz's film. Audiences see this when she provocatively describes her fertility to the childless Julius Caesar: 'I am the Nile. I will bear many sons. Isis has told me. My breasts are filled with love and life. My hips are rounded and well apart. Such women, they say, have sons.' In the parody of the Mankiewicz blockbuster, *Carry on Cleo*, straight-talking, warmongering Antony is reduced – on sight of Amanda Barrie's lithe Cleopatra in her bath – to growling lustfully, incoherently apologizing for the work he has been sent to do in deposing her, and agreeing to execute Ptolemy instead. While there are some limited variations in Cleopatra's beauty – which reflect different ideals of beauty for these writers, artists and directors, as well as the different genres and audiences they are aimed at – these texts demonstrate that she is universally conceived of as attractive. There is greater variation in terms of whether or not her allure results in sexual and political agency, with the Victorian and pornographic texts featured here stripping this out from their retelling of Shakespeare. The remainder of this chapter demonstrates Shakespeare's abiding presence in the Rices' novels, even as direct engagement with his play is frequently skirted by the writers.

Suffering: Cleopatra's Resurrection and 'Roman' Reputation

In terms of the second definition of passion, Cleopatra's suffering in the Rices' novels originates in part from her imperfect resurrection, which is physically painful.[20] Her mental anguish is longer lasting, as she has been given more of the elixir to treat the unrecovered areas of her body. Cleopatra is painfully aware of the gaps in her mind.[21] She asks Teddy to remind her, 'What is this thing that I am?'.[22] Her loss of memory regarding her son torments her most. Her physical and mental losses feed her murderous rage, which is dangerously coupled with supernatural strength that allows her to break the necks of her victims with ease and celerity. Yet the Rices' Cleopatra remains emotionally vulnerable, afraid that her amnesia is a sign of a madness that will engulf her completely and deny her the comfort of the sustained romantic relationship with Alex that she craves, dooming her to perpetual loneliness even as she is trapped interminably in an immortal body.[23]

However, Cleopatra's greater suffering stems from confronting the unfavourable representations of her in literature and culture, particularly those that are Roman in standpoint if not authorship, such as Plutarch's. The writer is described by Ramses as a 'liar! How dare the bastard say that Cleopatra had tried to seduce Octavian ... There was something about Plutarch which made him think of old men gossiping as they gathered on the benches in public squares. No gravitas to the history'.[24] Julie is prompted to deliver a feminist criticism of Plutarch when she reads some publicity for Shakespeare's *Antony and Cleopatra*, enjoying a run in London:

> She stood up and reached for Plutarch on the bookshelf ... Where was the story of Cleopatra? Plutarch had not devoted a full biography to her. No, her story was contained in that of Mark Antony, of course ... Cleopatra had been a great queen ... She had not only seduced Caesar and Antony, she

kept Egypt free of Roman conquest for decades ... Had Mark Antony been a little stronger, Octavian might have been overthrown. Even in her final days, however, she had been victorious in her own way ... She had tried out dozens of poisons on condemned prisoners, and then chosen the bite of a snake to end her life ... And so Octavian took possession of Egypt. But Cleopatra he could not have.[25]

As well as correcting what she sees as overestimation of Mark Antony, Julie emphasizes qualities she feels get buried in Plutarch's account but that testify to Cleopatra's equality with her male peers: her political and military leadership skills, the extent of her national and individual autonomy, and her empirical approach to researching the efficacy of poisons. Julie's reading demonstrates the way in which Roman-slanted histories have, according to the novels' key characters the Stratfords and Ramses, reduced her reputation to that of an Egyptian whore. This slur, among others, is revealed to Cleopatra herself shortly after her resurrection: she 'devoured the history books Teddy had bought for her. And it hadn't surprised her in the slightest how the Romans had told her story. A powerful whore, whose only true power lay in between her legs'.[26] Her critical stance on Roman historiography becomes known to her enemies, who seek to undermine the hopefulness and sense of self-worth she has built from critiquing her representations by expressing their scepticism in her attempts at revisionism. For example, they sarcastically invite her to 'lecture me more on your history as queen ... which aspects of your known story are truth, and which are fantasy created by an Empire that despised you and cheered your fall'.[27] Later, finding a way to appropriate advantageously that which she previously found dubious and defamatory in her legacy, she states, 'I know that I have charmed many men ... many rulers of Rome. I cannot remember how many exactly but the history books tell me I have done it and so I must be able to do it again.'[28]

The rendering of her sexual allure and wiles in the Roman-leaning histories is further degraded and parroted – to the horror of both Cleopatra and Ramses, with their first-hand knowledge of events in ancient Egypt and Rome – in the recollections of Oxford graduates such as Alex Savarell in the early twentieth century. Alex lists her qualities as taught to him thus: 'she was the trollop of the ancient word, a spendthrift, a temptress and an hysterical woman'.[29] Julie hushes Alex, insisting, 'I don't want to hear any more of your schoolboy history!', thereby unintendedly corroborating Alex's earlier assertion that 'you don't have to go to Oxford to hear mean things about Cleopatra' and confirming that disdain for Cleopatra is culturally widespread in the England of the novels, indeed systematized in its male-oriented educational institutions.[30] Indeed, the aspersions about Cleopatra put into Alex's mouth by the authors echo the verdicts of moralizing critics of the play such as John Dryden and Edward Dowden eminently available in the 1910s. Ramses has previously lashed out at the infidelity of the 'bastard' Plutarch's biography of Cleopatra.[31] On this occasion he counters Alex, insisting that the fault is in the readers – their limited powers of interpretation and inability to identify bias – not solely the text:

> She could've charmed God. Read between the lines of your Plutarch. The truth is there. She was a brilliant mind; she had a gift for languages and for governing which defied reason. The greatest men of the time paid court to her. Hers was a royal soul in every sense of the word. Why do you think Shakespeare wrote about her? Why do your schoolchildren know her name?[32]

Samir, another Egyptian and Egyptologist, joins in: 'Cleopatra was by any standards a formidable queen.' Ramses offers a parting shot: 'Egypt could use a Cleopatra now to rid it of British domination. She would have turned your soldiers packing, you can be sure.'[33] Here, even as they resist British colonialism and criticize Alex's British (mis)education, these Egyptian characters espouse an idealized view of Shakespeare and English education policy as a testimonial to Cleopatra's worth. They argue that neither the playwright nor the literary canon underpinning English education would immortalize a dissolute whore since they constitute global gold standards. Their support for both echoes the school inspector and critic Matthew Arnold's pronouncements on English education as involving 'the best that has been thought and said'. Their embracing of Shakespeare's play and canonical English literature is in stark contrast to their rejection of Plutarch's sensationalist and antagonistic treatment of Cleopatra, attributed to his Roman bias. These characters' dismissal of Plutarch is perceptive on Anne Rice's part as it contributes credibility to her depiction of England in 1914: it is redolent of the xenophobia that saw 'the national poet' Shakespeare emerge as a core ingredient in subject English in England around the First World War, replacing 'foreign' texts (i.e. the classics) and approaches such as philology.[34] Sentiments befitting the period in which the novels are set, the Western-educated, Egyptian characters' expression of them adds to the Rices' picture of the characters' complex and conflicted identities. Ramses and Samir are patriotically in favour of Egyptian independence but also collaborating with British archaeologists and, in Ramses' case, masquerading as a British expat.

Although Shakespeare is occasionally invoked by the Rices, nowhere in the novels does he come in for the savaging they mete out to Plutarch. Perhaps this is because Shakespeare provides the Rices with a model for identifying the Romans as responsible for Cleopatra's bad reputation. Shakespeare places criticism of Cleopatra in the Roman characters' mouths. Enobarbus reduces her to and objectifies her as a 'piece of work' (masterpiece), 'a new petticoat' (perhaps equivalent to our 'piece of skirt') and the 'Egyptian dish' (1.2.161, 176; 2.6.128). Antony expresses his awareness of her reputation among his countrymen when he demands of a messenger: 'Mince not the general tongue. Name Cleopatra as she is called in Rome' (1.2.112). Later, Antony – angered by her perceived over-familiarity with the (comparatively) lowly Thidias – upbraids her for her whoreish qualities: 'To flatter Caesar, would you mingle eyes / With one that ties his points?' (3.13.161–2). More explicitly, he labels her 'half blasted' (rotten), a 'boggler', 'a morsel, cold upon / Dead Caesar's trencher – nay ... a fragment / Of Gnaeus Pompey's' (3.13.110, 115, 121–3). In the next act, after she has retreated from battle, (in his mind) compelling him to follow suit, he further articulates the Roman association of whores with deception, particularly as practised by 'gipsies', and its application to Cleopatra: 'This foul Egyptian hath betrayed me' (4.12.10). He resumes this theme later, telling Eros: 'the Queen – / Whose heart I thought I had, for she had mine, / ... has / Packed cards with Caesar, and false-played my glory / Unto an enemy's triumph', 'O thy vile lady! She has robbed me of my sword' (4.14.15–20, 22–3).[35] The implication is that she has robbed him militarily (of victory), materially (of his sword), sexually (the sword has phallic connotations) and romantically (of his heart). Of course, this is not Antony's only, or predominant, view of Cleopatra. Rather, in Antony's rage, his deeply ingrained Roman prejudices against her are let fly. Shakespeare is excused by the Rices as merely 'dramatizing' Roman slanders against Cleopatra: giving voice to both sides of the warring parties through dramatic form, which makes 'Shakespeare's judgement of his characters less easy to discern'.[36] They may agree with critical interpretations of Shakespeare's nuance and even-handedness: 'Nothing purely good or evil can be found in the play and what seems admirable in one context is shown as ridiculous in another – or, rather, appears both admirable and ridiculous at one and the same time.'[37] The Rices' criticism of Plutarch's *Parallel Lives* in the novels condemns him for owning negative views of Cleopatra – such as laying the blame for Antony's decline 'squarely' on her – and for setting them forth as factual, as part of a scholarly biography.[38] However, it should be noted that the didactic purpose of Plutarch's work is to encourage readers to weigh up the merits and demerits of two historical personalities and to identify who is the better person, statesman and warrior, so as to equip readers with models of virtue to follow and of vice to avoid.[39] He 'is by no means a simple moralist': he also acknowledges their 'strengths and virtues – Antony's courage and magnanimity, Cleopatra's vitality, her magnetism'.[40] Unlike Plutarch, Shakespeare might be favoured by the Rices as an author who constitutes a model for placing Cleopatra centre stage. Shakespeare is friend, Plutarch foe as far as the Rices, or at least their characters, are concerned. However, notwithstanding his being briefly, directly invoked in the novels and his notions about the eponymous characters informing the Rices' writing, there are multiple instances in which they disavow the influence of Shakespeare's *Antony and Cleopatra* throughout, preferring to name other versions of the lovers' story. Unlike Shakespeare with Plutarch, they eschew adapting entire passages of text. Perhaps the duo in this way manifest *The Anxiety of Influence*, the authorial struggle inherent in engaging with a culturally and literarily dominant precursor: in this case, Shakespeare.[41] That Shakespeare's is the monolithic pre-text in our era is suggested by John Wilders: 'In attempting to write a play on such a celebrated subject, Shakespeare clearly set a challenge for himself. He rose to it so splendidly that in most of our minds Antony and Cleopatra actually were the people he created.'[42]

Shakespearian Creative and Critical Legacies

Almost unanimously well received by the significant characters in the book, and particularly beloved of Cleopatra and Alex, is Giuseppe Verdi's *Aida*. The opera is not ostensibly an adaptation of *Antony and Cleopatra*. Verdi deliberately specified a vast time period for the setting – 'ancient Egypt, in the time of the pharaohs' – and made 'no claims to authenticity' in his Italian Romanticist musical palette 'imbued with a convincingly mysterious and exotic hue' in order to avoid the opera being approached as 'anthropology or history' rather than 'myth'.[43] Indeed, *Aida* instead has readily identifiable parallels with another Egyptian love-triangle in the libretto for *La Nitteti*, of Italy's foremost writer of *opera seria* (the style of serious, purportedly noble, opera that predominated in eighteenth-century Europe), Pietro Metastasio. *Aida*'s creation in the late nineteenth century also represents a general vogue for Egyptology inspired by the immortalization of Antony and Cleopatra's fiery and tragic love story in literature. Verdi's composition will nonetheless readily evoke for many Shakespearian readers his knowledge of and passion for Shakespeare (including Verdi's pity at what he saw as the playwright's mistreatment by other librettists) as witnessed in his operatic adaptations of *Othello* and *Macbeth* as well as the comic opera *Falstaff*.[44] *Aida* is set in ancient Egypt and tells the story of the love between the eponymous Ethiopian princess enslaved by the Egyptians, with whom Ethiopia is at war, and the nation's military chief Radamès. In spite of her love for her father, and Radamès's otherwise loyal following of his king, their love flourishes. Amneris, the Egyptian princess, is also in love with Radamès and suspects a rival affection between Aida and Radamès. Jealous romantic and military plotting ensue, resulting in Radamès being sentenced to death in a sealed tomb – the twist being that Aida has secretly stowed herself in the tomb to die with him. The similarities between *Aida* and *Antony and Cleopatra* lie in the ancient Egyptian setting; the tragic love story between a warrior man and royal woman (who is in both – although to different extents and in markedly different roles – an outsider to Egypt, as a Greek or Ethiopian); the foregrounding of betrayals and divided loyalties between self and nation – the Metropolitan Opera's description of *Aida* as a peerless opera in 'its exploration of private emotion and public duty' could almost be taken from a critical introduction to Shakespeare's play;[45] rivalry for the warrior's hand in marriage; and the protagonists' suicidal behaviours leading to their deaths in a monumental Egyptian tomb.

There are some significant differences too. For instance, unlike Antony's or Romeo's, Radamès's death is arguably only suicide in that he knows the likely outcome of his conduct will be a death sentence. Nonetheless, Verdi's sympathetic portrayal of the faithful lovers, which foregrounds their romantic love and suffering – with no trace of stereotypes of, let alone 'austere' Roman scorn for, Egyptian 'erotic passion', 'sexual freedom', 'extravagance' and sensuousness – is accorded much greater approbation from the Rices' characters than Plutarch and other Roman-slanted histories.[46]

For example, the resurrected Cleopatra's first contact with *Aida* comes as she spies a newspaper advertisement for the opera. She snatches it up and stares at the 'quaintly Egyptian woman and her warrior lover, and the sketch of the three pyramids behind them and the fanlike Egyptian palms'. She gives an 'agitated moan' as she looks on the image – whether from longing or frustration at the partialness of her memory or at her misrepresentation is ambiguous.[47] Note that Aida is repeatedly misunderstood by the Rices' characters, or misread by the authors, as Egyptian, rather than an Ethiopian prisoner in Egypt as the libretto and productions make clear. The misreading may be deliberate on the Rices' part, perhaps to make an analogy with the story of Antony and Cleopatra, though it constitutes evidence of 'whitewashing', or at least 'lightwashing', something also discussed in relation to Shakespeare's Cleopatra.[48] The implication of the resurrected Cleopatra's response to the advertisement is that it fills her with a painful nostalgia for her past reign and her relationship with Antony and, perhaps, also Ramses (also her lover and a former military leader in his own right, with a name three letters shy of the opera's hero). Soon after this, an unspecified recording of the aria sung by Radamès, 'Celeste Aida' (Heavenly Aida), is played to Cleopatra by another character, who describes it to her as a song 'from a man to his Egyptian love', in an attempt to jog her memory of her previous life.[49] Later, in one of her victim's pockets she finds 'two small bits of paper with AIDA written on them. And OPERA'.[50] Cleopatra walks off from the scene of her crime with the tickets, curious to see the production, softly singing 'Celeste Aida' to herself. She sings it again to comfort herself when in physical pain and emotional turmoil before Ramses gives her a sufficient dose of the elixir, correctly administered orally as opposed to on the skin.[51] In *The Mummy*, Cleopatra attends the performance at the opera house in Cairo. This is the location for which Verdi's opera had been commissioned and was debuted in 1871, suggesting a knowing cultural reference on the part of Anne Rice. Cleopatra describes how 'the ugly little man sang the song ... his voice enormous, the melody enough to break the heart' (beyond this comment on this fictionalized Radamès's appearance, the cast, crew and production go unidentified).[52] At this point, readers are not given the lyrics of the aria in detail: it has only been established that it is a *romanza*, taking place in an ancient Egyptian setting and sung by a warrior to a royal woman. In *Ramses the Damned*, however, a Caruso recording of *Aida* is purchased by Alex's mother as a gift for him, transporting him back to holding the hand of Cleopatra, a 'magnificent jewelled creature, radiant with an energy that seemed almost otherwordly' in the Cairo opera house: his longing for her drives him to read the libretto of *Aida* in one go.[53] This same gift is heard playing by Alex at the end of the novel. The Italian lyrics are quoted at length as he tries to understand who is playing it, in a house he believed empty: 'Celeste Aida, forma divina / Mistico serto di luce e fior / ... Del mio pensiero / tu sei regina / tu di mia vita sei / lo splendor' (which, although it is not given in the book, translates as 'Heavenly Aida, divine form, mystical garland of light and flowers ... Of my thoughts, you are queen; Of my life, the splendour'). Following the source of the sound to the drawing room's phonograph reunites him with Cleopatra, who has secretly entered the house and put the record on. Cleopatra and Alex share a love of *Aida* because it offers them a redemptive version of Cleopatra as stable, noble and romantic rather than flighty, unprincipled and sexual, and thus (according to early twentieth-century social codes, however priggish and hypocritical) eminently more suitable for marriage into the British aristocracy. I will discuss metafictional aspects of the novels further in the conclusion, but it seems pertinent to note here briefly the introduction of a strong emphasis on this mother–son relationship in the collaborative novel by the mother-and-son authors of *Ramses the Damned*. Alex and his mother are working together to resurrect their stately home, his life after the collapse of his intended marriage to Julie and the car-crash 'death' of his lover, Cleopatra, as well as his memories from their fling through this 'Egyptian' opera; Christopher and Anne are working together to resurrect a plot and set of characters from ancient Egypt that have lain dormant for twenty-eight years. In terms of the plot, the mummy (Cleopatra) is recalled for the son by the mother's gift of a record; in terms of authorship, the mummy (both the character Cleopatra and the novelist Anne Rice) is renewed by the gift of co-authorship with the son (Christopher).

One of the exceptions to *Aida*'s acclaim in the novels comes when Ramses sees a poster for the production with what he perceives as 'a lurid, vulgar picture of ancient Egyptians entwined in each other's arms amid palms and pyramids'.[54] I have suggested throughout this chapter that there are resonances in the Rices' fiction with contemporary literary and cultural criticism, and this scene in the novel does imbue Ramses with an awareness of and disdain for Orientalism, the West's patronizing, frequently sexualized, representations of the East that would not look out of place in a discussion of Edward Said's seminal work of post-colonial criticism. Indeed, we are shown as a sign of his privilege and depravity that Henry routinely plays *Aida* on his gramophone, along with making his Egyptian concubine dress in (what he regards as) traditional costumes as part of the Oriental(ist) paradise he has created for himself in Cairo.[55] However, Ramses' ire at the production's publicity material needs to be contextualized within his own conflictedness about depictions of Cleopatra. This conflict is rooted in his desire for the original Cleopatra and his jealousy of her relationship with Antony, against which he had advised her, and leads to a further sense of her betrayal of him as both her lover and counsellor. His inner conflict is borne out in that sometimes Ramses agrees with Plutarch's and Shakespeare's Romans in their criticism of her luxuriousness identified by the novels in 'Roman' representations of her, and mouthed by Shakespeare's Roman characters as well as some of the Rices' unsympathetic ones, are explained away as products of her literal monstrosity and madness. Although her sexual allure and power have been depicted chauvinistically as metaphorically monstrous over the centuries, in the novels she is a physically monstrous hybrid of a beautiful young woman and rotten corpse. As an immortal, she is also imbued with monstrous strength to lift, throw and crush humans, and an insatiable appetite for food, drink and sex.[68] Her excessive love for Antony fits the early modern humoral theory's pathologizing of such strong emotion, and successive centuries have continued to deploy the association between love and insanity figuratively. In the novels, however, her madness stems from her pathological rage at Ramses forcing the elixir on her against her explicit instructions, her desire to revenge herself on him for this (and for refusing it to Antony) and the partial restoration of her brain tissue (and therefore also memory) due to the corrupt version of the elixir used ('the elixir itself ... is dangerous, more dangerous than you know').[69] Her mental impairment is attested to by her amnesia and compulsive desire for sex, frequently coupled with murder. Made literal, these characteristics of Cleopatra can be doubly excused: in the Rices' novels, they are not merely wilful misrepresentations of the historical Cleopatra, they are the fictional truth about her supernatural reincarnation in the early twentieth century, about the not-Cleopatra, a 'thing' masquerading in Cleopatra's familiar form, her soul split off into Sybil Parker.[70]

Conclusion

In this chapter, I have articulated some ways in which the contents of *The Mummy* and *Ramses the Damned* constitute a 'passion' of Cleopatra, giving a sympathetic account of her sexuality and suffering. I have also argued that *Ramses the*

Damned performs a resurrection of the oft-written and -filmed character, Cleopatra. This reanimation occurs on multiple levels with Anne Rice bringing back her character from *The Mummy*, almost three decades old, as well as the renewal of Cleopatra's legendary sexuality, which seems to 'breed' reincarnations because it is so ubiquitously and powerfully appealing. The appeal of writing about Cleopatra's sexuality seems to exist regardless of authors' sex or sexuality, as demonstrated by my consideration of multiple novels and films internationally: Anne Rice is a cis-gendered woman; Christopher Rice is a cis-gendered gay man. The collaboration between the mother and son could also be seen as having a regenerative force for these two authors. The collaboration with Christopher resurrects Anne's own 'salad days': *The Mummy* was published during a period when she was incredibly prolific, releasing more than a book a year, perhaps explaining why the promise that 'the adventures of Ramses the Damned shall continue' on the closing page of *The Mummy* took so long to be fulfilled. The collaboration liberates Christopher from some of the literary classifications, such as 'gay writer', of which he has spoken as constraining during his career.[71]

Throughout, I have demonstrated that the Rices blend notions from literary criticism and scholarship into their fictional narratives to tackle pejorative representations of Cleopatra in literature and culture, from Plutarch to the present. Shakespeare is included rather more approvingly than that biographer or stage productions. On occasion, he is invoked through a direct reference but more usually through the Rices' characterizations of the historical personalities. They also engage with Shakespeare indirectly by referencing his creative legacies such as *Aida*. Their apparent critical engagement is discernible in spite of Anne Rice's avowed personal disenchantment with the emphasis placed on literary criticism during her time as a doctoral student at the University of California, Berkeley: 'I wanted to be a writer, not a literature student', something similarly borne out in her son's junking two programmes of study in favour of honing his craft as, at first, a screenwriter.[72] Given their emphasis on the craft of writing, constructed in opposition to literary criticism, I want to conclude by considering some ways in which they enact metafictional writing; that is, fiction that purposefully reminds the reader of its own constructedness or literariness. True to her naming for the female oracles of ancient Greece and Rome, Sybil Parker seems to be an autobiographical mouthpiece for the Rices. She declares of her Egyptian novels that 'being freed from the burden of historical accuracy has allowed her to let her own childhood dreams of Egypt ... reign as queen over her creative process'.[73] The Rices remind their readers of their own poetic licence. In doing so, they problematize their endeavour to rehabilitate Cleopatra by reminding readers that they are adding yet another fictional representation to the existing mass. This metafictional moment ties the Rices back specifically to Shakespeare's Cleopatra, the iconic metatheatricality of that play, and establishes their shared concern with reputation and misrepresentation in his queen's declaration that:

saucy lictors
Will catch at us, like strumpets; and scald rhymers
Ballad us out o' tune: the quick comedians
Extemporally will stage us, and present
Our Alexandrian revels; Antony
Shall be brought drunken forth, and I shall see
Some squeaking Cleopatra boy my greatness
I' the posture of a whore.

(5.2.213–20)

8

Resources for Teaching and Studying *Antony and Cleopatra*

Paul Innes

Why are so many theatre audiences, readers, students and critics attracted to *Antony and Cleopatra*? This is not a question about the status of Shakespeare as a figure; there is no point in trying to summarize a centuries-long debate. *Antony and Cleopatra* can be viewed, interpreted and analysed in many ways, and no single book chapter can possibly do justice to them all. The task can seem daunting given the sheer amount of secondary material that is available about any Shakespeare play, but the effort is especially well worth making in the instance of this one. Almost by definition, therefore, the present essay involves partial choices. However, this is not a negative view of a seemingly intractable problem. *Antony and Cleopatra* lends itself to discussions of genre, ethnicity, culture, gender, empire, historical consciousness and performance, to name but a few. While many of these elements are present in other Shakespeare plays, this particular play affords many avenues of enquiry.

High-school teaching is often concerned with the usual Shakespearian suspects of a selected few comedies and tragedies. It is not difficult to see the reason for this; given constraints on time and resources, a play that needs extra information about Roman history and the Renaissance view of that history is unlikely to make it onto a national school curriculum. The play does appear more often on the university syllabus, although even here it often takes second or third place to more of the standard fare. It activates all sorts of anxieties about the pedagogical practice that lies behind curriculum design and the overall construction of the Shakespeare canon.[1]

Perhaps even more importantly in pragmatic terms, these issues cannot be separated from the whole environment that students inhabit. Despite the academic profession's commitment to learning for its own sake, students are becoming increasingly focused on what they need to learn and do to achieve the highest grades. This is something of an empty observation, since it has always been the case. However, it is much more at the forefront of current practice because of the commodification of higher education in many countries. Students are likely to have up to four part-time jobs at any one time, because they are paying for their education and need to make a living. This is the case even when they are in receipt of loans, because of course those will need to be repaid. Everyone in higher education knows that this is the reality for most students, but there is often little willingness to adapt the curriculum to swiftly changing contemporary needs. The effects on student well-being and mental health have been devastating. They still do choose their course of study because they are committed to that specific subject, but the foregoing has to be recognized because it is the immediate context within which a volume like the present one will be used by students. The current chapter seeks to provide selected resources that will meet the needs of the stressed student as well as of those more generally interested in *Antony and Cleopatra*. In fact, this volume provides an example of one of the major and perhaps most useful types of secondary critical material: the edited collection.

One can narrow the focus even further. Given the state of contemporary higher education, how exactly is this play valuable? Definitions of value will obviously vary, and so there is no exact answer to this vexed question, although it does have two parts. The first is the nature of the individual assignment, and the second is how that assignment fits into the module, course or programme as a whole. An awareness of both elements is crucial in understanding why any text or play is worth studying. Again, then, why study *Antony and Cleopatra*?

For most, the answer is simple: it is on a reading list and a deadline is looming, either examination or coursework. The latter now predominates because examinations depend on a single day that requires vast amounts of advance preparation, something that is often simply not possible for most contemporary students, and those revising *Antony and Cleopatra* for an examination are very unlikely indeed to be studying only this play, at least in the UK. Coursework assignments take many forms, such as comparisons of at least two plays. Essays are perhaps the most common assessment format, and this is exactly the attraction of *Antony and Cleopatra*: the earlier list of elements that could be used in an answer makes it an excellent play to choose for essays. This play is worth watching, reading, studying and analysing precisely because it raises many important cultural questions. Ultimately, this chapter is aimed squarely at the student who needs to get things done. The following material is not organized in alphabetical order, but for the purposes of a discursive tour. It is therefore intended to be much more than a simple annotated bibliography.

Scholarly Editions

The starting point is always the edition. In practice, the precise text tends to vary between students, who are much less concerned with the vagaries of editing than academics;

this section describes major current editions that include supplementary material of use in essay writing.

Antony and Cleopatra, ed. David Bevington (updated edn, Cambridge: Cambridge University Press, 2005).

In common with most other scholarly editions, this one (belonging to the New Cambridge Shakespeare series) has a long and useful Introduction, divided into nine sub-sections, three of which reference performance. The Introduction includes illustrations and line drawings, and appended at the end of the book are a section of textual analysis and a reading list. A full apparatus of footnotes accompanies the text on every page.

Antony and Cleopatra, ed. Emrys Jones (London: Penguin, 2005).

This is the play's entry into the ubiquitous Penguin Classics series. First published in 1977, this particular edition carries a further Introduction by René Weis. He also adds a section on the play in performance and a reading list; these usefully update Jones's text. Rather than accompanying notes, the Penguin series adopts the convention of a section of critical commentary that comes after the full text itself.

Antony and Cleopatra, ed. Ania Loomba (New York: Norton, 2011).

Though more expensive than others, the Norton Critical Editions are especially useful for students because each includes a large selection of secondary material. Accordingly, rather than a long Introduction, there is a short preface to the play; the text has footnotes on every page, mostly devoted to specific Renaissance word usage. This edition includes a chapter on sources, analogues and contexts, encompassing classical material such as Herodotus on Egypt and Plutarch's 'Life of Antony', as well as contemporary Renaissance references to the couple and extracts from the period's writings about women. There is a substantial selection of critical material, in addition to sections from adaptations in various genres. The volume concludes with a selected bibliography.

Antony and Cleopatra, ed. John Wilders (London and New York: Routledge for Arden Shakespeare, 1995).

This is the play's entry in the well-known scholarly Third Arden Shakespeare series. The long introduction has nine subsections. Six deal with major critical issues regarding the play, while the final three adopt the standard Arden approach to source material, date of composition and textual issues. The play is accompanied by full footnotes throughout.

Antony and Cleopatra in Monographs about Shakespeare and Rome

Book-length treatments of topics and plays that include *Antony and Cleopatra* inevitably come in different flavours, and quite a few have appeared since the 1970s. However, unlike the other types of material discussed in this chapter, these texts will be characterized in terms not only of what they say about the play but also how they treat Shakespeare's overall interest in ancient Rome. Some discuss his Roman reimaginings as a single epic; others focus more precisely upon the play as a dyad with *Julius Caesar*; and still others treat the various Roman plays, however defined, as modulations of an ongoing theme. The first few, by Robert S. Miola, Paul A. Cantor and Warren Chernaik, provide reasonably recent studies of issues that could be considered conventional. Some of the other material looks in different directions.

Robert S. Miola, *Shakespeare's Rome* (Cambridge: Cambridge University Press, 1983).

Miola's introduction is entitled 'The Roads to Rome', signalling a central concern with the place of Rome in Shakespeare's imagination. This is, however, contextualized in relation to contemporary English Renaissance uses of Rome: 'it seems clear that some consideration of Elizabethan classicism should preface consideration of Shakespeare's Rome' (3). The attitude to classical antecedents is characterized as having a rather haphazard approach to historicity:

> English classicism came to be ahistorical and eclectic in character, little concerned with understanding the past on its own terms. Shakespeare's anachronisms are to the point here, evidencing the age's disregard for historical accuracy, at least as we understand the concept. (9–10)

These two short quotations raise important issues not only of how Shakespeare's versions of Rome relate to others in the writings of his contemporaries but also how they might differ from ours. The term 'anachronism' is crucial here, alerting the reader to historical difference.

The chapter on *Antony and Cleopatra* is divided into an introductory passage, followed by seven sections. It locates the play as 'in many ways a sequel to *Julius Caesar*' (116), a common perspective – also touched upon in the Introduction to the present volume – that bases the relationship on the death of the republic and the birth of the empire: 'In addition to the popularity of subject matter, the two plays share a focus on the same critical juncture in Roman history: the decades encompassing the dissolution of Republic, and the birth of Empire' (116). The difference is that 'Rome in this play is not simply a city ... but an Empire, a world unto itself' (117).

The first section separates the worlds of Rome and Egypt via the figure of Cleopatra: 'Infinitely variable, she is the antithesis of Roman constancy and, therefore, perfectly fitted for her role as critic of Roman values' (119). Without explicitly stating the case, the book feminizes Egypt in relation to the Roman world by personifying Egypt as Cleopatra. This is a familiar position: 'Antony's leave-taking of Cleopatra, carefully prepared for by the conversation with Enobarbus, allows Cleopatra to display her power, pettiness, temper, and theatrical talents' (122). Cleopatra is passionate and irrational, a consummate actress, and Rome is by definition her binary opposite. Section two of the discussion concentrates on the Romans by way of contrast. As a major Roman political figure and general Antony is seen to have much in common with Octavius, while 'Unlike the contrast between Caesar and Antony, the contrast between Caesar and Cleopatra is clear-cut and unqualified' (129), reinforced by geographical and gendered difference. The third section spends time on Roman political infighting and 'bargaining' (134) by reference to Gnaeus Pompey, providing commentary on that old favourite of Shakespeare critics, the internally flawed protagonist: 'Before the outbreak of war and the Battle of Actium, Shakespeare shows Antony and Octavius to be flawed and ambivalent characters' (136). Section four concentrates on the importance of Cleopatra's gendered difference, suggesting that her 'attempt to play the man fails and results in death and disorder' (137). It is tempting to note that couching the result in terms of her failure effectively to be a man replicates an ages-old gendered hierarchy that privileges men, but of course the nascent Roman empire is resolutely patriarchal. Cleopatra is doomed to failure because the world in which she has to act is already coded politically and militarily as masculine.

Section five concentrates on the meanings generated by geographical difference: 'As in *Julius Caesar*, spatial and topographical metaphors express the transfer of power, this time from Antony to Octavius' (142). Nestling here, though, is an underlying insistence that what truly matters is the internal process constituting the tragic protagonist: 'Antony's rise from the nadir of misfortune and dishonor is a long spiritual process that begins with getting off the ground and ends with ascent to the tomb' (143), a vocabulary that is recalled in the following section when attention shifts to Cleopatra: 'Like Antony's falling on the sword, this falling begins a process of spiritual rising, an ascent that will result in transcendent reunion' (151). Political disaster allows the ineffable to be unmasked. The chapter ends with a return to the nature of Octavius's new Roman empire. However, it qualifies any binary opposition between the play's versions of Rome and Egypt: 'the dichotomy between these places and these values does not remain absolute and unqualified' (158).

Paul A. Cantor, *Shakespeare's Rome: Republic and Empire* (Chicago, IL: Chicago University Press, 2017).

This is the second edition of a book first published in 1976, together with a new preface. The first half reads *Coriolanus* as defining Shakespeare's understanding of republican politics, forming the basis for a comparison with the empire in *Antony and Cleopatra* in Part 2. Sometimes the pairing is modulated via *Julius Caesar*, a tendency that is enacted in full in Cantor's latest book on Rome, discussed below. The new preface sets the tone:

> In this book I work out the details of how the republican and imperial regimes operate, and I also do more of the kind of character analysis typical of most studies of the Roman plays, for example, discussing the pride of Coriolanus and the love of Antony and Cleopatra in ways that I do not in *Shakespeare's Roman Trilogy*. (4)

Many of his concerns are therefore similar to those of Miola, although there are important differences, especially when Cantor delineates the relationship between the public and private spheres.

Cantor is quite explicit about this from the outset of his material on *Antony and Cleopatra*:

> Antony and Cleopatra are not typical of lovers in general but claim a special status for their passion. In fact their insistence that they 'stand up peerless' (I.i.40) in the eyes of the whole word suggests that they have found an imperial form of love to correspond with the imperial form of politics that prevails in their era. (127)

He glosses the specific nature of their love on the next page: 'the early Roman Empire supplies the hothouse conditions necessary for such exotic flowers as the imperial love of Antony and Cleopatra to flourish' (128), and,'In the Empire, the rewards of public life begin to look hollow, whereas private life seems to offer new sources of satisfaction' (128). Politics, love and the relationship between them structure the second part of the book. The love between this pair is for Cantor already imbricated in an imperial world, and the connection between love and the nature of the empire's power is his main interest – he assumes that the Roman empire has already come into existence. In point of historical fact, of course, it is the demise of Antony and the supremacy of Octavius that ushers in the imperial era. Antony's death is required for the empire to emerge; this book defines Antony's character (and Cleopatra's) in relation to an emperor's dictates, so losing the political battle before the fact of military defeat.

The book accordingly insists throughout on the importance of 'desires' (134) and 'spiritual emptiness' (135), thereby personalizing the political in a way that is echoed to some extent by Miola. There is a similar treatment of topography: 'Merely locating the city of Rome in *Antony and Cleopatra* has become difficult, for it seems to have been swallowed up in the vast territory it conquered' (136). The effect of these imperial dislocations is shown by a case study of the character of Enobarbus (146–8), followed in the second chapter by further reference to the figure of Antony, who 'has no such blind attachment to the Roman cause, and sees more clearly than most of his contemporaries the questionable aspects of public life in the Empire' (155). The inevitable destruction of Antony's cause is rooted in his character psychology as a manifestation of new modes of being in a post-republican world, producing something akin to a death drive (164ff). In the final chapter, tragedy arises because 'Antony and Cleopatra want to excel in love just as the Republican Romans want to excel in war' (186), and 'as the play progresses it becomes clear that Antony has staked his whole sense of his worth as a man on the fact that Cleopatra loves him' (188). These two short passages could serve as working definitions of the book's critical position on the play.

Paul A. Cantor, *Shakespeare's Roman Trilogy: The Twilight of the Ancient World* (Chicago, IL: University of Chicago Press, 2017).

Cantor's second book on Shakespeare and Rome extends and refines nascent elements from the first. His Nietzschean philosophical underpinnings are made more explicit, introducing *Julius Caesar* more fully as it mediates between the ancient republic and the newly emerging empire; he pays relatively little attention to *Antony and Cleopatra*, which occupies the final chapter. Refiguring the focus of his first book, the Introduction to this one sees the emergence of the empire as a radical departure from the republican view of the city as sufficient in and of itself; the drive to empire produces a set of logical consequences.

The chapter on *Antony and Cleopatra* shows this process at work, returning to the play by relocating some of the concerns of its predecessor. It argues for the centrality of the Mediterranean world to Shakespeare's imagination, the corollary being the critical importance of Rome in his conception. The chapter just prior to this one discusses Rome's role in shaping English Renaissance notions of the imperial state as a precursor to the emerging British empire (195–6), with the material on the play itself tellingly subtitled 'Empire, Globalization and the Clash of Civilizations'. It is a short piece (210–24), comparing conceptions of empire in the Renaissance via Rome to modern global politics: globalization 'constantly awakens new desires in the process of satisfying old ones; it dissolves old orders even as it brings new ones into being' (224). The book therefore replays the methodology of its predecessor: politics and desire are intertwined.

Warren Chernaik, *The Myth of Rome in Shakespeare and His Contemporaries* (Cambridge: Cambridge University Press, 2011).

Chernaik provides a variation on a by now familiar theme, the relationship between love and politics:

> Throughout *Antony and Cleopatra*, Cleopatra keeps up a running commentary on conventional Roman notions of heroism and masculinity, and the virtues of the cold, efficient Octavius Caesar are less attractive and dramatically interesting than the vices of his rival Antony. (3)

Here again the focus is on Antony's politically self-destructive behaviour, as noted by Cleopatra. However, there is a slippage as Chernaik shifts from Cleopatra's viewpoint to a generalized statement about dramatic power. It is inevitable that Octavius's Egyptian rival has a negative view of his version of Rome, but her role takes over critical discourse as well.

The chapter on the play is entitled 'O'erflowing the Measure: *Antony and Cleopatra*', recalling the conventional critical assumptions already noted; they achieve boundless love even as they are destroyed. It begins with Scarus's choral speech about Antony's conduct at the Battle of Actium, showing that Antony lacks political and military judgement (135). The first section is entitled 'Tragic Cleopatras', following on logically enough from the implications of Antony's desertion of his navy. This part of the chapter refers to other English Renaissance texts concerning Cleopatra in addition to Shakespeare's version, contextualizing the issues. The third section is concerned with Roman values, concentrating on the power relationships between the play's important Roman figures.

The final section is entitled 'Immortal Longings', emphasizing the importance of the grandstanding love of the protagonists. The structure of Chernaik's argument is most instructive: it begins with one character's denigration of the effects of the couple's love on Antony's capacity for action; it then moves through a historical contextualization of the story as it was understood in the English Renaissance, especially upon the stage; and it ends by means of their love's transcendence of mere politics and an emerging imperial state. In this reading, the doomed love of the protagonists becomes profound. A common theme is emerging in these four books, couched in ways that seem reassuringly modern: the personal love between Cleopatra and Antony is tragically elevated above the mundane world.

Coppélia Kahn, *Roman Shakespeare: Warriors, Wounds and Women* (London and New York: Routledge, 1997).

Belonging to a series of feminist analyses of Shakespeare, Kahn's book departs radically from the seemingly standard critical line even though it predates Chernaik's by over a decade. Her Introduction investigates the kind of 'anachronism' mentioned by Miola, but with a difference: 'Through a kind of cross-pollination that isn't simply anachronism, Englishness appears in Roman settings, and Romanness is anglicized' (4). Kahn reformulates what later cultures like our own might see as anachronistic, registering a sense of the productive possibilities afforded by the dynamic relationship between ancient Rome and the English Renaissance. She comments on both Roman and Renaissance politics in Shakespeare's approach to Rome: 'Skillfully deploying details culled from Livy or Plutarch, he evokes the workings of a republic or an empire, making them intelligible to the subjects of a monarchy' (14). Her insistence on the primacy of the political in Shakespeare's conception of Rome differentiates her book from the others just discussed; even more marked is her investigation of gender relations within this context.

She investigates them, however, in a perhaps unexpected manner. One might naively assume that a feminist analysis would concentrate on Cleopatra, especially given the conventional critical tendency to oppose her femininity to the rational masculine world of Rome. However, Kahn focuses upon Antony, with her chapter on the play entitled 'Antony's Wound'. She delineates a more 'deconstructionist' approach, refusing to characterize Rome and Egypt as simple binary opposites:

Such a stance ignores the historical specificity of the narrative Shakespeare dramatizes, and the political circumstances determining the creation of that narrative. Furthermore, it fails to take full account of Antony's ambivalence and the more radical instabilities of his subjectivity. (111)

Kahn analyses Antony's 'subjectivity' as deeply unstable, influenced by both Rome and Egypt, comprising an ambivalence that structures the interplay between the time periods in Shakespeare's drama. This is a feminist understanding of masculinity as historically and culturally produced. The vocabulary retains traces of a less 'materialist' approach by utilizing subjectivity rather than the terminology of the subject, but even so Kahn is clearly trying to show how Antony is constructed (or over-determined) by conflicting cultural imperatives.

This chapter carefully locates issues that an older critical tradition would call Antony's 'character' by relating its effects to Shakespeare's uses of Plutarch:

> As Linda Fitz demonstrates, Shakespeare's departures from Plutarch's account 'mitigate Cleopatra's culpability' for Antony's defeat (1977: 310). More than that, his play dramatizes the Roman construction of her agency as such – as an ideological reading of events that differs from what can be known about them but effectively becomes what is known about them.[2] (117)

Such an emphasis on the importance of Antony destabilizes any easy assumption of a binary opposition between Rome and Egypt because he oscillates between them. It also implicitly reinforces the importance of Antony as part of the play's eponymous pairing, restoring him to something like parity in the face of a critical tradition that often gets carried away by the figure of Cleopatra, whose position is also shown to be ideologically constructed.

As with many other critics who have written on this play, Kahn ends her chapter with death, in this case that of Antony.

But she does so in a way that denies a simple identification of Antony with Egypt in the form of Cleopatra:

> But even in her arms, with death upon him, he portrays himself as 'a Roman by a Roman / Valiantly vanquished' (4.15.59–60), countering the undertow of her attraction for him by evoking a reciprocity with Caesar that, even though fatal, insures Romanness. (137)

Even at the moment of Antony's death, then, and in a refreshing departure from the critical tradition, Kahn insists on the tension between Rome and Egypt that constructs Antony's 'subjectivity'.

Lisa S. Starks-Estes, *Violence, Trauma and* Virtus *in Shakespeare's Roman Poems and Plays: Transforming Ovid* (Basingstoke: Palgrave Macmillan, 2014).

This is a major publication in the fast-developing field of literary trauma studies. In accordance with a post-Freudian psychosexual understanding of trauma, literature and plays are read for signs of post-traumatic stress. This absolutely requires characters to be treated like real people so that they can be analysed as surface manifestations of deeply buried elements of the human psyche. Starks-Estes is clear about this procedure in Shakespeare, by focusing on his uses of Ovid:

> In his Roman poems and plays, in which matters of violence and its effects are heightened, Shakespeare creatively transforms Ovidian subjects to grapple with them, foregrounding the trauma inherent in subjectivity and shifting conceptions of the self. (3)

The self itself is the ultimate subject of study, the fundamental centre of cultural endeavour, and her book reads how Shakespeare grapples with selfhood and identity. Accordingly, Starks-Estes defines the Ovidian project as registering 'the traumatic effects of violence, the shattering of the self' (13). The literary self that Ovid invents is constituted in opposition to the powerful tradition of the epic (11–13), the tension between the two going on to inform later writers like Shakespeare.

This book is well aware of possible challenges to its central position, defined as 'employing psychoanalysis and contemporary trauma theory, combined with materialist approaches' (16). There is a tendency for psychoanalytical readings to dispense with historical or cultural specificity because they are merely surface variations of deeper truths. Although Starks-Estes invokes 'materialist approaches', a reader would have to dig through the book very deeply indeed to try to find any materialist examples. Her book is therefore similar to many other monographs that provide a literary analysis, with performance considered to be of secondary importance.

The Introduction sets up the central emphasis on the sense of self. The individual chapters modulate this critical position via various texts, including *Antony and Cleopatra*. Starks-Estes revealingly gives this chapter the title of 'Dido and Aeneas "Metamorphis'd": Ovid, Marlowe, and the Masochistic Scenario in *Antony and Cleopatra*'. The emphasis is resolutely on the personal desires of the main characters and the relationship between them, extending to lesser figures too: 'Moreover, Enobarbus' setting is strikingly similar to that of desire itself, particularly as conceived of early modern discourses of love sickness and later psychoanalytical theory' (101), which, of course, suggests that cultural elements separated by well over 300 years are uncannily similar. Starks-Estes uses the work of Gilles Deleuze to characterize the masochistic drive of desire as she moves on from Enobarbus to the two lovers (102). Overall, she replays in more avowedly psychoanalytical terms the tragic dichotomy already noted in the conventional critical tradition: 'Triumphant figures of Ovidian transformation, Antony and Cleopatra's deaths may be seen as a happy ending – at least for the anti-Augustan tradition' (108). Here again a modern re-reading of the play sees the personal as much more important than the political; such an observation would no doubt delight a psychoanalytic critic.

Paul Innes, *Shakespeare's Roman Plays* (London: Palgrave Macmillan, 2015).

This volume takes stock of developments in critical theory to interrogate many of the assumptions that lie behind the critical tradition, at least as they manifest in writing about Shakespeare and Rome. The Introduction is very short because the emphasis is on the individual plays, each treated separately from the others. There is no overarching narrative of Shakespeare's engagement with the classical past; since Shakespeare has been dead for 400 years, using the plays to reconstruct his thoughts would seem to be rather pointless. Part of the reason for this is that these are plays; the medium itself renders any retrospective very problematic indeed. Trying to locate meaning in the figure of the author would at best produce a partial reconstruction that says more about the critic's assumptions than it ever could about Shakespeare. The book is accordingly very suspicious of totalizing narratives.

The chapter on *Antony and Cleopatra* has three main concerns, and each considers some of the elements familiar from previous criticism. The first is the play's representations of Cleopatra, which are interrogated in terms of the Virgilian epic tradition that has been so powerful in the production of discourses of empire. The chapter investigates this tradition's denoting of Cleopatra as an Orientalized and feminized other, analysing her instead in relation to Roman politics via Antony. Although Cleopatra did make politically astute use of the trappings of the pharaohs, she was nevertheless the heiress of a fundamentally Greek elite culture. A progeny of the Ptolemies, she descends from one of Alexander the Great's foremost generals, a member of the dynasty that sought to establish pre-eminent control over Greek learning and culture via the institution of the Great Library. Unlike Starks-Estes' book, this book sees the figuration of Cleopatra very much as a Virgilian construction, following the crucial trajectory established in the *Aeneid*. The distinction necessarily and inevitably undercuts any assumption of a binary opposition between Egypt and

Rome. Much like Antony, then, Cleopatra is perceived to be a site for the contestation of classical values.

The second major element of the chapter is a return to anachronism, in an attempt to theorize the historical consciousness that lies behind English Renaissance attempts to manage the history of Rome. Anachronism is reconfigured as a peculiarly modern invention, which does not exist in that form during the Renaissance. Instead, following some of the observations made by Kahn, this book seeks to uncover a dynamic interplay between classical and contemporary notions of Rome. The perception is that both are operating at the same time, in all sorts of dazzling, conflicted and confusing ways, as the play tries to make sense of Roman history to fit its own very current cultural concerns. This doubled perspective is labelled 'anamorphic', a term derived from art history.

The third issue dealt with in this chapter is the fact that these are plays. Performance theory is seen as a corrective to conventional criticism that reads the plays exclusively as literature. Many critics do of course mention performances, either in Shakespeare's time, our own, or both, but it is very often lip-service. The analysis here balances Cleopatra's cultural importance with Antony's stage presence, especially in the public theatres of Renaissance London. Any such reconstruction is entirely provisional, of course, but at least it attempts to move beyond a narrowly literary conception of the play. Lurking beneath these critical manoeuvres is an awareness that Shakespeare's plays were reconstituted as literature by subsequent cultures.[3]

Antony and Cleopatra in Other Monographs

It is not surprising that a play at the nexus of so many critical views about major cultural issues also appears in writing concerned with topics other than Shakespeare and Rome. What follows is a sample of such work, chosen for the way these contributions interact with major questions of critical theory, not just literary enquiry. Not all have individual chapters on this play, but they do provide important perspectives in addition to the more traditional ones.

Jonathan Dollimore, *Radical Tragedy: Religion, Ideology and Power in the Drama of Shakespeare and His Contemporaries* (2nd edn, Hertfordshire: Harvester Wheatsheaf, 1989).[4]

First published in 1984, *Radical Tragedy* is an important corrective to criticism that views tragedy as somehow inherent to the protagonist, usually manifested in Shakespearian criticism as the well-known formulation of the tragic flaw. Dollimore eschews this emphasis on a historically recently constructed individualism, instead producing a Hegelian theorizing of tragedy as a social form. This provides a nuanced view of the forces that constitute Antony's position:

> heroic *virtus* may appear to be identical with the dominant material forces and relations of power. But this is never actually so: they were only ever coterminous and there is always the risk that a new historical conjuncture will throw them into misalignment. This is what happens in *Antony and Cleopatra*; Antony, originally identified in terms of both *virtus* and those dominant forces and relations, is destroyed by their emerging disjunction. (206)

Dollimore defines the interest of this conflict of forces for the English Renaissance slightly earlier in his discussion, noting that plays like this one were 'Staged in a period in which there occurred the unprecedented decline of the power, military and political, of the titular aristocracy' (204). Even though he is a Roman triumvir, Antony is nonetheless imbricated in this Renaissance play as a member of the aristocracy, because these are the circumstances within which he is constructed. By extension, then, it could be argued that Octavius Caesar wins because he is more successful at managing the contradictions produced both by the nascent Roman empire and its English Renaissance reconfiguration. Within this context, Dollimore's reformulation of tragedy as fundamentally social refuses to grant Antony's death any transcendent power: 'As effective power slips from Antony he becomes obsessed with reasserting his sense of himself' (210). He further supplements this observation on the next page: '*Virtus*, divorced from the power structure, has left to it only the assertion of a negative, inverted autonomy' (211). Such a perspective radically questions the modern privileging of the supposedly autonomous subject, in a return to the social conditions that precede it.

Ania Loomba, *Gender, Race, Renaissance Drama* (Oxford: Oxford University Press, 1989).

Loomba's book does not contain a chapter specifically on *Antony and Cleopatra*, instead referencing the play as she moves across thematically topical chapters. This permits a more dispersed analysis, allowing her to relate the observations of her individual chapters to the general terrain outlined in the book's title. It is a necessary move because she wishes to discuss not just the three issues of gender, race and performance but how they intertwine. The most sustained encounter with *Antony and Cleopatra* comes in a chapter entitled 'Theatre and the Space of the Other', in a section subtitled 'Spatial Politics'. Loomba sets up the standard stereotypical opposition between masculine Rome and feminine Egypt, but, in a move similar to that of Dollimore, she notes how the figure of Antony fragments after Actium:

> Without power, without space, without Rome and without Cleopatra, Antony disintegrates. It is important that Cleopatra's transformation into the 'whore' and 'witch' occurs precisely at this point: the language of what Antony perceives as a betrayal reduces Cleopatra's 'infinite variety' to both patriarchal and racist stereotypes. (127)

Here is another important corrective to critical convention: Antony himself decries and derides Cleopatra in the language constructed for her by their Roman opponents. This demonstrates the ideological nature of that discourse precisely because it is so partial; it also deals a body blow to criticism that sees their love at the end as somehow transcendent. Loomba's characterization of Cleopatra similarly comprises contradictory elements; not only are these to be expected in a critical analysis of her as a figure, they are managed in this book by interrogating the discourse that previously constructed her personality. This section on the play finishes by describing the performed contradictory elements of the play's ending as 'false resolutions' (129).

Pauline Kiernan, *Shakespeare's Theory of Drama* (Cambridge: Cambridge University Press, 1998).

Kiernan's book ends with a chapter entitled '*Antony and Cleopatra* as a Defence of Drama'. This balances her first main chapter, which takes a challenging look at dramatic works in an era that produced Philip Sidney's *Defence of Poesy*. She emphasizes the importance, fleeting though it is, of the body in performance, the physicality of acting:

> For Shakespeare's audience, the historical Cleopatra can never appear 'indeed'. The meeting at Cydnus between the two famous lovers is an event in history that history itself has made irretrievable. What spectators at the Globe in the seventeenth century, and spectators at the new Globe in the twentieth century, can see is Shakespeare's Cleopatra: there, she appears 'indeed'. In Plutarch's narrative, Cleopatra's physicality is nowhere described; in Enobarbus' report, little other than her physicality is described. (158–9)

For Kiernan, the moment of performance puts in question the competing discourses, historical and contemporary, adhering to the performing body of the actor, and perhaps even obliterating them (although of course traces do survive). It is almost impossible for late modern audiences not to be aware of both the historical Cleopatra and also Shakespeare's version of her even as they watch another unfolding for their own cultural moment. Kiernan suggests that performance is layered almost like an archaeology of stage presences. It is this immediate context in her chapter that sets the scene for the discussion of Cleopatra, Antony and Octavius Caesar that follows, especially and most importantly the interrelationships among all of them. She resolutely insists on the crucial importance of physicality in all of this:

> a plain utterance is heightened and intensified by the simple, physical act of it being spoken as an exclamation. It is language at its most prosaic describing the most commonplace of human actions. But what it conveys, and conveys most powerfully, is the sense of a human body: the man's solid weight of flesh and bone is what we are aware of. (174)

It is no coincidence that this play provides the pinnacle for Kiernan's argument about the primary importance of performance. After all, the Renaissance dramatists' penchant for self-reflective statements is particularly acute in *Antony and Cleopatra*. What criticism like this does is remind us that these plays are also, crucially, about themselves in performance.[5]

Edited Collections

These take two forms: books like this containing new essays, and collections of previously published chapters and essays. The first type is relatively rare when compared with the second, but both are invaluable resources because they bring together a large amount of material on the same topic. They tend to be produced in major series such as the Longman Critical Readers or the Arden Early Modern Drama Guides (previously Continuum Renaissance Drama). Such series can be treasure troves of information on all sorts of subjects, Shakespeare aside.

John Drakakis (ed.), *Antony and Cleopatra: Contemporary Critical Essays* (Basingstoke: Macmillan, 1994).

The original Macmillan Casebook series contains a great deal of older literary critical material; the New Casebooks provide much more recent criticism in one convenient place. They fall into the second category defined above, since they collect already published information, albeit with a new editorial introduction. Mostly, these take the form of essays that have been influenced in some way or another by elements of critical theory, and this one is no exception. It contains twelve pieces, reprinted in the form of essays, although some of them were originally published as book chapters. In the words of the Introduction:

> The first six essays in the present collection, ranging from John Danby's attempt to problematize the act of judgement in *Antony and Cleopatra*, through Janet Adelman's and Phyllis Rackin's focus on the rhetorical function of poetry, to Terence Hawkes's account of its social context, and then beyond to Neville Davies's and Margot Heinemann's varying accounts of the play's negotiations of 'history', all in their different ways mark a distinct departure from those traditional approaches which privilege transcendental themes, and which express an uncritical fascination with the seductive allure of Cleopatra. (17–18)

None of these essays, therefore, is taken from the monographs that are described in this particular chapter of the current volume, precisely because they are oppositional in tone to the received wisdom of conventional criticism. The rest of

Drakakis's Introduction investigates why this should be so, forming a context for the other essays collected in his collection.

Naomi Conn Liebler (ed.), *The Female Tragic Hero in English Renaissance Drama* (Basingstoke: Palgrave Macmillan, 2002).

Liebler's collection contains one essay that relates Shakespeare's play to two other Renaissance dramas about Cleopatra, plus one that is fully concerned with Shakespeare's play. Liebler's primary interest in editing this collection is stated in her Introduction:

> What has been missing from feminist criticism of tragedy, especially, is a reading of women as such actors and agents, as tragic heroes, protagonists positioned in their plays in precisely (or nearly so) the same ways as Hamlet, Othello, King Lear, Dr. Faustus, and Macbeth. This volume aims to supply that reading by exploring the dimensions of a feminist tragic heroic discourse. (2)

Regarding *Antony and Cleopatra*, such a project sidesteps many of the issues that have been raised in the current chapter, because Liebler's book is itself produced by a very specific kind of critical discourse: 'Tragedy always tells the tale of a culture in crisis; it depends no less on what happens in domestic arenas than it does on what happens on battlefields' (3).

The two investigations of the figure of Cleopatra in this collection fully accord with this editorial position. In her essay on three versions of Cleopatra, Mimi Still Dixon notes the resonances produced by the queen's theatricality:

> Shakespeare's *Antony and Cleopatra* is a complex play in part because it foregrounds these issues of sexual power and visual perspective, of subjects and objects and knowledge relations. By doing so, it avoids the simple resolutions of the moralizing or romanticizing representation. (75)

Such a critical gesture therefore refuses the usual closure enacted upon the play as privileging the fecund power of love over the dearth of politics. Dixon shows how the figure of Cleopatra ultimately undoes such simplistic assumptions:

> Cleopatra, of course, is the supremely self-conscious object. She exploits her power as visual object with her unrelenting theatrics. Her personal and political strategies depend on the power of theatrical spectacle. (76)

This formulation comes very close indeed to the kind of performative power ascribed to Cleopatra by Kiernan. Dixon is effectively proposing that a notable, and culturally variable, confluence of effects is produced by the extraordinary affective power of gender in performance.

Kay Stanton provides the second essay in the collection that discusses *Antony and Cleopatra*. Unlike Dixon, she is interested in Cleopatra's mythic resonances. Her starting point reaffirms the editorial gloss already noted in Liebler's Introduction: 'male and female literary critics have resisted granting Shakespeare's Cleopatra full status as tragic hero' (93), and, again, 'The same Greco-Roman tradition that would propagandize against the historical Cleopatra as "prostitute queen" also defined and refined the genre of tragedy' (93). Stanton shows that the rules of the game are already fixed against personages such as Cleopatra, although she sees Shakespeare's play as in some sense reacting in performance against that tradition.

Journal Articles

No book chapter can possibly cover the volume and range of articles on a play such as *Antony and Cleopatra*. However, this is where the internet starts to flavour critical material because of the availability of essays in digital formats. This is especially important because of the difficulty in easily accessing paper copies of journals, not all of which are carried even by university libraries, which are in many cases reallocating their budgets from print to electronic. The two main collections of peer-reviewed academic journals are Project Muse (https://muse.jhu.edu) and JSTOR (https://www.jstor.org). Much depends on precisely which of several journal collections that exist within both is available to a particular library; what this means in practice is that access to journals depends on which virtual collection has been purchased. Their online availability, however, makes them at least as important as edited collections, because they provide instant digital versions of many items at the same time, and these can be searched for specific phrases or texts. JSTOR has recently gone further in this regard, with a new search engine capable of enumerating all of the essays in the collection containing a set phrase. For example, one could take a speech from *Antony and Cleopatra* and look for any essay that quotes that passage. Many of these will be older critical essays, but the utility of such a process is obvious.

Historical Information

Shakespeare's primary source is of course Plutarch; see Early English Books Online – Text Creation Partnership: http://quod.lib.umich.edu/e/eebo/A09802.0001.001?view=toc. A useful modern edition is *Plutarch: Lives of the Noble Grecians and Romans*, ed. Arthur Clough (Oxford: Benediction Classics, 2010). The section on Antony is on 854–9. *The Comparison of Demetrius and Antony* that follows (890–1) paints Antony in an unflattering light.

The most thorough recent historical biography of the famous couple is Adrian Goldsworthy, *Antony and Cleopatra* (London: Weidenfeld & Nicolson, 2010).

A recent overview of Shakespeare's engagement with the classics can be found in Colin Burrow, *Shakespeare and*

Classical Antiquity (Oxford: Oxford University Press, 2013). His position is summarized as follows:

> Shakespeare knew quite a lot of classical literature. Given his education and the period in which he lived it would be surprising if he did not.
>
> Shakespeare did interesting things with that classical learning, and understanding what he did with his knowledge, rather than just trying scrupulously to assess its exact extent, is central to an understanding of his work.
>
> The ways Shakespeare used his classical learning changed throughout his career, in response to his contemporaries (including Ben Jonson), to new reading, and to the demands of different generic and theatrical settings. (2)

Burrow's book is organized thematically rather than by individual plays, with references to *Antony and Cleopatra* throughout. The most sustained comes in his chapter on Plutarch (207–11). The play provides him with a test case for the ways in which Shakespeare mined his Plutarch for dramatic ideas.

It should be apparent that this chapter is not an annotated bibliography; hence, it should be much more useful for students in particular to have a sense of the main arguments made in critical material and of how this material is informed by different currents of critical theory, and so this constitutes a guided, discursive tour. However, there is one important consideration that has been in the background throughout: critics always have an axe to grind, even if simply in response to another critical position. Theorized material can be especially difficult to read if one does not know where it is coming from, and that goes for this chapter as well.

Ultimately, the best thing to do when engaging in detail with a play like *Antony and Cleopatra* is just to watch it, or listen to an audio version, letting the words wash over you. Digital availability makes the plays so much more easily accessible, whether it be on DVD (as with recent performances recorded at the Globe in 2014 and at the Royal Shakespeare Theatre in 2017) or through an online resource such as Digital Theatre Plus (https://www.digitaltheatreplus.com/education) or on YouTube. Recordings of performances are especially useful for students in non-English-speaking countries in that they have subtitles. All of this seems obvious, but as always, there is a catch: no performance is neutral, just as no critic is neutral. Choices are made at all levels. For example, in Trevor Nunn's 1974 television version, Cleopatra's sumptuous Egypt is denoted by multicoloured drapes and a suggestion of a hot, sandy environment, while Rome is cold and sterile, a pure white ambience fitting for men in togas. There is little sense of Cleopatra's Greek origins, and in this respect the production follows an age-old critical line. There is one good thing about all of this: if you can include performance details in an essay, you are likely to make a positive impression on your marker. Or, if you wish, you can just enjoy the play for its own sake.

Apart from hosting full video and radio performances (both amateur and professional) as well as clips of single scenes, YouTube is worth mentioning further in that it offers an incredibly wide array of resources, ranging from recorded university lectures to interviews with actors and directors about the challenges the play poses in performance, to summaries of the plays for the laziest students who cannot even bring themselves to read (or watch) the entire play. As a free resource, accessible from anywhere in the world, YouTube has inevitably changed and will certainly continue to shape the landscape of teaching Shakespeare, especially for students living in non-English-speaking countries, who can benefit from access to the plays in ways that would have been inconceivable, say, only twenty years ago.

NOTES

Introduction

1. Sarah Hatchuel, *Shakespeare and the Cleopatra/Caesar Intertext: Sequel, Conflation, Remake* (Madison, WI: Fairleigh Dickinson University Press, 2011), 2.
2. Andrew Gurr, *The Shakespeare Company, 1594–1642* (Cambridge: Cambridge University Press, 2004), 175.
3. Hatchuel, *Shakespeare and the Cleopatra/Caesar Intertext*, 2, 7. All parenthetical references to the play are to William Shakespeare, *Antony and Cleopatra*, ed. John Wilders (London: Routledge for Arden Shakespeare, 1995).
4. Hatchuel, *Shakespeare and the Cleopatra/Caesar Intertext*, xv.
5. Hatchuel, *Shakespeare and the Cleopatra/Caesar Intertext*, 20.
6. All parenthetical references to the play are to William Shakespeare, *Julius Caesar*, ed. David Daniell (Walton-on-Thames: Nelson for Arden Shakespeare, 1998).
7. Robert S. Miola, *Shakespeare's Rome* (Cambridge: Cambridge University Press, 1983), 117.
8. On Antony's 'latent', 'deep-seated feeling of comparative inadequacy' with Caesar, see also John E. Curran Jr's discussion in *Character and the Individual Personality in English Renaissance Drama: Tragedy, History, Tragicomedy* (Newark, DE: University of Delaware Press, 2014), 291–311, at 294–5, as well as his chapter in this volume, 136–40.
9. John Roe, *Shakespeare and Machiavelli* (Cambridge: Brewer, 2002), 206.
10. David Bevington, 'Introduction', in William Shakespeare, *Antony and Cleopatra* (updated edn, Cambridge: Cambridge University Press, 2005), 1–80, at 17–19.
11. Bevington, 'Introduction', 25.

12 Ernst Honigmann, *Shakespeare: Seven Tragedies Revisited* (Basingstoke: Palgrave, 2002), 152.

13 Curran, *Character and the Individual Personality*, 307.

14 Curran, *Character and the Individual Personality*, 307.

15 Curran, *Character and the Individual Personality*, 305.

16 On Caesar's *celeritas*, see Luca Grillo, *The Art of Caesar's Bellum Civile: Literature, Ideology, and Community* (Cambridge: Cambridge University Press, 2012), 14–36; Michael Lovano, *All Things Julius Caesar: An Encyclopedia of Caesar's World and Legacy* (Santa Barbara, CA: ABC-CLIO, 2015), 258.

17 David Daniell, 'Introduction', in Shakespeare, *Julius Caesar*, 1–147, at 125.

18 'paragon, v.', *OED Online* (July 2018), Oxford University Press. Available at http://www.oed.com/view/Entry/137416?rskey=9aDtfE&result=2&isAdvanced=false (accessed 25 September 2018); 'paragon, n. and adj.', *OED Online* (July 2018), Oxford University Press. Available at http://www.oed.com/view/Entry/137415?rskey=9aDtfE&result=1&isAdvanced=false (accessed 25 September 2018).

19 Curran, *Character and the Individual Personality*, 303.

20 Curran, *Character and the Individual Personality*, 303.

21 Andrew Hadfield, *Shakespeare and Republicanism* (Cambridge: Cambridge University Press, 2005), 226.

22 Andrew Hiscock, *The Uses of This World: Thinking Space in Shakespeare, Marlowe, Cary, and Jonson* (Cardiff: University of Wales Press, 2004), 93–4.

23 John Wilders, 'Introduction', in Shakespeare, *Antony and Cleopatra*, 1–84 (at 43); Barbara L. Parker, *Plato's Republic and Shakespeare's Rome: A Political Study of the Roman Works* (Newark, DE: University of Delaware Press, 2004), 108–9.

24 Bevington, 'Introduction', 21.

Chapter 1

1 Janet Adelman, *The Common Liar: An Essay on* Antony and Cleopatra (New Haven, CT: Yale University Press, 1973), 30.

2   All parenthetical references to the play are to William Shakespeare, *Antony and Cleopatra*, ed. John Wilders (London and New York: Routledge for Arden Shakespeare, 1995).

3   John Dryden, *All for Love; or, The World Well Lost*, ed. N. J. Andrews (London: Methuen, 2004), 10.

4   Dryden, *All for Love*, 20.

5   Dryden, *All for Love*, 20.

6   Nicholas Rowe, *Some Account of the Life, &c of Mr. William Shakespeare* (1709), in Brian Vickers (ed.), *William Shakespeare: The Critical Heritage*, 6 vols (London: Routledge and Kegan Paul, 1974–81), II, 190–202, at 198.

7   Rowe, *Some Account of the Life*, 198.

8   Rowe, *Some Account of the Life*, 199.

9   Anon., *An Examen of the New Comedy, Call'd 'The Suspicious Husband' with Some Observations upon Our Dramatick Poetry and Authors* (1747), in Brian Vickers (ed.), *William Shakespeare: The Critical Heritage*, 6 vols (London: Routledge and Kegan Paul, 1974–81), III, 259–70, at 270.

10 Anon., *An Examen of the New Comedy*, 270.

11 William Dodd, *The Beauties of Shakespeare* (1752), in Brian Vickers (ed.), *William Shakespeare: The Critical Heritage*, 6 vols (London: Routledge and Kegan Paul, 1974–81), III, 464–77, at 471.

12 John Hall, *Some Remarks upon the New-Revived Play of* Antony and Cleopatra, in Brian Vickers (ed.), *William Shakespeare: The Critical Heritage*, 6 vols (London: Routledge and Kegan Paul, 1974–81), IV, 403–4, at 403.

13 Hall, *Some Remarks*, 403.

14 Hall, *Some Remarks*, 403.

15 Hall, *Some Remarks*, 404.

16 Samuel Johnson, *The Plays of William Shakespeare* (1765), in Brian Vickers (ed.), *William Shakespeare: The Critical Heritage*, 6 vols (London: Routledge and Kegan Paul, 1974–81), V, 55–176, at 148.

17 Johnson, *The Plays of William Shakespeare*, 148.

18 Johnson, *The Plays of William Shakespeare*, 148.

19 William Duff, *Critical Observations on the Writings of the Most Celebrated Original Geniuses in Poetry* (1770), in Brian Vickers (ed.), *William Shakespeare: The Critical Heritage*, 6 vols (London: Routledge and Kegan Paul, 1974–81), V, 367–73, at 370.

20 Samuel Taylor Coleridge, in John Russell Brown (ed.), *Antony and Cleopatra: A Selection of Critical Essays* (London: Macmillan, 1969), 28.

21 Coleridge, in Brown, *Antony and Cleopatra*, 28–9.

22 William Hazlitt, in John Russell Brown (ed.), *Antony and Cleopatra: A Selection of Critical Essays* (London: Macmillan, 1969), 34.

23 Hazlitt, in Brown, *Antony and Cleopatra*, 31.

24 Hazlitt, in Brown, *Antony and Cleopatra*, 32.

25 Hazlitt, in Brown, *Antony and Cleopatra*, 32.

26 Edward Dowden, *Shakspere: A Critical Study of His Mind and Art* (London: Kegan Paul, 1909), 306–7. First published 1875.

27 Dowden, *Shakspere*, 307.

28 Dowden, *Shakspere*, 312.

29 Dowden, *Shakspere*, 312.

30 A. C. Bradley, *Shakespearean Tragedy: Lectures on Hamlet, Othello, King Lear, Macbeth* (2nd edn, London: Macmillan, 1950), 282.

31 Bradley, *Shakespearean Tragedy*, 40, 55, 213.

32 Bradley, *Shakespearean Tragedy*, 2.

33 A. C. Bradley, 'Shakespeare's *Antony and Cleopatra*' (1905), in John Russell Brown (ed.), *Antony and Cleopatra: A Selection of Critical Essays* (London: Macmillan, 1969), 63–85, at 65.

34 Bradley, 'Shakespeare's *Antony and Cleopatra*', 66–7.

35 Bradley, 'Shakespeare's *Antony and Cleopatra*', 69.

36 Bradley, 'Shakespeare's *Antony and Cleopatra*', 85.

37 Mungo William MacCallum, *Shakespeare's Roman Plays and Their Background* (London: Macmillan, 1910), 317.

38 MacCallum, *Shakespeare's Roman Plays*, 316–17.

39 MacCallum, *Shakespeare's Roman Plays*, 317.

40 MacCallum, *Shakespeare's Roman Plays*, 343.
41 MacCallum, *Shakespeare's Roman Plays*, 447.
42 MacCallum, *Shakespeare's Roman Plays*, 447–8.
43 Bradley, 'Shakespeare's *Antony and Cleopatra*', 68.
44 Harley Granville-Barker, *Prefaces to Shakespeare* (London: Batsford, 1972), 367.
45 Granville-Barker, *Prefaces to Shakespeare*, 371.
46 Granville-Barker, *Prefaces to Shakespeare*, 434.
47 Granville-Barker, *Prefaces to Shakespeare*, 435.
48 Granville-Barker, *Prefaces to Shakespeare*, 435.
49 Granville-Barker, *Prefaces to Shakespeare*, 441.
50 Granville-Barker, *Prefaces to Shakespeare*, 441.
51 G. Wilson Knight, *The Wheel of Fire: Interpretations of Shakespearian Tragedy* (London: Methuen, 1965), 15.
52 G. Wilson Knight, *The Imperial Theme: Further Interpretations of Shakespeare's Tragedies Including the Roman Plays* (London: Methuen, 1965), 200.
53 Knight, *The Imperial Theme*, 204–5.
54 Knight, *The Imperial Theme*, 205.
55 Knight, *The Imperial Theme*, 263.
56 Knight, *The Imperial Theme*, 326.
57 Ernest Schanzer, *The Problem Plays of Shakespeare* (London: Routledge & Kegan Paul, 1963), 182.
58 Schanzer, *The Problem Plays of Shakespeare*, 183.
59 Schanzer, *The Problem Plays of Shakespeare*, 133.
60 Schanzer, *The Problem Plays of Shakespeare*, 133.
61 Schanzer, *The Problem Plays of Shakespeare*, 133.
62 Schanzer, *The Problem Plays of Shakespeare*, 133.
63 Schanzer, *The Problem Plays of Shakespeare*, 145.
64 Schanzer, *The Problem Plays of Shakespeare*, 146.
65 Derek Traversi, *Shakespeare: The Roman Plays* (London: Hollis & Carter, 1963), 79.
66 Traversi, *Shakespeare: The Roman Plays*, 79.

67 Traversi, *Shakespeare: The Roman Plays*, 203.

68 Maurice Charney, *Shakespeare's Roman Plays: The Function of Imagery in the Drama* (Cambridge, MA: Harvard University Press, 1961), 6.

69 Charney, *Shakespeare's Roman Plays*, 11.

70 Charney, *Shakespeare's Roman Plays*, 114.

71 Charney, *Shakespeare's Roman Plays*, 114.

72 J. L. Simmons, *Shakespeare's Pagan World: The Roman Tragedies* (Charlottesville, VA: University Press of Virginia, 1973), 3.

73 Simmons, *Shakespeare's Pagan World*, 3.

74 Simmons, *Shakespeare's Pagan World*, 14–15.

75 Simmons, *Shakespeare's Pagan World*, 16.

76 Simmons, *Shakespeare's Pagan World*, 17.

77 Simmons, *Shakespeare's Pagan World*, 162.

78 Simmons, *Shakespeare's Pagan World*, 162.

79 Paul A. Cantor, *Shakespeare's Rome: Republic and Empire* (Ithaca, NY: Cornell University Press, 1976), 27.

80 Cantor, *Shakespeare's Rome*, 52.

81 Cantor, *Shakespeare's Rome*, 128.

82 Adelman, *The Common Liar*, 1.

83 Adelman, *The Common Liar*, 12.

84 Adelman, *The Common Liar*, 53.

85 Adelman, *The Common Liar*, 103.

86 Robert S. Miola, *Shakespeare's Rome* (Cambridge: Cambridge University Press, 1983), 11.

87 Miola, *Shakespeare's Rome*, 17.

88 Miola, *Shakespeare's Rome*, 17.

89 Miola, *Shakespeare's Rome*, 116.

90 Miola, *Shakespeare's Rome*, 134.

91 Miola, *Shakespeare's Rome*, 158.

92 Vivian Thomas, *Shakespeare's Roman Worlds* (London and New York: Routledge, 1989), 1.

93 Thomas, *Shakespeare's Roman Worlds*, 1.

94 Thomas, *Shakespeare's Roman Worlds*, 2.

95 Thomas, *Shakespeare's Roman Worlds*, 2.

96 Thomas, *Shakespeare's Roman Worlds*, 93.

97 Geoffrey Miles, *Shakespeare and the Constant Romans* (Oxford: Oxford University Press, 1996), 175.

98 Miles, *Shakespeare and the Constant Romans*, 185.

99 Miles, *Shakespeare and the Constant Romans*, 187.

100 J. Leeds Barroll, *Shakespearean Tragedy: Genre, Tradition, and Change in Antony and Cleopatra* (Washington, DC: Folger Shakespeare Library, 1984), 19.

101 Barroll, *Shakespearean Tragedy*, 19.

102 Barroll, *Shakespearean Tragedy*, 20.

103 Barroll, *Shakespearean Tragedy*, 90.

104 Barroll, *Shakespearean Tragedy*, 132–3.

105 Barroll, *Shakespearean Tragedy*, 288.

106 Jonathan Dollimore, *Radical Tragedy: Religion, Ideology and Power in the Drama of Shakespeare and His Contemporaries* (3rd edn, Basingstoke: Palgrave Macmillan, 2010), 4.

107 Dollimore, *Radical Tragedy*, 205–6.

108 Dollimore, *Radical Tragedy*, 210.

109 Dollimore, *Radical Tragedy*, 211.

110 Dollimore, *Radical Tragedy*, 217.

111 Leonard Tennenhouse, *Power on Display: The Politics of Shakespeare's Genres* (New York: Methuen, 1986), 4.

112 Tennenhouse, *Power on Display*, 144.

113 Tennenhouse, *Power on Display*, 144.

114 Tennenhouse, *Power on Display*, 146.

115 H. Neville Davies, 'Jacobean *Antony and Cleopatra*', in John Drakakis (ed.), *Antony and Cleopatra: Contemporary Critical Essays* (Basingstoke: Macmillan, 1994), 126–65, at 127.

116 Davies, 'Jacobean *Antony and Cleopatra*', 138.

117 Ania Loomba, *Gender, Race, Renaissance Drama* (Oxford: Oxford University Press, 1989), 125.

118 Loomba, *Gender, Race, Renaissance Drama*, 125.

119 Loomba, *Gender, Race, Renaissance Drama*, 126.

120 Loomba, *Gender, Race, Renaissance Drama*, 125.

121 Loomba, *Gender, Race, Renaissance Drama*, 127.

122 Loomba, *Gender, Race, Renaissance Drama*, 130.

123 Loomba, *Gender, Race, Renaissance Drama*, 129–30.

124 Loomba, *Gender, Race, Renaissance Drama*, 130.

125 Jyotsna G. Singh, 'Renaissance Anti-theatricality, Anti-feminism, and Shakespeare's *Antony and Cleopatra*', in John Drakakis (ed.), *Antony and Cleopatra: Contemporary Critical Essays* (Basingstoke: Macmillan, 1994), 308–28, at 308.

126 Singh, 'Renaissance Anti-theatricality', 309.

127 Laura Levine, *Men in Women's Clothing: Anti-Theatricality and Effeminization, 1579–1642* (Cambridge: Cambridge University Press, 1994), 56–7.

128 Levine, *Men in Women's Clothing*, 65.

129 Levine, *Men in Women's Clothing*, 64.

130 Janet Adelman, *Suffocating Mothers: Fantasies of Maternal Origin in Shakespeare's Plays, Hamlet to The Tempest* (London and New York: Routledge, 1992), 10.

131 Adelman, *Suffocating Mothers*, 10.

132 Adelman, *Suffocating Mothers*, 165.

133 Adelman, *Suffocating Mothers*, 176.

134 Adelman, *Suffocating Mothers*, 176.

135 Adelman, *Suffocating Mothers*, 177.

136 Adelman, *Suffocating Mothers*, 177–8.

137 Coppélia Kahn, *Roman Shakespeare: Warriors, Wounds and Women* (London and New York: Routledge, 1997), 1.

138 Kahn, *Roman Shakespeare*, 18.

139 Kahn, *Roman Shakespeare*, 110.

140 Kahn, *Roman Shakespeare*, 112.

141 Kahn, *Roman Shakespeare*, 112.

142 Kahn, *Roman Shakespeare*, 137.

143 Kahn, *Roman Shakespeare*, 137.

144 Linda Charnes, *Notorious Identity: Materializing the Subject in Shakespeare* (Cambridge, MA: Harvard University Press, 1993), 1.

145 Charnes, *Notorious Identity*, 106.

146 Charnes, *Notorious Identity*, 110.

147 Charnes, *Notorious Identity*, 111.

148 Charnes, *Notorious Identity*, 111.

149 Adelman, *The Common Liar*, 170.

150 Adelman, *The Common Liar*, 170–1.

Chapter 2

1 This chapter examines a number of productions I chose according to a shaping idea of showing how the play relates to the historical development of staging Shakespeare in London and Stratford-upon-Avon with a specific focus on its relation to other media, in particular cinema; hence, the chapter does not seek to provide a complete survey of the performance history of the play. Margaret Lamb, *Antony and Cleopatra on the English Stage* (London: Associated University Presses, 1980) is essential to retrace the history of *Antony and Cleopatra* on the British stage up to 1980. For an update to 2005, which also considers the other side of the Atlantic, see Sara Munson Deats, 'Shakespeare's Anamorphic Drama: A Survey of *Antony and Cleopatra* in Criticism, on Stage, and on Screen', in Sara Munson Deats (ed.), *Antony and Cleopatra: New Critical Essays* (London and New York: Routledge, 2005), 1–93.

2 All parenthetical references to the play are to William Shakespeare, *Antony and Cleopatra*, ed. John Wilders (London and New York: Routledge for Arden Shakespeare, 1995).

3 John Gillies, *Shakespeare and the Geography of Difference* (Cambridge: Cambridge University Press, 1994), 52–69; Gilberto Sacerdoti, '*Antony and Cleopatra* and the Overflowing of the Roman Measure', in Maria Del Sapio Garbero (ed.), *Identity, Otherness, and Empire in Shakespeare's Rome* (Farnham: Ashgate, 2009), 107–18.

4 Márta Minier, 'Interdisciplinary Considerations about a Subgenre of the Contemporary Biographical Drama: Celebrity and Fandom in Recent Adaptations of Famous Lives for the Stage', *Critical Stages*, 112 (2015). Available at http://www.critical-stages.org/12/interdisciplinary-considerations-about-a-subgenre-of-the-contemporary-biographical-drama-celebrity-and-fandom-in-recent-adaptations-of-famous-lives-for-the-stage (accessed 10 June 2018).

5 See Márta Minier and Maddalena Pennacchia, 'Interdisciplinary Perspectives on the Biopic: An Introduction', in Márta Minier and Maddalena Pennacchia (eds.), *Adaptation, Intermediality and the British Celebrity Biopic* (Farnham: Ashgate, 2014), 1–31.

6 Maria Del Sapio Garbero, 'Fostering the Question "Who Plays the Host?"', in Maria Del Sapio Garbero (ed.), *Identity, Otherness, and Empire in Shakespeare's Rome* (Farnham: Ashgate, 2009), 91–104, at 99.

7 Elisabeth Bronfen, 'Hybrid Spaces in *Antony and Cleopatra*', in Ina Habermann and Michelle Witen (eds.), *Shakespeare and Space: Theatrical Explorations of the Spatial Paradigm* (Basingstoke: Palgrave Macmillan, 2016), 103–20.

8 Harley Granville-Barker, *Prefaces to Shakespeare*, 4 vols (London: Batsford, 1972), II, 83.

9 David Bevington, 'Introduction', in William Shakespeare, *Antony and Cleopatra* (Cambridge: Cambridge University Press, 1990), 1–70, at 2.

10 Michael Neill, 'Introduction', in William Shakespeare, *The Tragedy of Anthony and Cleopatra* (Oxford: Oxford University Press, 1994), 1–130, at 20.

11 'Killigrew's Patent, 25 April 1662', in David Thomas (ed.), *Restoration and Georgian England, 1660–1788* (Cambridge: Cambridge University Press, 1989), 18.

12 Allardyce Nicoll, *A History of Restoration Drama* (Cambridge: Cambridge University Press, 1928), 315–16.

13 Andrew Gurr, 'London's Blackfriars Playhouse and the Chamberlain's Men', in Paul Menzer (ed.), *Inside Shakespeare: Essays on the Blackfriars Stage* (Selinsgrove, PA: Susquehanna University Press, 2006), 17–34, at 26.

14 Lamb, *Antony and Cleopatra on the English Stage*, 39.
15 John Dryden, *All for Love; or, The World Well Lost*, ed. N. J. Andrew (New York: Norton, 1975), 1.1.77.
16 Dryden, *All for Love*, 1.1.105–6.
17 Lamb, *Antony and Cleopatra on the English Stage*, 39.
18 Lamb, *Antony and Cleopatra on the English Stage*, 42.
19 Deats, 'Shakespeare's Anamorphic Drama', 37.
20 Lamb, *Antony and Cleopatra on the English Stage*, 46.
21 Dennis Kennedy, *Looking at Shakespeare: A Visual History of Twentieth-Century Performance* (2nd edn, Cambridge: Cambridge University Press, 2001), 25.
22 Lamb, *Antony and Cleopatra on the English Stage*, 46–8.
23 J. L. Styan, *The English Stage: A History of Drama and Performance* (Cambridge: Cambridge University Press, 1996), 304.
24 Kennedy, *Looking at Shakespeare*, 26.
25 Neill, 'Introduction', 33.
26 Lamb, *Antony and Cleopatra on the English Stage*, 96, 91.
27 Neill, 'Introduction', 40.
28 J. L. Styan, *The Shakespeare Revolution: Criticism and Performance in the Twentieth Century* (Cambridge: Cambridge University Press, 1977), 47–63.
29 Granville-Barker, *Prefaces to Shakespeare*, 94–5.
30 Granville-Barker, *Prefaces to Shakespeare*, 97.
31 Lamb, *Antony and Cleopatra on the English Stage*, 102.
32 Granville-Barker, *Prefaces to Shakespeare*, 125.
33 Lamb, *Antony and Cleopatra on the English Stage*, 132.
34 Deats, 'Shakespeare's Anamorphic Drama', 49.
35 Carol Chillington Rutter, *Enter the Body: Women and Representation on Shakespeare's Stage* (London and New York: Routledge, 2001), 75.
36 Michael Scott, *Antony and Cleopatra: Text and Performance* (Basingstoke: Macmillan, 1983), 44.
37 Virginia Mason Vaughan, *Antony and Cleopatra: Language and Writing* (London: Bloomsbury Arden Shakespeare, 2016), 140.

38 Janet Adelman, *The Common Liar: An Essay on* Antony and Cleopatra (New Haven, CT: Yale University Press, 1973).
39 Deats, 'Shakespeare's Anamorphic Drama', 67.
40 Deats, 'Shakespeare's Anamorphic Drama', 69.
41 Rutter, *Enter the Body*, 60.
42 Scott, *Antony and Cleopatra*, 47.
43 Lamb, *Antony and Cleopatra on the English Stage*, 173–8.
44 Gregory Doran, 'Gregory Doran 2006 Production: Q & A with Gregory Doran'. Available at https://www.rsc.org.uk/antony-and-cleopatra/past-productions/gregory-doran-2006-production (accessed 30 August 2018).
45 Lamb, *Antony and Cleopatra on the English Stage*, 180–5.
46 Doran, 'Q & A with Gregory Doran'.
47 Styan, *The Shakespeare Revolution*, 180–205.
48 James C. Bulman, 'Queering the Audience: All-Male Casts in Recent Productions of Shakespeare', in Barbara Hodgdon and W. B. Worthen (eds.), *A Companion to Shakespeare and Performance* (Malden, MA: Blackwell, 2005), 564–87, at 565.
49 Georgia E. Brown, 'Interview with Giles Block, Director of the 1999 Production of *Antony and Cleopatra* at Shakespeare's Globe in London', in Sara Munson Deats (ed.), *Antony and Cleopatra: New Critical Essays* (London and New York: Routledge, 2005), 309–24, at 309.
50 Bulman, 'Queering the Audience', 585.
51 Michael J. Collins, '*Antony and Cleopatra* – Review', *Shakespeare Bulletin*, 24 (2006): 112–15, at 115, 113.
52 Roberta Barker, '"Deared by Being Lacked": The Realist Legacy and the Art of Failure in Shakespearean Performance', in James C. Bulman (ed.), *The Oxford Handbook of Shakespeare and Performance* (Oxford: Oxford University Press, 2017), 46–63, at 56.
53 Barker, 'Deared by Being Lacked', 58.
54 Francesca T. Royster, *Becoming Cleopatra: The Shifting Image of an Icon* (Basingstoke: Palgrave Macmillan, 2003), 58–92; Paolo Cherchi Usai, *Georges Méliès* (Milan: Il Castoro, 2009), 118; Linda Hutcheon and Siobhan O'Flynn, *A Theory of Adaptation* (2nd edn, London and New York: Routledge, 2013), 6–9.

55 Roberta E. Pearson and William Uricchio, 'The Bard in Brooklyn: Vitagraph's Shakespearean Productions', in Luke McKernan and Olwen Terris (eds.), *Walking Shadows: Shakespeare in the National Film and Television Archive* (London: British Film Institute, 1994), 201–6, at 201. On the use of Shakespeare to lend respectability to the film industry, see Judith Buchanan, *Shakespeare on Silent Film: An Excellent Dumb Discourse* (Cambridge: Cambridge University Press, 2009); Deborah Cartmell and Imelda Whelehan, *Screen Adaptation: Impure Cinema* (Basingstoke: Palgrave Macmillan, 2010), 28–40.

56 Quoted in Robert Hamilton Ball, *Shakespeare on Silent Film: A Strange Eventful History* (London and New York: Routledge, 2013), 47–8.

57 Ball, *Shakespeare on Silent Film*, 38–60.

58 The print I had the opportunity to see is owned by the Centro di Cinematografia Sperimentale in Rome, ENIC (Ente Nazionale Industrie Cinematografiche).

59 Ball, *Shakespeare on Silent Film*, 167.

60 Maria Wyke, *The Roman Mistress: Ancient and Modern Representations* (Oxford: Oxford University Press, 2002), 251.

61 Douglas Brode, *Shakespeare in the Movie: From the Silent Era to Shakespeare in Love* (Oxford: Oxford University Press, 2000), 195–202.

62 Christine Geraghty, *Now a Major Motion Picture: Film Adaptations of Literature and Drama* (Plymouth: Rowman & Littlefield, 2008), 15. For a detailed discussion of Mankiewicz's *Cleopatra*, see Sarah Hatchuel, 'Cleopatra in Cinematic Conflations: Subversion or Containment', in Sarah Hatchuel and Nathalie Vienne-Guerrin (eds.), *Shakespeare on Screen: The Roman Plays* (Mont-Saint-Aignan: Publications des Universités de Rouen et du Havre, 2009), 239–70, at 240–5.

63 Samuel Crowl, 'A World Elsewhere: The Roman Plays on Film and Television', in Anthony Davies and Stanley Wells (eds.), *Shakespeare and the Moving Image: The Plays on Film and Television* (Cambridge: Cambridge University Press, 1994), 146–62, at 162n17.

64 Michael Brooke, *The Spread of the Eagle* (1963). Available at http://www.screenonline.org.uk/tv/id/466545/index.html (accessed 27 June 2018).

65 Brooke, *The Spread of the Eagle*.
66 Crowl, 'A World Elsewhere', 153–4.
67 David Fuller, 'Passion and Politics: *Antony and Cleopatra* in Performance', in Sara Munson Deats (ed.), *Antony and Cleopatra: New Critical Essays* (London and New York: Routledge, 2005), 111–35, at 120.
68 James C. Bulman, 'The BBC Shakespeare and "House Style"', *Shakespeare Quarterly*, 35 (1984): 571–81, at 572.
69 J. David Bolter and Richard Grusin, *Remediation: Understanding New Media* (Cambridge, MA: MIT Press, 1999), 15.
70 James C. Bulman, 'Introduction: Cross-Currents in Performance Criticism', in James C. Bulman (ed.), *The Oxford Handbook of Shakespeare and Performance* (Oxford: Oxford University Press, 2017), 1–9, at 6–7.
71 Thomas Cartelli, 'High-Tech Shakespeare in a Mediatized Globe: Ivo van Hove's *Roman Tragedies* and the Problem of Spectatorship', in James C. Bulman (ed.), *The Oxford Handbook of Shakespeare and Performance* (Oxford: Oxford University Press, 2017), 267–83, at 267.
72 Cartelli, 'High-Tech Shakespeare', 272.
73 Barker, 'Deared by Being Lacked', 57.
74 The first digitally live broadcast cinema had been experimented by the New York Metropolitan Opera at the end of 2006 for a performance of Wolfgang Amadeus Mozart's *The Magic Flute*. See Martin Barker, *Live to Your Local Cinema: The Remarkable Rise of Livecasting* (Basingstoke: Palgrave Macmillan, 2013).
75 See Maddalena Pennacchia, 'Intermedial Products for Digital Natives: British Theatre-Cinema on Italian Screens', *Intermédialités*, 30–1 (2017). Available at https://www.erudit.org/en/journals/im/2017-n30-31-im03868/1049952ar.
76 The xylograph can be seen in Giorgio de Vincenti, 'Il kolossal storico-romano nell'immaginario del Novecento', *Bianco e nero*, 49 (1988): 7–29.
77 Ben Lawrence, '*Antony and Cleopatra*: First Look at the NT Production Starring Ralph Fiennes and Sophie Okonedo',

Telegraph, 18 June 2018. Available at https://www.telegraph.co.uk/theatre/what-to-see/antony-cleopatra-first-look-nt-production-starring-ralph-fiennes (accessed 19 July 2018).

Chapter 3

1 Janet Adelman, *The Common Liar: An Essay on* Antony and Cleopatra (New Haven, CT: Yale University Press, 1973); Robert S. Miola, *Shakespeare's Rome* (Cambridge: Cambridge University Press, 1983); Linda Charnes, *Notorious Identity: Materializing the Subject in Shakespeare* (Cambridge, MA: Harvard University Press, 1993); Coppélia Kahn, *Roman Shakespeare: Warriors, Wounds and Women* (London and New York: Routledge, 1997). All parenthetical references to the play are to William Shakespeare, *Antony and Cleopatra*, ed. John Wilders (London and New York: Routledge for Arden Shakespeare, 1995).

2 Adelman, *The Common Liar*, 53.

3 John H. Astington, 'Venus on the Thames', *Shakespeare Studies*, 39 (2011): 117–32, at 118.

4 Astington, 'Venus on the Thames', 118.

5 Astington, 'Venus on the Thames', 119, 124–5.

6 Astington, 'Venus on the Thames', 130, 126.

7 Catherine Belsey, 'The Elephants' Graveyard Revisited: Shakespeare at Work in *Antony and Cleopatra*, *Romeo and Juliet* and *All's Well That Ends Well*', *Shakespeare Survey* 68 (2015): 62–72, at 64–5.

8 Belsey, 'The Elephants' Graveyard Revisited', 65–6.

9 Robert A. Logan, *Shakespeare's Marlowe: The Influence of Christopher Marlowe on Shakespeare's Artistry* (Aldershot: Ashgate, 2007), 176.

10 Logan, *Shakespeare's Marlowe*, 184.

11 Logan, *Shakespeare's Marlowe*, 184.

12 Logan, *Shakespeare's Marlowe*, 184.

13 Lisa S. Starks, 'Immortal Longings: The Erotics of Death in Shakespeare's *Antony and Cleopatra*', in Sara Munson Deats

(ed.), *Antony and Cleopatra: New Critical Essays* (London and New York: Routledge, 2005), 243–58, at 244.

14   Starks, 'Immortal Longings', 244, 253.

15   David Read, 'Disappearing Act: The Role of Enobarbus in *Antony and Cleopatra*', *Studies in Philology*, 110 (2013): 562–83, at 564, 567.

16   Read, 'Disappearing Act', 582–3.

17   Eric Langley, *Narcissism and Suicide in Shakespeare and His Contemporaries* (Oxford: Oxford University Press, 2009), 179–80.

18   Langley, *Narcissism and Suicide*, 181, 185.

19   Langley, *Narcissism and Suicide*, 189.

20   Barbara L. Parker, *Plato's* Republic *and Shakespeare's Rome: A Political Study of the Roman Works* (Newark, DE: University of Delaware Press, 2004), 105, 103.

21   Jacqueline Vanhoutte, 'Antony's "Secret House of Death": Suicide and Sovereignty in *Antony and Cleopatra*', *Philological Quarterly*, 79 (2000): 153–75, at 158–9, 163.

22   Vanhoutte, 'Antony's "Secret House of Death"', 167.

23   Vanhoutte, 'Antony's "Secret House of Death"', 167.

24   Vanhoutte, 'Antony's "Secret House of Death"', 171.

25   David Bevington, '*Antony and Cleopatra* and Midlife Crisis', in Jean-Cristophe Mayer (ed.), *Lectures de Shakespeare: Antony and Cleopatra* (Rennes: Presses Universitaires de Rennes, 2000), 55–68, at 59.

26   Bevington, '*Antony and Cleopatra* and Midlife Crisis', 58, 62.

27   Bevington, '*Antony and Cleopatra* and Midlife Crisis', 65.

28   David Schalkwyk, 'Is Love an Emotion? Shakespeare's *Twelfth Night* and *Antony and Cleopatra*', *symplokē*, 18 (2010): 99–130, at 119.

29   Schalkwyk, 'Is Love an Emotion?', 119.

30   Schalkwyk, 'Is Love an Emotion?', 119.

31   Gail Kern Paster, *Humoring the Body: Emotions and the Shakespearean Stage* (Chicago, IL: University of Chicago Press, 2004), 164.

32 Paster, *Humoring the Body*, 179.

33 Paster, *Humoring the Body*, 166.

34 Paster, *Humoring the Body*, 168, 177.

35 Daniel Cadman, '"Quick Comedians": Mary Sidney, Samuel Daniel and the *Theatrum Mundi* in Shakespeare's *Antony and Cleopatra*', *Actes des Congrès de la Société Française Shakespeare*, 33 (2015): 1–13, at 2. Available at http://shakespeare.revues.org/3536 (accessed 25 July 2017).

36 Cadman, 'Quick Comedians', 5.

37 Cadman, 'Quick Comedians', 5, 10.

38 Mimi Still Dixon, '"Not Know Me Yet?": Looking at Cleopatra in Three Renaissance Tragedies', in Naomi Conn Liebler (ed.), *The Female Tragic Hero in English Renaissance Drama* (Basingstoke: Palgrave, 2002), 71–91, at 77.

39 Dixon, 'Not Know Me Yet?', 85–6.

40 Warren Chernaik, *The Myth of Rome in Shakespeare and His Contemporaries* (Cambridge: Cambridge University Press, 2011), 140.

41 Chernaik, *The Myth of Rome*, 156.

42 Chernaik, *The Myth of Rome*, 158, 162, 164.

43 Alison V. Scott, *Literature and the Idea of Luxury in Early Modern England* (Farnham: Ashgate, 2015), 66.

44 Scott, *Literature and the Idea of Luxury*, 79, 82.

45 Scott, *Literature and the Idea of Luxury*, 82.

46 Pascale Aebischer, 'The Properties of Whiteness: Renaissance Cleopatras from Jodelle to Shakespeare', *Shakespeare Survey* 65 (2012): 221–38, at 222.

47 Aebischer, 'The Properties of Whiteness', 222.

48 Aebischer, 'The Properties of Whiteness', 237–8.

49 Aebischer, 'The Properties of Whiteness', 237–8.

50 Ania Loomba, *Shakespeare, Race, and Colonialism* (Oxford: Oxford University Press, 2002), 133, 125.

51 Loomba, *Shakespeare, Race, and Colonialism*, 133.

52 Loomba, *Shakespeare, Race, and Colonialism*, 133–4.

53 Loomba, *Shakespeare, Race, and Colonialism*, 134.
54 Mary Thomas Crane, 'Roman World, Egyptian Earth: Cognitive Difference and Empire', *Comparative Drama*, 43 (2009): 1–17, at 1–2.
55 Crane, 'Roman World, Egyptian Earth', 2, 7.
56 Crane, 'Roman World, Egyptian Earth', 2.
57 Arthur L. Little Jr, *Shakespeare Jungle Fever: National-Imperial Revisions of Race, Rape, and Sacrifice* (Stanford, CA: Stanford University Press, 2000), 107–9.
58 Little, *Shakespeare Jungle Fever*, 128, 126.
59 Little, *Shakespeare Jungle Fever*, 142.
60 Little, *Shakespeare Jungle Fever*, 117.
61 Paul A. Cantor, '*Antony and Cleopatra*: Empire, Globalization, and the Clash of Civilizations', in Bruce E. Altschuler and Michael A. Genovese (eds.), *Shakespeare and Politics: What a Sixteenth-Century Playwright Can Tell Us about Twenty-First-Century Politics* (London: Paradigm, 2014), 65–83, at 67.
62 Cantor, '*Antony and Cleopatra*', 67, 73.
63 Cantor, '*Antony and Cleopatra*', 76, 69–70.
64 Richmond Barbour, *Before Orientalism: London's Theatre of the East, 1576–1626* (Cambridge: Cambridge University Press, 2003), 59.
65 Barbour, *Before Orientalism*, 67.
66 Arthur Lindley, 'Antony, Cleopatra, the Market, and the End(s) of History', in Lloyd Davis (ed.), *Shakespeare Matters: History, Teaching, Performance* (Newark, DE: University of Delaware Press, 2003), 62–73, at 62.
67 Lindley, 'Antony, Cleopatra, the Market', 62.
68 Lindley, 'Antony, Cleopatra, the Market', 63.
69 Lindley, 'Antony, Cleopatra, the Market', 63.
70 Andrew Hiscock, *The Uses of This World: Thinking Space in Shakespeare, Marlowe, Cary, and Jonson* (Cardiff: University of Wales Press, 2004), 95.
71 Hiscock, *The Uses of This World*, 102.
72 Hiscock, *The Uses of This World*, 89, 99–100.

73 William Junker, 'The Image of Both Theaters: Empire and Revelation in Shakespeare's *Antony and Cleopatra*', *Shakespeare Quarterly*, 66 (2015): 167–87, at 174, 172.

74 Junker, 'The Image of Both Theaters', 172–3.

75 Junker, 'The Image of Both Theaters', 177.

76 Anthony Miller, *Roman Triumphs and Early Modern English Culture* (Basingstoke: Palgrave, 2001), 133–4, 136.

77 Miller, *Roman Triumphs and Early Modern English Culture*, 128.

78 Lisa Hopkins, 'Cleopatra and the Myth of Scota', in Sara Munson Deats (ed.), *Antony and Cleopatra: New Critical Essays* (London and New York: Routledge, 2005), 231–42, at 232–3, 236.

79 Hopkins, 'Cleopatra and the Myth of Scota', 232.

80 Hopkins, 'Cleopatra and the Myth of Scota', 232.

81 Michael Platt, *Rome and Romans according to Shakespeare* (Salzburg: Institut für Englische Sprache und Literatur, 1976).

82 Parker, *Plato's Republic and Shakespeare's Rome*, 93, 107–8, 95.

83 Parker, *Plato's Republic and Shakespeare's Rome*, 96, 108.

84 Parker, *Plato's Republic and Shakespeare's Rome*, 105.

85 Andrew Hadfield, *Shakespeare and Republicanism* (Cambridge: Cambridge University Press, 2005), 226.

86 Hadfield, *Shakespeare and Republicanism*, 226.

87 Hadfield, *Shakespeare and Republicanism*, 226.

88 Richard Strier, *The Unrepentant Renaissance: From Petrarch to Shakespeare to Milton* (Chicago, IL: University of Chicago Press, 2011), 114.

89 Strier, *The Unrepentant Renaissance*, 117–19.

90 Strier, *The Unrepentant Renaissance*, 123, 125.

91 Akiko Kusunoki, *Gender and Representations of the Female Subject in Early Modern England: Creating Their Own Meanings* (Basingstoke: Palgrave Macmillan, 2015), 27.

92 Kusunoki, *Gender and Representations*, 28–30, 32.

93 Camilla Caporicci, '"Gods and Goddesses – All the Whole Synod of Them!": Shakespeare's References to the Gods in *Antony and Cleopatra*', *Textus: English Studies in Italy*, 29 (2) (2016): 83–102, at 88, 90.

94 Caporicci, 'Gods and Goddesses', 100.

95 John Roe, *Shakespeare and Machiavelli* (Cambridge: Brewer, 2002), 181.

96 Roe, *Shakespeare and Machiavelli*, 206, 181.

97 Tanya Pollard, '"A Thing like Death": Sleeping Potions and Poisons in *Romeo and Juliet* and *Antony and Cleopatra*', *Renaissance Drama*, 32 (2003): 95–121, at 95.

98 Pollard, 'A Thing like Death', 108, 110.

99 Pollard, 'A Thing like Death', 108, 115.

100 Pollard, 'A Thing like Death', 116–17.

101 Alan Stewart, *Shakespeare's Letters* (Oxford: Oxford University Press, 2008), 95.

102 Stewart, *Shakespeare's Letters*, 101.

103 Stewart, *Shakespeare's Letters*, 94, 114.

104 Stewart, *Shakespeare's Letters*, 99–100.

105 Carol Chillington Rutter, '"Hear the Ambassadors!": Marking Shakespeare's Venice Connection', *Shakespeare Survey* 66 (2013): 265–86, at 270.

106 Rutter, 'Hear the Ambassadors!'.

107 Rutter, 'Hear the Ambassadors!', 271.

108 Lloyd Davis, Peter J. Smith, and Greg Walker, 'From Revelation to Commodity: Performing Messengers, Language and News from the York Cycle to Ben Jonson', *Cahiers Élisabéthains*, 70 (2006): 1–13, at 6.

109 Davis et al., 'From Revelation to Commodity', 6–8.

110 Peter A. Parolin, '"Cloyless Sauce": The Pleasurable Politics of Food in *Antony and Cleopatra*', in Sara Munson Deats (ed.), *Antony and Cleopatra: New Critical Essays* (London and New York: Routledge, 2005), 213–29, at 213.

111 Parolin, 'Cloyless Sauce', 214, 226.

112 Parolin, 'Cloyless Sauce', 222.

113 Parolin, 'Cloyless Sauce', 214, 223.

114 Jennifer Park, 'Discandying Cleopatra: Preserving Cleopatra's Infinite Variety in Shakespeare's *Antony and Cleopatra*', *Studies in Philology*, 113 (2016): 595–633, at 598.

115 Park, 'Discandying Cleopatra', 598–9.

116 Park, 'Discandying Cleopatra', 618.

117 Gilberto Sacerdoti, '*Antony and Cleopatra* and the Overflowing of the Roman Measure', in Maria Del Sapio Garbero (ed.), *Identity, Otherness, and Empire in Shakespeare's Rome* (Farnham: Ashgate, 2009), 107–18, at 113.

118 Sacerdoti, '*Antony and Cleopatra*', 109, 116.

119 Adrian Streete, 'The Politics of Ethical Presentism: Appropriation, Spirituality and the Case of *Antony and Cleopatra*', *Textual Practice*, 22 (2008): 405–31, at 405–8.

120 Streete, 'The Politics of Ethical Presentism', 421, 423, 425–6.

Chapter 4

1 All parenthetical references to the play are to William Shakespeare, *Antony and Cleopatra*, ed. John Wilders (London and New York: Routledge for Arden Shakespeare, 1995).

2 Janet Adelman, *The Common Liar: An Essay on* Antony and Cleopatra (New Haven, CT: Yale University Press, 1973), 40.

3 On the tensions inherent in Renaissance discourses of exemplarity see, e.g., Timothy Hampton, *Writing from History: The Rhetoric of Exemplarity in Renaissance Literature* (Ithaca, NY: Cornell University Press, 1990).

4 Sarah Hatchuel, *Shakespeare and the Cleopatra/Caesar Intertext: Sequel, Conflation, Remake* (Madison, WI: Fairleigh Dickinson University Press, 2011), 8–9.

5 Paul A. Cantor, *Shakespeare's Rome: Republic and Empire* (2nd edn; Chicago, IL: University of Chicago Press, 2017). Other useful book-length studies in this vein that include

sustained discussion of *Antony and Cleopatra* include Robert S. Miola, *Shakespeare's Rome* (Cambridge: Cambridge University Press, 1983), and Warren Chernaik, *The Myth of Rome in Shakespeare and His Contemporaries* (Cambridge: Cambridge University Press, 2011).

6 Adelman, *The Common Liar*; Linda Charnes, *Notorious Identity: Materializing the Subject in Shakespeare* (Cambridge, MA: Harvard University Press, 1993), 103–47.

7 For an authoritative historical account, see Christopher Pelling, 'The Triumviral Period', in Alan K. Bowman, Edward Champlin and Andrew Lintott (eds.), *The Cambridge Ancient History*, X: *The Augustan Empire, 43 BC–AD 69* (2nd edn, Cambridge: Cambridge University Press, 1996), 1–69, at 1.

8 I mean decorum in the sense laid out in Cicero's *De officiis*, as naming a quality of public seemliness assumed both to accompany and to be integral to civic virtue. Tom McAlindon's book-length study of *Shakespeare and Decorum* (London: Macmillan, 1973) is about decorum as a rhetorical concept demonstrated by Shakespeare and his characters. While this study corroborates my sense of the importance of Cicero, including for *Antony and Cleopatra*, its approach and objectives are therefore quite a bit different from my own.

9 Adelman, *The Common Liar*, 53–101, was certainly correct to read the play as being about the ambiguity and polyvocality of the tradition that grew up around these figures in Augustan Rome and subsequently. See also Heather James's acute reading of the way the play 'historicizes the Augustan record, revealing how the ideologically charged narrative of Antony and Cleopatra's defeat is cast as a cornerstone of the new Roman state', in her *Shakespeare's Troy: Drama, Politics, and the Translation of Empire* (Cambridge: Cambridge University Press, 1997), 121. I am suggesting here that Shakespeare also understood the triumviral moment as a special moment in which Roman identity was up for grabs.

10 Citation from William Shakespeare, *Julius Caesar*, ed. David Daniell (Walton-on-Thames: Nelson for Arden Shakespeare, 1998).

11 Geoffrey Miles, *Shakespeare and the Constant Romans* (Oxford: Clarendon Press, 1996), 18.

12 Shadi Bartsch, *The Mirror of the Self: Sexuality, Self-Knowledge, and the Gaze in the Early Roman Empire* (Chicago, IL: University of Chicago Press, 2006), esp. 115–38, 216–29. Bartsch notes that the 'normative republican usage' of the word *persona*, when to describe social roles, 'almost always points to a public role that is not felt to be a concealment of some truer or inner private self' (223; emphasis in original). On the importance of public performance within Roman political life, see also Geoffrey S. Sumi, *Ceremony and Power: Performing Politics in Rome between Republic and Empire* (Ann Arbor, MI: University of Michigan Press, 2005).

13 *Marcus Tullius Ciceroes Thre Bokes of Duties, to Marcus His Sonne, Turned Oute of Latine into English*, by Nicolas Grimald, ed. Gerald O'Gorman (Cranbury: Associated University Presses, 1990); I quote from 86 and 205 respectively. The latter quotation is of one of the marginal notes from Grimald's *Cicero*, and in this edition these are printed in an appendix at the end of the volume.

14 *De re publica*, 2.69: 'ut numquam a se ipso instituendo contemplandoque discedat, ut ad imitationem sui vocet alios, ut sese splendore animi et vitae suae sicus speculum praebeat civibus'. I quote from the Loeb Classical Library volume (213) containing Cicero's *On the Republic and On the Laws*, ed. Jeffrey Henderson, trans. Clinton Walker Keyes (Cambridge, MA: Harvard University Press, 2000).

15 A quick search of EEBO-TCP indicates that glowing eyes are often associated with inhumanity in early modern literature, as when the Cretan Minotaur is described as having a face in which 'eyes glowed like a furnace of kindled fire' or when Thomas Dekker describes a cook 'whose eies glowed with the heat of the fier … poaking in at the mouth of an Oven, torturing soules as it were in the Single furnace of Lucifer'. See, respectively, the nearly anonymous translation (by L. A.) of Marcos Martínez, *The Eighth Booke of the Myrror of Knighthood Being the Third of the Third Part. Englished out of the Spanish Tongue* (London, 1599), sig. X2, and Thomas Dekker, *The Belman of London Bringing to Light the Most*

Notorious Villanies That Are Now Practised in the Kingdome (London, 1608), sig. B4v.

16 On spectacle and mimesis, see especially Jonathan Gil Harris, '"Narcissus in thy Face": Roman Desire and the Difference It Fakes in *Antony and Cleopatra*', *Shakespeare Quarterly*, 45 (1994): 408–25.

17 Charnes, *Notorious Identity*, 112.

18 Miles, *Shakespeare and the Constant Romans*, 180.

19 *Marcus Tullius Ciceroes thre bokes of duties*, 86; Miles, *Shakespeare and the Constant Romans*, 179.

20 Miola, *Shakespeare's Rome*, 158. Brent Dawson reads the play as being about 'the language of imperial worldhood' in '"The World Transformed": Multiple Worlds in *Antony and Cleopatra*', *Renaissance Drama*, 43 (2015): 173–91, at 179.

21 Compare, for instance, two interesting recent essays that make similarly deconstructive moves to very different effect: Mary Thomas Crane, 'Roman World, Egyptian Earth: Cognitive Difference and Empire in Shakespeare's *Antony and Cleopatra*', *Comparative Drama*, 43 (1) (2009): 1–17; and Colby Gordon, 'Shakespearean Futurity: Soft Cities in *Antony and Cleopatra*', *postmedieval*, 6 (2015): 429–38.

22 Coppélia Kahn, *Roman Shakespeare: Warriors, Wounds and Women* (London and New York: Routledge, 1997), 110, describes the play as 'an attempt to transmute Roman matter and style into a glittering if unstable alloy of mettle and mutability, a Rome drawn to, repelled by, and finally fused with what is Other to it'.

23 Though the play begins with the image of Antony gazing on Cleopatra's 'tawny front' and so losing his Roman virtue, its depiction of Cleopatra's skin colour is somewhat inconsistent, as Adelman, *The Common Liar*, 184–8, noted long ago. Such inconsistencies do not seem to diminish the importance to the play of Cleopatra's alterity, and so I find Joyce Green MacDonald's argument, in *Women and Race in Early Modern Texts* (Cambridge: Cambridge University Press, 2002), 45–67, persuasive: 'the play is so convinced of the cosmic import of Cleopatra's racial difference … that it cannot be bothered to be consistent about her skin color. Its view of what her race

means is so large as to render mere consistency of physical description irrelevant' (60). For an alternative approach – one that sees racial markers as performative and that locates Shakespeare's Cleopatra in relation to earlier dramatic versions of the character in neo-classical plays, see Pascale Aebischer, 'The Properties of Whiteness: Renaissance Cleopatras from Jodelle to Shakespeare', *Shakespeare Survey* 65 (2012): 221–38.

24 See Benjamin Isaac, *The Invention of Racism in Classical Antiquity* (Princeton, NJ: Princeton University Press, 2004), 225–47.

25 Among the first items discussed in Plutarch's life is Antony's friendship with Curio who – in North's Elizabethan translation, quoted from Geoffrey Bullough, *Narrative and Dramatic Sources of Shakespeare*, 8 vols (London and New York: Routledge, 1957–75), V, 255 – 'was a dissolute man' and who 'to have Antonius the better at his commaundement, trained him on into great follies, and vain expenses upon women, in rioting and banketing'. Christopher Pelling discusses this aspect of the comparison between Plutarch and Shakespeare in his authoritative edition of Plutarch, *Life of Antony* (Cambridge: Cambridge University Press, 1988), 39–40. On Plutarch's depiction of 'integrated characters' – characters whose core characteristics are relatively durable and cluster together – see also Christopher Pelling, 'Aspects of Plutarch's Characterisation', *Illinois Classical Studies*, 13 (1988): 257–74. Though that portion of Appian's history that might have focused upon Antony and Cleopatra in Egypt has been lost, Appian tends to see erotic desire as destructive and as characteristic of losing Romanness, and it is possible to read Cleopatra's impact upon Antony as corrupting him away from Romanness in the portions of the history that we do have. Of course, there is no shortage of possible sources, going back to Augustan propaganda, for the idea of Cleopatra as seducing Antony away from Roman rectitude. On Appian, though, see Luke Pitcher, 'The Erotics of Appian', in Kathryn Welch (ed.), *Appian's Roman History: Empire and Civil War* (Swansea: Classical Press of Wales, 2015), 205–19.

26 Ania Loomba, *Shakespeare, Race, and Colonialism* (Oxford: Oxford University Press, 2002), 133.

27 I quote from the Loeb Classical Library edition (vols 221 and 293) of Cicero, *The Verrine Orations*, trans. L. H. G. Greenwood, 2 vols (Cambridge, MA: Harvard University Press, 1928–35).

28 John Richardson, *The Language of Empire: Rome and the Idea of Empire from the Third Century BC to the Second Century AD* (Cambridge: Cambridge University Press, 2008), 63–116; C. E. W. Steel, *Cicero, Rhetoric, and Empire* (Oxford: Oxford University Press, 2001), 21–74.

29 *Marcus Tullius Ciceroes thre bokes of duties*, 90. I have modernized the use of i/j in these quotations.

30 *Marcus Tullius Ciceroes thre bokes of duties*, 121.

31 Plutarch, *Life of Antony*, 16.

32 I quote from Adelman, *The Common Liar*, 103. See Charnes, *Notorious Identity*, especially 142–7; James, *Shakespeare's Troy*, especially 144–7; and Arthur L. Little Jr, *Shakespeare Jungle Fever: National-Imperial Re-visions of Race, Rape, and Sacrifice* (Stanford, CA: Stanford University Press, 2000), 143–76.

33 On the date of Seneca's treatise, see Susanna Braund's introduction to her edition of Seneca's *De clementia* (Oxford: Oxford University Press, 2009), 1–92 (16).

34 Leah Whittington, *Renaissance Suppliants: Poetry, Antiquity, Reconciliation* (Oxford: Oxford University Press, 2016), 51; but see 50–81. See also Melissa Barden Dowling, *Clemency and Cruelty in the Roman World* (Ann Arbor, MI: University of Michigan Press, 2006).

35 The idea that an ethics founded on self-mastery developed in a compensatory manner during the early years of the principate was popularized by Michel Foucault in *The Care of the Self: The History of Sexuality*, III, trans. Robert Hurley (New York: Vintage Books, 1988). He argues, for instance, that 'the first two centuries of the imperial epoch can be seen as … a kind of golden age in the cultivation of the self' (45). See also the clarifying and refining discussion in Matthew B. Roller, *Constructing Autocracy: Aristocrats and Emperors in Julio-*

Claudian Rome (Princeton, NJ: Princeton University Press, 2001), 64–126.

36 Bartsch, *The Mirror of the Self*, 191.

37 The early modern notion that Stoicism's inward-looking emphasis on self-cultivation might be a technique of self-protection in response to tyranny and other forms of political instability does not originate with Shakespeare, of course. Rather, it is an idea developed as part of the pan-European vogue for neo-Stoicism associated with the work of Justus Lipsius in the late sixteenth century and one that had previously been explored in Roman-themed plays like Samuel Daniel's *Tragedie of Cleopatra* (1594) and Ben Jonson's *Sejanus His Fall* (1605).

38 Michael Shapiro, 'Boying Her Greatness: Shakespeare's Use of Coterie Drama in *Antony and Cleopatra*', *Modern Language Review*, 77 (1982): 1–15. Shakespeare's more concrete borrowings from neo-classical plays about Antony and Cleopatra are also canvassed by Bullough, *Narrative and Dramatic Sources*, V, 222–39.

39 Samuel Daniel, *Delia and Rosamund Augmented: Cleopatra* (London, 1594), sigs. N5v and N4v, respectively. Daniel continually edited his play, but the tenor of the last act remains the same across all the different versions of the play. Even in the 1607 version of the play, in which Daniel converts the last act from a messenger's account of Cleopatra's final moments to a dramatic scene with Cleopatra herself onstage, many of the same speeches are preserved, as is the neo-Stoic tenor of the queen's refusal to go along with Caesar.

40 I develop this point in greater detail in 'Seneca and English Political Culture', in R. Malcolm Smuts (ed.), *The Oxford Handbook of the Age of Shakespeare* (Oxford: Oxford University Press, 2016), 306–21.

41 Daniel Cadman, *Sovereigns and Subjects in Early Modern Neo-Senecan Drama: Republicanism, Stoicism, and Authority* (Farnham: Ashgate, 2015).

42 T. S. Eliot, *Selected Essays* (New York: Harcourt, Brace & World, 1964), 110.

43 Little, *Shakespeare Jungle Fever*, 169.

Chapter 5

1 All parenthetical references to the play are to William Shakespeare, *Antony and Cleopatra*, ed. John Wilders (London and New York: Routledge for Arden Shakespeare, 1995).

2 See the English continuation of Appian, *An Aunciend Historie and Exquisite Chronicle of the Romanes Warres* (London, 1578), 397–8. See also Jan H. Blits, *New Heaven, New Earth: Shakespeare's Antony and Cleopatra* (Lanham, MD: Lexington, 2009), 1–12; Alex Schulman, *Rethinking Shakespeare's Political Philosophy: From Lear to Leviathan* (Edinburgh: Edinburgh University Press, 2014), 80–91.

3 For theatricality in the play, see Northrop Frye, '*Antony and Cleopatra*', in Harold Bloom (ed.), *William Shakespeare's Antony and Cleopatra: New Edition* (New York: Bloom's Literary Criticism, 2011), 69–71. For the intellectual context, see Daniel Cadman, '"Quick Comedians": Mary Sidney, Samuel Daniel and the *Theatrum Mundi* in Shakespeare's *Antony and Cleopatra*', *Actes des Congrès de la Société Française Shakespeare*, 33 (2015): 1–13. Available at http://shakespeare.revues.org/3536 (accessed 21 January 2018). For the fusion of performing and feeling, see Jyotsna G. Singh, '"Come, Eros, Eros!" Rereading Emotion and Affect in Shakespeare's *Antony and Cleopatra*', in Ronda Arab, Michelle M. Dowd and Adam Zucker (eds.), *Historical Affects and the Early Modern Theater* (London and New York: Routledge, 2015), 96–108.

4 Marilyn L. Williamson, *Infinite Variety: Antony and Cleopatra in Renaissance and Earlier Tradition* (Mystic, CT: Lawrence Verry, 1974), 181–216; Alan Bloom, *Shakespeare on Love and Friendship* (Chicago, IL: University of Chicago Press, 2000), 29–57; Gordon Braden, 'Plutarch, Shakespeare, and the Alpha Males', in Charles Martindale and A. B. Taylor (eds.), *Shakespeare and the Classics* (Cambridge: Cambridge University Press, 2004), 188–205.

5 Michael Goldman, *Acting and Action in Shakespearean Tragedy* (Princeton, NJ: Princeton University Press, 1985), 112–39, especially 112.

6   John E. Curran Jr, *Character and the Individual Personality in English Renaissance Drama: Tragedy, History, Tragicomedy* (Newark, DE: University of Delaware Press, 2014), 291–311.

7   Thomas M. Greene, 'Pressures of Context in *Antony and Cleopatra*', in Harold Bloom (ed.), *William Shakespeare's Antony and Cleopatra: New Edition* (New York: Bloom's Literary Criticism, 2011), 119–38; Warren Chernaik, *The Myth of Rome in Shakespeare and His Contemporaries* (Cambridge: Cambridge University Press, 2011), 148–64.

8   See T. J. B. Spencer (ed.), *Shakespeare's Plutarch* (Harmondsworth: Penguin, 1964), 215–16. All references to Plutarch's *Lives* are from this edition. On daemons see Curran, *Character and the Individual Personality*, 294–6.

9   See Rick Bowers, '"The Luck of Caesar": Winning and Losing in *Antony and Cleopatra*', *English Studies*, 79 (1998): 522–35 (on Soothsayer, 526).

10 See Curran, *Character and the Individual Personality*, 301–4; John E. Curran Jr, 'Fletcher, Massinger, and Roman Imperial Character', *Comparative Drama*, 43 (2009): 317–54, at 320–7.

11 On 'reconstruction', see Judith Anderson, *Biographical Truth: The Representation of Historical Persons in Tudor-Stuart Writing* (New Haven, CT: Yale University Press, 1984).

12 Melanchthon, *Philosophiae Moralis Epitome*, in *Opera quae supersunt Omnia*, XVI, ed. H. E. Bindseil (New York: Johnson Reprint, 1963), 57–8. See Curran, *Character and the Individual Personality*, 299–300.

13 For Julius's self-emulation, see Spencer, *Shakespeare's Plutarch*, 79; for Alexander, 31. See Braden, 'Plutarch, Shakespeare, and the Alpha Males', 195–9.

14 See James C. Bulman, *The Heroic Idiom of Shakespearean Tragedy* (Newark, DE: University of Delaware Press, 1985), 191–213.

15 Cicero, *De officiis*, 1.30–3, trans. Walter Miller (Cambridge, MA: Harvard University Press, 1990), 106–25.

16 John of Salisbury, *Policraticus*, 1–4, 3.8–10, ed. K. S. B. Keats-Rohan (Turnhout: Corpus Christianorum, 1993), 190–201.

17 Pierre de La Primaudaye, *The French Academie* (London, 1586), 471–2.

18 Suetonius, 'The Deified Augustus', in *The Lives of the Caesars*, trans. J. C. Rolfe, 2 vols (Cambridge, MA: Harvard University Press, 1989), I, 281.

19 Suetonius, 'The Deified Augustus', I, 243.

20 Spencer, *Shakespeare's Plutarch*, 273. See Appian, *An Auncient Historie*, 391, and Wilders's note.

21 Peggy Muñoz Simonds, '"To the Very Heart of Loss": Renaissance Iconography in Shakespeare's *Antony and Cleopatra*', *Shakespeare Studies*, 22 (1994): 220–76, at 249.

22 Spencer, *Shakespeare's Plutarch*, 261–2.

23 Antony's soldiership is praised (2.1.35–6) but called into doubt (3.1, esp. by Ventidius 16–17); see Spencer, *Shakespeare's Plutarch*, 219.

24 *Hercules Furens*, 62–88, esp. 84–5, *Hercules Oetaeus*, 55–6, 62–3, in *Seneca's Tragedies*, trans. Frank Justus Miller, 2 vols (Cambridge, MA: Harvard University Press, 1979), I, 8–11; II, 190–1.

25 *Hercules Oetaeus*, 1683–5, in *Seneca's Tragedies*, II, 318–19.

26 Mary Sidney, *Antonius*, 1217–46, 1878, in *The Collected Works of Mary Sidney Herbert, Countess of Pembroke*, ed. Margaret P. Hannay, Noel J. Kinnamon and Michael G. Brennan, 2 vols (Oxford: Clarendon Press, 1998), I, 186, 203.

27 Janet Adelman, *The Common Liar: An Essay on* Antony and Cleopatra (New Haven, CT: Yale University Press, 1973), 134–7.

28 Spencer, *Shakespeare's Plutarch*, 274–5; Wilders' note to 4.3.21. On Hercules and Bacchus, also see Julia Griffin's chapter in this volume, 165–9.

29 For a feminist perspective, see Carol Cook, 'The Fatal Cleopatra', in Shirley Nelson Garner and Madelon Sprengnether (eds.), *Shakespearean Tragedy and Gender* (Bloomington, IN: Indiana University Press, 1996), 241–67.

30 On young Antony's having been 'trained' for debauchery, see Spencer, *Shakespeare's Plutarch*, 175.

31 Thomas Rogers, *A Philosophicall Discourse, Entituled, The Anatomie of the Minde* (London, 1576), fol. 98.

32 See H. W. Fawkner, *Shakespeare's Hyperontology: Antony and Cleopatra* (Rutherford, NJ: Fairleigh Dickinson, 1990), 30–3.

33 John Fletcher and Philip Massinger, *The False One*, 5.4.15–34, 4.2.94–123 (104), ed. Robert K. Turner, in *The Dramatic Works in the Beaumont and Fletcher Canon*, ed. Fredson Bowers, 10 vols (Cambridge: Cambridge University Press, 1992), VIII, 194–5, 177.

34 See Cadman, 'Quick Comedians'; for Cleopatra and Fortune, see Simonds, 'To the Very Heart of Loss', 226–45.

35 Sidney, *Antonius*, 1815–20, in *The Collected Works*, I, 202.

36 Fletcher and Massinger, *The False One*, 4.2.126–7, in *Dramatic Works*, VIII, 178.

37 This in disagreement with Derick R. C. Marsh, *Passion Lends Them Power: A Study of Shakespeare's Love Tragedies* (Manchester: Manchester University Press, 1976), 142–3; Bloom, *Shakespeare on Love*, 37–8; Peter Holbrook, *Shakespeare's Individualism* (Cambridge: Cambridge University Press, 2010), 180–1.

Chapter 6

1 Thomas North, *The Lives of the Noble Grecians and Romanes Compared Together by That Grave Learned Philosopher and Historiographer Plutarke of Chaeronea* [...] (London: Thomas Vautroullier, 1579), n.p. Richard Field brought out a second edition in 1595: see below. Another epigraph for this paper might be a remark by F. O. Matthiessen, *Translation: An Elizabethan Art* (Cambridge, MA: Harvard University Press, 1931), 75: 'It is extraordinary how North's inaccuracies sometimes improve the context rather than injure it.'

2 Translation and editing had begun in the late fourteenth century, but the first complete translations appear between 1559 and 1572: besides Amyot's French, there are two Latin translations.

3   North claimed to have translated the work 'out of French into Englishe' (title-page); scholars have debated whether he was in fact being too modest. (He had also two Latin versions available to consult.)

4   By the time of *Antony and Cleopatra* (assuming a date of 1606–7), three editions of North had appeared: 1579, 1595 and 1603; it is not certain which Shakespeare was following. He must have used the 1579 edition at least at the beginning of his relationship with Plutarch; the wording is largely identical, though there are differences. The Shakespeare Birthplace Trust owns a copy of 1579 with an inscription by Alice, Countess of Derby, to someone called William (the page is damaged, and the surname is lost): this may be Shakespeare's own copy – or it may not. The 1603 edition adds a (spurious) *Life of Octavian*, which some think Shakespeare used for writing the play.

5   In using this perhaps old-fashioned terminology, I do not mean either to ignore or to oppose the subtler terms, 'kinds of memory and forgetting', offered by Raphael Lyne in the fine chapter devoted to the play in his *Memory and Intertextuality in Renaissance Literature* (Cambridge: Cambridge University Press, 2016), 160–205. This chapter will focus more narrowly on the results of the selection, or forgetting; the psychology behind it is much less my concern.

6   All parenthetical references to the play are to William Shakespeare, *Antony and Cleopatra*, ed. John Wilders (London and New York: Routledge for Arden Shakespeare, 1995).

7   All parenthetical references to North's version of Plutarch's *Life of Antony* are taken from Geoffrey Bullough, *Narrative and Dramatic Sources of Shakespeare*, V (London: Routledge & Kegan Paul, 1964).

8   All references to the 1574 edition of Amyot's *Les Vies des Hommes Illustres, Grecs et Romans, comparées l'une avec l'autre par Plutarque* – the one North probably used – will be given in parentheses in the text. Gordon Braden, 'Shakespeare', in Mark Beck (ed.), *A Companion to Plutarch* (Malden, MA: Wiley-Blackwell, 2014), 577–91, at 587, points out the adaptation of this gloss.

9   See, in particular, John Denton, 'Wearing a Gown in the Market Place or a Toga in the Forum: Coriolanus from Plutarch to Shakespeare via Renaissance Translation', in Grazia Caliumi (ed.), *Shakespeare e la sua eredità* (Parma: Zara, 1993), 97–109.

10 The French, though still quite clotted, is less so, avoiding the first and the fourth of those 'him's: '*luy* mandant qu'il *l*'avoit irrité, pour autant qu'il faisoit trop du superbe, & l'avoit eu en mespris, mesmement lors qu'il estoit facile & aisé d'aigrir pour la misere en laquelle il se trouvoit' (1143). The Greek is much clearer, thanks largely to its inflections – *grapsas hōs entruphōn kai periphronōn paroxuneien auton, euparoxunton hupo kakōn onta* – literally, 'writing how he-being-proud-and-disdainful had provoked him-being-easily-angered-by-misfortunes'. Sometimes, though, Plutarch himself uses unsignposted and confusing pronouns; see the description of Eros and Antony together attempting Antony's suicide (North, 309): this is discussed by Lyne, *Memory and Intertextuality*, 170–1.

11 *Plutarch's Lives*, trans. Bernadotte Perrin (Cambridge, MA: Harvard University Press, 1920), XI, 305 (73.2).

12 William Shakespeare, *Anthony and Cleopatra*, ed. Michael Neill (Oxford: Oxford University Press, 1994), 260.

13 *Plutarch: Life of Antony*, ed. Christopher Pelling (Cambridge: Cambridge University Press, 1988), 299.

14 David Green, *Plutarch Revisited: A Study of Shakespeare's Last Roman Tragedies* (Salzburg: Institut für Anglistik und Amerikanistik, 1979), 91.

15 Stephen Oakley, 'Single Combat in the Roman Republic', *Classical Quarterly*, 35 (1985): 392–410, especially the end.

16 Susanne Wofford, 'Antony's Egyptian Bacchanals: Heroic and Divine Impersonation in Shakespeare's Plutarch and *Antony and Cleopatra*', *Poetica: An International Journal of Linguistic-Literary Studies*, 48 (1997): 33–67, at 33. The 'humiliating defeat' that Wofford mentions is not Actium (already behind him, in both Plutarch's sequence) but his final defeat, in the abortive naval engagement that Shakespeare's Antony describes at 4.12.9ff. For an extended and very fine treatment of this scene, see Lyne, *Memory and Intertextuality*, 163–6.

17 Lyne, *Memory and Intertextuality*, 163.
18 Lyne, *Memory and Intertextuality*, 163.
19 On Hercules and Bacchus, also see John E. Curran Jr's chapter in this volume, 133–54.
20 There are nearly 200 mentions of trumpet/trumpets in the plays; thirteen of hautboys. *Henry VI, Part 2* begins with trumpets followed by hautboys; apart from this, all the uses of them seem to be late: *Macbeth, Antony and Cleopatra, Coriolanus, Timon of Athens, Henry VIII*. (I draw no conclusions from this.)
21 Bruce Smith, *The Acoustic World of Early Modern England* (Chicago, IL: University of Chicago Press, 1999), 244–5. See also Gary Taylor, 'Divine [ ]sences', *Shakespeare Survey 54* (2001): 13–30, at 29: 'hautboys produce sounds loud enough and shrill enough to penetrate the wooden barrier and reach every ear in the audience'.
22 William Shakespeare, *Timon of Athens*, ed. Anthony B. Dawson and Gretchen E. Minton (London: Bloomsbury Arden Shakespeare, 2008).
23 They must also have had the power to be sinister. Consider use of them in William Shakespeare, *Macbeth*, ed. Sandra Clark and Pamela Mason (London: Bloomsbury Arden Shakespeare, 2015), to introduce the apparitions (4.1.105). From the sinister to the melancholy is a short step, if one is facing the right way.
24 See, for a discussion of the music in the barge scene, F. W. Sternfeld, *Music in Shakespearean Tragedy* (London: Routledge & Kegan Paul, 1963), 222–4. He speaks of Shakespeare's 'musical economy' in this and the Hercules scene.
25 Wofford, 'Antony's Egyptian Bacchanals', 57, referring to Antony's later raging about the 'shirt of Nessus' (4.12.43).
26 *The Thirteene Books of Aeneidos* (1600), n.p.
27 *The Thirteene Books of Aeneidos* (1600), n.p.
28 For a fine recent study of Shakespeare's debt to Virgil, the subject of increasing interest, see Colin Burrow, *Shakespeare and Classical Antiquity* (Oxford: Oxford University Press, 2013), Chapter 2. In the acute words of Leah Whittington, 'Shakespeare's Virgil: Empathy and *The Tempest*', in John Cox

and Patrick Gray (eds.), *Shakespeare and Renaissance Ethics* (Cambridge: Cambridge University Press, 2014), 98–120, at 103, 'if Virgil's presence is difficult to trace, it is because critics are not always looking in the right place'.

29 John Dryden, *All for Love* (1678), 5.1.503–5, in Sandra Clark (ed.), *Shakespeare Made Fit: Restoration Adaptations of Shakespeare* (London: Dent, 1997), 288.

30 Eliot discussed Shakespeare's wording and compared it with Dryden's in a radio talk on 'Dryden the Dramatist' given in 1931; his discussion is discussed no less brilliantly by Christopher Ricks in *T. S. Eliot and Prejudice* (Berkeley, CA: University of California Press, 1988), 159–62. As Lyne (*Memory and Intertextuality*, 172) remarks, discussing the scene himself, 'In such critical company it feels rash to add anything further'; however, we both attempt to do so.

31 Given how like a typographical error this looks, it is worth remarking that the pronoun at least remains unchanged in all later editions of North's *Plutarch*.

32 Citation from William Shakespeare, *Cymbeline*, ed. Valerie Wayne (London: Bloomsbury Arden Shakespeare, 2017).

33 Etymologically, to watch is to be awake; the derived sense of being aware of something by regarding it is dated by the *OED* to the sixteenth century. In many cases, Shakespeare implies both senses of the word: see, for example, William Shakespeare, *A Midsummer Night's Dream*, ed. Sukanta Chaudhuri (London: Bloomsbury Arden Shakespeare, 2017), 2.1.177, 'I'll watch Titania when she is asleep' – the first example the *OED* gives of sense 11.a: 'To keep a person in view in order to observe any actions, movements, or changes that may occur'. The fact that Titania, like Innogen, is asleep, and thus unable to avoid her wakeful watcher, shows the rather sinister connection between the two senses.

34 As Iachimo moves from memory to invention, the same story runs in his creator's mind, pressing again: 'If you seek / For further satisfying, under her breast – / Worthy the pressing – lies a mole, right proud / Of that most delicate lodging. By my life, / I kissed it, and it gave me present hunger / To feed again, though full' (2.4.133–8). Or, as Enobarbus said: 'she makes hungry / Where most she satisfies' (2.2.247–8).

35 Shakespeare uses 'report' in *Antony and Cleopatra* and *Coriolanus*, two of his three Plutarchan plays, more than in any other except *Cymbeline*, which has more by 25 per cent than its nearest rival (*Coriolanus*). The word 'rare' occurs eleven times in *Cymbeline* – 30 per cent more than any other play.

36 Amyot has 'quelque fray et quelque trace' (657): 'fray' is a medieval French word for 'track', which North clearly misunderstood as 'frais' = 'fresh'.

37 The closest parallel is the dying speech of Hotspur in William Shakespeare, *King Henry IV, Part 1*, ed. David Scott Kastan (London: Thomson for Arden Shakespeare, 2002), 5.4.85: '[I am] food for –'. Prince Henry finishes it for him, as Charmian does for Cleopatra; Hotspur's speech left much less to Hal's imagination than Cleopatra's did to Charmian's.

38 From a search through EEBO-TCP, this seems to be the only occurrence of the word 'rarest' in all of North's *Plutarch*.

39 Apart from having a name that ends 'o' rather than 'us', Iachimo carries ducats: modern Italian currency. Much has been written about the technique of anachronism in *Cymbeline*: see, for example, Peter A. Parolin, 'Anachronistic Italy: Cultural Alliances and National Identity in *Cymbeline*', *Shakespeare Studies*, 30 (2002): 188–218.

Chapter 7

1 Melissa Parker, 'Anne Rice Interview: *Vampire Chronicles* Author Talks Latest Installment, *Blood Communion*, and Catholic Clergy Scandal', *Smashing Interviews*. Available at http://smashinginterviews.com/interviews/authors/anne-rice-interview-vampire-chronicles-author-talks-latest-installment-blood-communion-and-catholic-clergy-scandal (accessed 31 January 2019).

2 'About Christopher'. Available at http://www.christopherricebooks.com/biography-photos (accessed 31 January 2019).

3 Anne Rice, *The Mummy* (New York: Ballantine, 1989), 231, 243.

4   Rice, *The Mummy*, 339–40, 354.
5   Anne Rice and Christopher Rice, *Ramses the Damned: The Passion of Cleopatra* (New York: Anchor, 2017), 60.
6   Rice and Rice, *Ramses the Damned*, 369.
7   Rice and Rice, *Ramses the Damned*, 265, 274.
8   Rice and Rice, *Ramses the Damned*, 71.
9   Rice, *The Mummy*, 373, 429, 437, 438, 446, 456.
10 Rice and Rice, *Ramses the Damned*, 79, 274, 356.
11 Rice, *The Mummy*, 305, 318; Rice and Rice, *Ramses the Damned*, 23.
12 William Shakespeare, *Antony and Cleopatra*, ed. Jonathan Bate and Eric Rasmussen (London: Royal Shakespeare Company/Macmillan, 2009), 9.
13 Shakespeare, *Antony and Cleopatra*, 137, 141. All parenthetical references to the play are to William Shakespeare, *Antony and Cleopatra*, ed. John Wilders (London and New York: Routledge for Arden Shakespeare, 1995).
14 Rice, *The Mummy*, 280.
15 Rice and Rice, *Ramses the Damned*, 272.
16 Rice and Rice, *Ramses the Damned*, 272.
17 Rice and Rice, *Ramses the Damned*, 132.
18 Henry Rider Haggard, *Cleopatra* (Auckland: Floating Press, 2012), 197.
19 Shakespeare, *Antony and Cleopatra*, ed. Bate and Rasmussen, 173.
20 Rice, *The Mummy*, 362.
21 Rice, *The Mummy*, 365.
22 Rice and Rice, *Ramses the Damned*, 179.
23 Rice and Rice, *Ramses the Damned*, 307, 205.
24 Rice and Rice, *Ramses the Damned*, 175.
25 Rice and Rice, *Ramses the Damned*, 307, 205.
26 Rice and Rice, *Ramses the Damned*, 52.
27 Rice and Rice, *Ramses the Damned*, 206–7.
28 Rice and Rice, *Ramses the Damned*, 296.

29 Rice, *The Mummy*, 213.
30 Rice, *The Mummy*, 213.
31 Rice, *The Mummy*, 175.
32 Rice, *The Mummy*, 213.
33 Rice, *The Mummy*, 213.
34 Christopher Baldick, *The Social Mission of English Criticism* (Oxford: Clarendon Press, 1983), 87–8.
35 Shakespeare, *Antony and Cleopatra*, ed. Bate and Rasmussen, 4.
36 John Wilders, 'Introduction' to William Shakespeare, *Antony and Cleopatra* (London and New York: Routledge for Arden Shakespeare, 1995), 1–84, at 1, 38.
37 Wilders, 'Introduction', 49.
38 Wilders, 'Introduction', 38.
39 Wilders, 'Introduction', 60.
40 Wilders, 'Introduction', 60, 38.
41 Harold Bloom, *The Anxiety of Influence* (Oxford: Oxford University Press, 1973).
42 Wilders, 'Introduction', 1.
43 Metropolitan Opera, *Aida*, Metopera. Available at https://www.metopera.org/season/2018-19-season/aida/ (accessed 19 July 2018).
44 Gary Wills, 'Shakespeare and Verdi in the Theater', *New York Review of Books*, 24 November 2011. Available at https://www.nybooks.com/articles/2011/11/24/shakespeare-and-verdi-theater (accessed 19 July 2018).
45 Metopera.
46 Shakespeare, *Antony and Cleopatra*, ed. Bate and Rasmussen, 7–8.
47 Rice, *The Mummy*, 307.
48 Ben Child Bate, '"Whitewashing" Row over Scarlett Johansson's *Ghost in the Shell* Role Reignites', *Guardian*, 15 April 2016. Available at https://www.theguardian.com/film/2016/apr/15/scarlettjohanssons-role-in-ghost-in-the-shell-ignites-twitter-storm (accessed 25 July 2018).

49 Rice, *The Mummy*, 310.
50 Rice, *The Mummy*, 341.
51 Rice, *The Mummy*, 369.
52 Rice, *The Mummy*, 441.
53 Rice and Rice, *Ramses the Damned*, 346.
54 Rice, *The Mummy*, 268.
55 Rice, *The Mummy*, 266.
56 Rice, *The Mummy*, 254.
57 Rice and Rice, *Ramses the Damned*, 79; Rice, *The Mummy*, 254.
58 Rice, *The Mummy*, 26, 455.
59 Wilders, 'Introduction', 31.
60 Wilders, 'Introduction', 2.
61 Rice, *The Mummy*, 57.
62 Shakespeare, *Antony and Cleopatra*, ed. Bate and Rasmussen, 156; Wilders, 'Introduction', 4, 17.
63 Rice, *The Mummy*, 16, 45, 57, 80.
64 Rice and Rice, *Ramses the Damned*, 29.
65 Rice and Rice, *Ramses the Damned*, 52.
66 Rice and Rice, *Ramses the Damned*, 79, 274, 356.
67 Rice, *The Mummy*, 400.
68 Rice, *The Mummy*, 314, 402; Rice and Rice, *Ramses the Damned*, 26.
69 Rice, *The Mummy*, 350; see also Rice and Rice, *Ramses the Damned*, 340.
70 Rice, *The Mummy*, 286.
71 Robert Birnbaum, 'Author Interview: Christopher Rice', *Identity Theory*. Available at http://www.identitytheory.com/christopher-rice (accessed 26 July 2018).
72 Anna Metcalfe, 'Small Talk: Anne Rice', *Financial Times*, 15 November 2010. Available at https://www.ft.com/content/d15d15e4-ede9-11df-8616-00144feab49a (accessed 19 July 2018).
73 Rice and Rice, *Ramses the Damned*, 173.

Chapter 8

1. A collection about the implications of teaching Renaissance dramatists including Shakespeare is Andrew Hiscock and Lisa Hopkins (eds.), *Teaching Shakespeare and Early Modern Dramatists* (Basingstoke: Palgrave Macmillan, 2007). Since 2012, the British Shakespeare Association has been running a journal entitled *Teaching Shakespeare: Policy; Pedagogy; Practice*, edited by Sarah Olive. It is open to all areas concerned with Shakespeare and teaching, including those that have traditionally been frowned upon by the more exclusive academic circles. See also Bridget Escolme, Antony and Cleopatra: *A Guide to the Text and Its Theatrical Life* (Basingstoke: Palgrave Macmillan, 2006).
2. The reference is to Linda T. Fitz, 'Egyptian Queens and Male Reviewers', *Shakespeare Quarterly*, 28 (1977): 297–316.
3. But see Lukas Erne, *Shakespeare as Literary Dramatist* (Cambridge: Cambridge University Press, 2003).
4. This chapter is also anthologized in Graham Holderness, Bryan Loughrey and Andrew Murphy (eds.), *Shakespeare: The Roman Plays* (London: Longman, 1996).
5. The work of Bill Worthen provides a similar emphasis upon the centrality of performance. Specifically with reference to *Antony and Cleopatra*, see W. B. Worthen, 'The Weight of Antony: Staging "Character" in *Antony and Cleopatra*', *Studies in English Literature, 1500–1900* (1986): 295–308.

BIBLIOGRAPHY

Adelman, Janet. *The Common Liar: An Essay on Antony and Cleopatra* (New Haven, CT: Yale University Press, 1973).

Adelman, Janet. *Suffocating Mothers: Fantasies of Maternal Origin in Shakespeare's Plays, Hamlet to The Tempest* (London and New York: Routledge, 1992).

Aebischer, Pascale. 'The Properties of Whiteness: Renaissance Cleopatras from Jodelle to Shakespeare', *Shakespeare Survey* 65 (2012): 221–38.

Amyot, Jacques. *Les Vies des hommes illustres, Grecs et Romans, comparées l'une avec l'autre par Plutarque* (Paris, 1574).

Appian. *An Aunciente Historie and Exquisite Chronicle of the Romanes Warres* (London, 1578).

Arnold, Matthew. *Culture and Anarchy* (London: Nelson, 1869).

Astington, John H. 'Venus on the Thames', *Shakespeare Studies*, 39 (2011): 117–32.

Baldick, Christopher. *The Social Mission of English Criticism* (Oxford: Clarendon Press, 1983).

Barbour, Richmond. *Before Orientalism: London's Theatre of the East, 1576–1626* (Cambridge: Cambridge University Press, 2003).

Barker, Martin. *Live to Your Local Cinema: The Remarkable Rise of Livecasting* (Basingstoke: Palgrave Macmillan, 2013).

Barker, Roberta. '"Deared by Being Lacked": The Realist Legacy and the Art of Failure in Shakespearean Performance', in James C. Bulman (ed.), *The Oxford Handbook of Shakespeare and Performance* (Oxford: Oxford University Press, 2017), 46–63.

Barroll, J. Leeds. *Shakespearean Tragedy: Genre, Tradition, and Change in Antony and Cleopatra* (Washington, DC: Folger Shakespeare Library, 1984).

Bartsch, Shadi. *The Mirror of the Self: Sexuality, Self-Knowledge, and the Gaze in the Early Roman Empire* (Chicago, IL: University of Chicago Press, 2006).

Cantor, Paul A. *Shakespeare's Rome: Republic and Empire* (2nd edn; Chicago, IL: University of Chicago Press, 2017).
Caporicci, Camilla. '"Gods and Goddesses – All the Whole Synod of Them!": Shakespeare's References to the Gods in *Antony and Cleopatra*', *Textus: English Studies in Italy*, 29 (2) (2016): 83–102.
Cartelli, Thomas. 'High-Tech Shakespeare in a Mediatized Globe: Ivo Van Hove's *Roman Tragedies* and the Problem of Spectatorship', in James C. Bulman (ed.), *The Oxford Handbook of Shakespeare and Performance* (Oxford: Oxford University Press, 2017), 267–83.
Cartmell, Deborah, and Imelda Whelehan. *Screen Adaptation: Impure Cinema* (Basingstoke: Palgrave Macmillan, 2010).
Charnes, Linda. *Notorious Identity: Materializing the Subject in Shakespeare* (Cambridge, MA: Harvard University Press, 1993).
Charney, Maurice. *Shakespeare's Roman Plays: The Function of Imagery in the Drama* (Cambridge, MA: Harvard University Press, 1961).
Cherchi Usai, Paolo. *Georges Méliès* (Milan: Il Castoro, 2009).
Chernaik, Warren. *The Myth of Rome in Shakespeare and His Contemporaries* (Cambridge: Cambridge University Press, 2011).
Child, Ben. '"Whitewashing" Row over Scarlett Johansson's *Ghost in the Shell* Role Reignites'. *Guardian*, 15 April 2016. Available at https://www.theguardian.com/film/2016/apr/15/scarlett-johanssons-role-in-ghost-in-the-shell-ignites-twitter-storm (accessed 25 July 2018).
Cicero. *De officiis*, trans. Walter Miller (Cambridge, MA: Harvard University Press, 1990).
Cicero. *Marcus Tullius Ciceroes thre bokes of duties, to marcus his sonne, turned oute of latine into English, by Nicolas Grimalde*, ed. Gerald O'Gorman (Cranbury: Associated University Presses, 1990).
Cicero. *On the Republic; On the Laws*, ed. Jeffrey Henderson, trans. Clinton Walker Keyes (Cambridge, MA: Harvard University Press, 2000).
Cicero. *The Verrine Orations*, trans. L. H. G. Greenwood, 2 vols (Cambridge, MA: Harvard University Press, 1928–35).
Collins, Michael J. '*Antony and Cleopatra* – Review', *Shakespeare Bulletin*, 24 (2006): 112–15.

Cook, Carol. 'The Fatal Cleopatra', in Shirley Nelson Garner and Madelon Sprengnether (eds.), *Shakespearean Tragedy and Gender* (Bloomington, IN: Indiana University Press, 1996), 241–67.

Crane, Mary Thomas. 'Roman World, Egyptian Earth: Cognitive Difference and Empire in Shakespeare's *Antony and Cleopatra*', *Comparative Drama*, 43 (2009): 1–17.

Crowl, Samuel. 'A World Elsewhere: The Roman Plays on Film and Television', in Anthony Davies and Stanley Wells (eds.), *Shakespeare and the Moving Image: The Plays on Film and Television* (Cambridge: Cambridge University Press, 1994), 146–62.

Curran, John E., Jr. *Character and the Individual Personality in English Renaissance Drama: Tragedy, History, Tragicomedy* (Newark, DE: University of Delaware Press, 2014).

Curran, John E., Jr. 'Fletcher, Massinger, and Roman Imperial Character', *Comparative Drama*, 43 (2009): 317–54.

Daniell, David. 'Introduction', in William Shakespeare, *Julius Caesar* (Walton-on-Thames: Nelson for Arden Shakespeare, 1998), 1–147.

Davies, H. Neville. 'Jacobean *Antony and Cleopatra*', in John Drakakis (ed.), *Antony and Cleopatra: Contemporary Critical Essays* (Basingstoke: Macmillan, 1994), 126–65.

Davis, Lloyd, Peter J. Smith and Greg Walker. 'From Revelation to Commodity: Performing Messengers, Language and News from the York Cycle to Ben Jonson', *Cahiers Élisabéthains*, 70 (2006): 1–13.

Dawson, Brent. '"The World Transformed": Multiple Worlds in *Antony and Cleopatra*', *Renaissance Drama*, 43 (2015): 173–91.

de Vincenti, Giorgio. 'Il kolossal storico-romano nell'immaginario del Novecento', *Bianco e nero*, 49 (1988): 7–29.

Deats, Sara Munson. 'Shakespeare's Anamorphic Drama: A Survey of *Antony and Cleopatra* in Criticism, on Stage, and on Screen', in Sara Munson Deats (ed.), *Antony and Cleopatra: New Critical Essays* (London and New York: Routledge, 2005), 1–93.

Dekker, Thomas. *The Belman of London Bringing to Light the Most Notorious Villanies that Are Now Practised in the Kingdome* (London, 1608).

Del Sapio Garbero, Maria. 'Fostering the Question "Who Plays the Host?"', in Maria Del Sapio Garbero (ed.), *Identity, Otherness, and Empire in Shakespeare's Rome* (Farnham: Ashgate, 2009), 91–104.

Denton, John. 'Wearing a Gown in the Market Place or a Toga in the Forum: *Coriolanus* from Plutarch to Shakespeare via Renaissance Translation', in Grazia Caliumi (ed.), *Shakespeare e la sua eredità* (Parma: Zara, 1993), 97–109.

Dixon, Mimi Still. '"Not Know Me Yet?" Looking at Cleopatra in Three Renaissance Tragedies', in Naomi Conn Liebler (ed.), *The Female Tragic Hero in English Renaissance Drama* (Basingstoke: Palgrave, 2002), 71–91.

Dollimore, Jonathan. *Radical Tragedy: Religion, Ideology and Power in the Drama of Shakespeare and His Contemporaries* (3rd edn, Basingstoke: Palgrave Macmillan, 2010).

Doran, Gregory. 'Gregory Doran 2006 Production: Q & A with Gregory Doran'. Available at https://www.rsc.org.uk/antony-and-cleopatra/past-productions/gregory-doran-2006-production (accessed 30 August 2018).

Dowden, Edward. *Shakspere: A Critical Study of His Mind and Art* (London: Kegan Paul, 1909).

Dowling, Melissa Barden. *Clemency and Cruelty in the Roman World* (Ann Arbor, MI: University of Michigan Press, 2006).

Drakakis, John (ed.). *Antony and Cleopatra: Contemporary Critical Essays* (Basingstoke: Macmillan, 1994).

Dryden, John. *All for Love* (1678), in Sandra Clark (ed.), *Shakespeare Made Fit: Restoration Adaptations of Shakespeare* (London: Dent, 1997).

Dryden, John. *All for Love; or, The World Well Lost*, ed. N. J. Andrew (London: Methuen, 2014).

Eliot, T. S. *Selected Essays* (New York: Harcourt, Brace and World, 1964).

Escolme, Bridget. *Antony and Cleopatra: A Guide to the Text and Its Theatrical Life* (Basingstoke: Palgrave Macmillan, 2006).

Fawkner, H. W. *Shakespeare's Hyperontology: Antony and Cleopatra* (Rutherford: Fairleigh Dickinson University Press, 1990).

Fitz, Linda T. 'Egyptian Queens and Male Reviewers', *Shakespeare Quarterly*, 28 (1977): 297–316.

Fletcher, John, and Philip Massinger. *The False One*, ed. Robert K. Turner, in *The Dramatic Works in the Beaumont and Fletcher Canon*, ed. Fredson Bowers, VIII, 113–221 (Cambridge: Cambridge University Press, 1992).

Foucault, Michel. *The Care of the Self: The History of Sexuality*, III, trans. Robert Hurley (New York: Vintage, 1988).

Frye, Northrop. *Antony and Cleopatra*, in Harold Bloom (ed.), *William Shakespeare's Antony and Cleopatra: New Edition* (New York: Bloom's Literary Criticism, 2011), 65–80.

Fuller, David. 'Passion and Politics: *Antony and Cleopatra* in Performance', in Sara Munson Deats (ed.), *Antony and Cleopatra: New Critical Essays* (London and New York: Routledge, 2005), 111–35.

Geraghty, Christine. *Now a Major Motion Picture: Film Adaptations of Literature and Drama* (Plymouth: Rowman & Littlefield, 2008).

Gillies, John. *Shakespeare and the Geography of Difference* (Cambridge: Cambridge University Press, 1994).

Goldman, Michael. *Acting and Action in Shakespearean Tragedy* (Princeton, NJ: Princeton University Press, 1985).

Goldsworthy, Adrian. *Antony and Cleopatra* (London: Weidenfeld & Nicolson, 2010).

Gordon, Colby. 'Shakespearean Futurity: Soft Cities in *Antony and Cleopatra*', *postmedieval*, 6 (2015): 429–38.

Granville-Barker, Harley. *Prefaces to Shakespeare*, 4 vols (London: Batsford, 1972).

Green, David. *Plutarch Revisited: A Study of Shakespeare's Last Roman Tragedies* (Salzburg: Institut für Anglistik und Amerikanistik, 1979).

Greene, Thomas M. 'Pressures of Context in *Antony and Cleopatra*', in Harold Bloom (ed.), *William Shakespeare's Antony and Cleopatra: New Edition* (New York: Bloom's Literary Criticism, 2011), 119–38.

Grillo, Luca. *The Art of Caesar's* Bellum Civile: *Literature, Ideology, and Community* (Cambridge: Cambridge University Press, 2012).

Gurr, Andrew. 'London's Blackfriars Playhouse and the Chamberlain's Men', in Paul Menzer (ed.), *Inside Shakespeare: Essays on the Blackfriars Stage* (Selinsgrove: Susquehanna University Press, 2006), 17–34.

Gurr, Andrew. *The Shakespeare Company, 1594–1642* (Cambridge: Cambridge University Press, 2004).

Hadfield, Andrew. *Shakespeare and Republicanism* (Cambridge: Cambridge University Press, 2005).

Haggard, Henry Rider. *Cleopatra* (Auckland: Floating Press, 2012).

Hampton, Timothy. *Writing from History: The Rhetoric of Exemplarity in Renaissance Literature* (Ithaca, NY: Cornell University Press, 1990).

Harris, Jonathan Gil. '"Narcissus in thy Face": Roman Desire and the Difference It Fakes in *Antony and Cleopatra*', *Shakespeare Quarterly*, 45 (1994): 408–25.

Hatchuel, Sarah. 'Cleopatra in Cinematic Conflations: Subversion or Containment', in Sarah Hatchuel and Nathalie Vienne-Guerrin (eds.), *Shakespeare on Screen: The Roman Plays* (Mont-Saint-Aignan: Publications des Universités de Rouen et du Havre, 2009), 239–70.

Hatchuel, Sarah. *Shakespeare and the Cleopatra/Caesar Intertext: Sequel, Conflation, Remake* (Madison, WI: Fairleigh Dickinson University Press, 2011).

Hiscock, Andrew. *The Uses of This World: Thinking Space in Shakespeare, Marlowe, Cary, and Jonson* (Cardiff: University of Wales Press, 2004).

Hiscock, Andrew, and Lisa Hopkins (eds.). *Teaching Shakespeare and Early Modern Dramatists* (Basingstoke: Palgrave Macmillan, 2007).

Holbrook, Peter. *Shakespeare's Individualism* (Cambridge: Cambridge University Press, 2010).

Holderness, Graham, Bryan Loughrey and Andrew Murphy (eds.). *Shakespeare: The Roman Plays* (London: Longman, 1996).

Honigmann, Ernst. *Shakespeare: Seven Tragedies Revisited* (Basingstoke: Palgrave, 2002).

Hopkins, Lisa. 'Cleopatra and the Myth of Scota', in Sara Munson Deats (ed.), *Antony and Cleopatra: New Critical Essays* (London: Routledge, 2005), 231–42.

Hutcheon, Linda, and Siobhan O'Flynn. *A Theory of Adaptation* (2nd edn, London and New York: Routledge, 2013).

Innes, Paul. *Shakespeare's Roman Plays* (London: Palgrave Macmillan, 2015).

Isaac, Benjamin. *The Invention of Racism in Classical Antiquity* (Princeton, NJ: Princeton University Press, 2004).

James, Heather. *Shakespeare's Troy: Drama, Politics, and the Translation of Empire* (Cambridge: Cambridge University Press, 1997).

John of Salisbury, *Policraticus* 1–4, ed. K. S. B. Keats-Rohan (Turnhout: Corpus Christianorum, 1993).

Junker, William. 'The Image of Both Theaters: Empire and Revelation in Shakespeare's *Antony and Cleopatra*', *Shakespeare Quarterly*, 66 (2015): 167–87.

Kahn, Coppélia. *Roman Shakespeare: Warriors, Wounds and Women* (London and New York: Routledge, 1997).

Kennedy, Dennis. *Looking at Shakespeare: A Visual History of Twentieth-Century Performance* (2nd edn, Cambridge: Cambridge University Press, 2001).

Kiernan, Pauline. *Shakespeare's Theory of Drama* (Cambridge: Cambridge University Press, 1998).

Knight, G. Wilson. *The Imperial Theme: Further Interpretations of Shakespeare's Tragedies Including the Roman Plays* (London: Methuen, 1965).

Knight, G. Wilson. *The Wheel of Fire: Interpretations of Shakespearian Tragedy* (London: Methuen, 1965).

Kusunoki, Akiko. *Gender and Representations of the Female Subject in Early Modern England: Creating Their Own Meanings* (Basingstoke: Palgrave Macmillan, 2015).

La Primaudaye, Pierre de. *The French Academie* (London, 1586).

Lamb, Margaret. *Antony and Cleopatra on the English Stage* (London: Associated University Press, 1980).

Langley, Eric. *Narcissism and Suicide in Shakespeare and His Contemporaries* (Oxford: Oxford University Press, 2009).

Lawrence, Ben. '*Antony and Cleopatra*: First Look at the NT Production Starring Ralph Fiennes and Sophie Okonedo', *Telegraph*, 18 June 2018. Available at https://www.telegraph.co.uk/theatre/what-to-see/antony-cleopatra-first-look-nt-production-starring-ralph-fiennes/ (accessed 19 July 2018).

Levine, Laura. *Men in Women's Clothing: Anti-Theatricality and Effeminization, 1579–1642* (Cambridge: Cambridge University Press, 1994).

Liebler, Naomi Conn (ed.). *The Female Tragic Hero in English Renaissance Drama* (Basingstoke: Palgrave Macmillan, 2002).

Lindley, Arthur. 'Antony, Cleopatra, the Market, and the End(s) of History', in Lloyd Davis (ed.), *Shakespeare Matters: History, Teaching, Performance* (Newark, DE: University of Delaware Press, 2003), 62–73.

Little, Arthur L., Jr. *Shakespeare Jungle Fever: National-Imperial Revisions of Race, Rape, and Sacrifice* (Stanford, CA: Stanford University Press, 2000).

Logan, Robert A. *Shakespeare's Marlowe: The Influence of Christopher Marlowe on Shakespeare's Artistry* (Aldershot: Ashgate, 2007).

Loomba, Ania. *Gender, Race, Renaissance Drama* (Oxford: Oxford University Press, 1989).
Loomba, Ania. *Shakespeare, Race, and Colonialism* (Oxford: Oxford University Press, 2002).
Lovano, Michael. *All Things Julius Caesar: An Encyclopedia of Caesar's World and Legacy* (Santa Barbara, CA: ABC-CLIO, 2015).
Lyne, Raphael. *Memory and Intertextuality in Renaissance Literature* (Cambridge: Cambridge University Press, 2016).
MacCallum, Mungo William. *Shakespeare's Roman Plays and Their Background* (London: Macmillan, 1910).
Marsh, Derick R. C. *Passion Lends Them Power: A Study of Shakespeare's Love Tragedies* (Manchester: Manchester University Press, 1976).
Martínez, Marcos. *The Eighth Booke of the Myrror of Knighthood Being the Third of the Third Part. Englished out of the Spanish Tongue*, trans. L. A. (London, 1599).
Matthiessen, F. O. *Translation: An Elizabethan Art* (Cambridge, MA: Harvard University Press, 1931).
McAlindon, Tom. *Shakespeare and Decorum* (London: Macmillan, 1973).
McDonald, Joyce Green. *Women and Race in Early Modern Texts* (Cambridge: Cambridge University Press, 2002).
Melanchthon, Philip. *Philosophiae moralis epitome*, in *Opera quae supersunt omnia*, XVI, ed. H. E. Bindseil (New York: Johnson Reprint, 1963).
Metcalfe, Anna. 'Small Talk: Anne Rice', *Financial Times*, 15 November 2010. Available at https://www.ft.com/content/d15d15e4-ede9-11df-8616-00144feab49a (accessed 17 September 2018).
Metropolitan Opera. '*Aida*'. Metopera. Available at https://www.metopera.org/season/2018-19-season/aida/ (accessed 19 July 2018).
Miles, Geoffrey. *Shakespeare and the Constant Romans* (Oxford: Clarendon Press, 1996).
Miller, Anthony. *Roman Triumphs and Early Modern English Culture* (Basingstoke: Palgrave, 2001).
Minier, Márta. 'Interdisciplinary Considerations about a Subgenre of the Contemporary Biographical Drama: Celebrity and Fandom in Recent Adaptations of Famous Lives for the Stage', *Critical*

Stages, 112 (2015). Available at http://www.critical-stages .org/12/interdisciplinary-considerations-about-a-subgenre-of-the-contemporary-biographical-drama-celebrity-and-fandom-in-recent-adaptations-of-famous-lives-for-the-stage (accessed 10 June 2018).

Minier, Márta, and Maddalena Pennacchia. 'Interdisciplinary Perspectives on the Biopic: An Introduction', in Márta Minier and Maddalena Pennacchia (eds.), *Adaptation, Intermediality and the British Celebrity Biopic* (Farnham: Ashgate, 2014), 1–32.

Miola, Robert S. *Shakespeare's Rome* (Cambridge: Cambridge University Press, 1983).

Neill, Michael. 'Introduction', in William Shakespeare, *The Tragedy of Anthony and Cleopatra* (Oxford: Oxford University Press, 1994), 1–130.

Nicoll, Allardyce. *A History of Restoration Drama* (Cambridge: Cambridge University Press, 1928).

North, Thomas. *The Lives of the Noble Grecians and Romanes Compared Together by That Grave Learned Philosopher and Historiographer Plutarke of Chaeronea* [...] (London: Thomas Vautroullier, 1579).

Oakley, Stephen. 'Single Combat in the Roman Republic', *Classical Quarterly*, 35 (1985): 392–410.

Park, Jennifer. 'Discandying Cleopatra: Preserving Cleopatra's Infinite Variety in Shakespeare's *Antony and Cleopatra*', *Studies in Philology*, 113 (2016): 595–633.

Parker, Barbara L. *Plato's Republic and Shakespeare's Rome: A Political Study of the Roman Works* (Newark, DE: University of Delaware Press, 2004).

Parker, Melissa. 'Anne Rice Interview: *Vampire Chronicles* Author Talks Latest Installment, *Blood Communion*, and Catholic Clergy Scandal', *Smashing Interviews*, 1 October 2018. Available at http://smashinginterviews.com/interviews/authors/anne-rice-interview-vampire-chronicles-author-talks-latest-installment-blood-communion-and-catholic-clergy-scandal (accessed 31 January 2019).

Parolin, Peter A. 'Anachronistic Italy: Cultural Alliances and National Identity in *Cymbeline*', *Shakespeare Studies*, 30 (2002): 188–218.

Parolin, Peter A. '"Cloyless Sauce": The Pleasurable Politics of Food in *Antony and Cleopatra*', in Sara Munson Deats (ed.), *Antony and Cleopatra: New Critical Essays* (London and New York: Routledge, 2005), 213–29.

Paster, Gail Kern. *Humoring the Body: Emotions and the Shakespearean Stage* (Chicago, IL: University of Chicago Press, 2004).
Pearson, Roberta E., and William Uricchio. 'The Bard in Brooklyn: Vitagraph's Shakespearean Productions', in Luke McKernan and Olwen Terris (eds.), *Walking Shadows: Shakespeare in the National Film and Television Archive* (London: British Film Institute, 1994), 201–6.
Pelling, Christopher. 'Aspects of Plutarch's Characterisation', *Illinois Classical Studies*, 13 (1988): 257–74.
Pelling, Christopher. 'The Triumviral Period', in Alan K. Bowman, Edward Champlin and Andrew Lintott (eds.), *The Cambridge Ancient History*, X: *The Augustan Empire, 43 BC–AD 69* (Cambridge: Cambridge University Press, 1996), 1–69.
Pennacchia, Maddalena. 'Intermedial Products for Digital Natives: British Theatre-Cinema on Italian Screens', *Intermédialités*, 30–1 (2017). Available at https://www.erudit.org/en/journals/im/2017-n30-31-im03868/1049952ar (accessed 7 June 2019).
Perry, Curtis. 'Seneca and English Political Culture', in R. Malcolm Smuts (ed.), *The Oxford Handbook of the Age of Shakespeare* (Oxford: Oxford University Press, 2016), 306–21.
Pitcher, Luke. 'The Erotics of Appian', in Kathryn Welch (ed.), *Appian's Roman History: Empire and Civil War* (Swansea: Classical Press of Wales, 2015), 205–19.
Platt, Michael. *Rome and Romans according to Shakespeare* (Salzburg: Institut für Englische Sprache und Literatur, 1976).
Plutarch. *Life of Antony*, ed. Christopher Pelling (Cambridge: Cambridge University Press, 1988).
Plutarch. *Lives of the Noble Grecians and Romans*, ed. Arthur Clough (Oxford: Benediction Classics, 2010).
Plutarch. *Plutarch's Lives*, trans. Bernadotte Perrin, 11 vols (Cambridge, MA: Harvard University Press, 1914–26).
Plutarch. *Shakespeare's Plutarch*, ed. T. J. B. Spencer (Harmondsworth: Penguin, 1964).
Pollard, Tanya. '"A Thing like Death": Sleeping Potions and Poisons in *Romeo and Juliet* and *Antony and Cleopatra*', *Renaissance Drama*, 32 (2003): 95–121.
Read, David. 'Disappearing Act: The Role of Enobarbus in *Antony and Cleopatra*', *Studies in Philology*, 110 (2013): 562–83.
Rice, Anne. *The Mummy* (New York: Ballantine, 1989).

Rice, Anne, and Christopher Rice. *Ramses the Damned: The Passion of Cleopatra* (New York: Anchor, 2017).
Richardson, John. *The Language of Empire: Rome and the Idea of Empire from the Third Century BC to the Second Century AD* (Cambridge: Cambridge University Press, 2008).
Ricks, Christopher. *T. S. Eliot and Prejudice* (Berkeley, CA: University of California Press, 1988).
Roe, John. *Shakespeare and Machiavelli* (Cambridge: Brewer, 2002).
Rogers, Thomas. *A Philosophicall Discourse, Entituled, The Anatomie of the Minde* (London, 1576).
Roller, Matthew B. *Constructing Autocracy: Aristocrats and Emperors in Julio-Claudian Rome* (Princeton, NJ: Princeton University Press, 2001).
Royster, Francesca T. *Becoming Cleopatra: The Shifting Image of an Icon* (Basingstoke: Palgrave Macmillan, 2003).
Rutter, Carol Chillington. *Enter the Body: Women and Representation on Shakespeare's Stage* (London and New York: Routledge, 2001).
Rutter, Carol Chillington. '"Hear the Ambassadors!" Marking Shakespeare's Venice Connection', *Shakespeare Survey* 66 (2013): 265–86.
Sacerdoti, Gilberto. '*Antony and Cleopatra* and the Overflowing of the Roman Measure', in Maria Del Sapio Garbero (ed.), *Identity, Otherness, and Empire in Shakespeare's Rome* (Farnham: Ashgate, 2009), 107–18.
Said, Edward, *Orientalism* (New York: Pantheon, 1978).
Schalkwyk, David. 'Is Love an Emotion? Shakespeare's *Twelfth Night* and *Antony and Cleopatra*', *symplokē*, 18 (2010): 99–130.
Schanzer, Ernest. *The Problem Plays of Shakespeare* (London: Routledge & Kegan Paul, 1963).
Schulman, Alex. *Rethinking Shakespeare's Political Philosophy: From Lear to Leviathan* (Edinburgh: Edinburgh University Press, 2014).
Scott, Alison V. *Literature and the Idea of Luxury in Early Modern England* (Farnham: Ashgate, 2015).
Scott, Michael. *Antony and Cleopatra: Text and Performance* (Basingstoke: Macmillan, 1983).
Seneca. *De clementia*, ed. Susanna Braund (Oxford: Oxford University Press, 2009).
Seneca. *Hercules Furens*, in *Seneca's Tragedies*, trans. Frank Justus Miller, 2 vols (Cambridge, MA: Harvard University Press, 1979), I, 1–119.

Seneca. *Hercules Oetaeus*, in *Seneca's Tragedies*, trans. Frank Justus Miller, 2 vols (Cambridge, MA: Harvard University Press, 1979), II, 183–341.
Shakespeare, William. *Antony and Cleopatra*, ed. Jonathan Bate and Eric Rasmussen (London: Royal Shakespeare Company/ Macmillan, 2009).
Shakespeare, William. *Antony and Cleopatra*, ed. David Bevington (updated edn, Cambridge: Cambridge University Press, 2005).
Shakespeare, William. *Antony and Cleopatra*, ed. Emrys Jones, with an introduction by René Weis (London: Penguin, 2005).
Shakespeare, William. *Antony and Cleopatra*, ed. Ania Loomba (New York: Norton, 2011).
Shakespeare, William. *Antony and Cleopatra*, ed. John Wilders (London and New York: Routledge for Arden Shakespeare, 1995).
Shakespeare, William. *Cymbeline*, ed. Valerie Wayne (London: Bloomsbury Arden Shakespeare, 2017).
Shakespeare, William. *Julius Caesar*, ed. David Daniell (Walton-on-Thames: Nelson for Arden Shakespeare, 1998).
Shakespeare, William. *King Henry IV, Part 1*, ed. David Scott Kastan (London: Thomson for Arden Shakespeare, 2002).
Shakespeare, William. *Macbeth*, ed. Sandra Clark and Pamela Mason (London: Bloomsbury Arden Shakespeare, 2015).
Shakespeare, William. *A Midsummer Night's Dream*, ed. Sukanta Chaudhuri (London: Bloomsbury Arden Shakespeare, 2017).
Shakespeare, William. *Timon of Athens*, ed. Anthony B. Dawson and Gretchen E. Minton (London: Bloomsbury Arden Shakespeare, 2008).
Shapiro, Michael. 'Boying Her Greatness: Shakespeare's Use of Coterie Drama in *Antony and Cleopatra*', *Modern Language Review*, 77 (1982): 1–15.
Shaughnessy, Robert. 'On Location', in Barbara Hodgdon and W. B. Worthen (eds.), *A Companion to Shakespeare and Performance* (Malden, MA: Blackwell, 2005), 79–100.
Sidney, Mary. *Antonius*, in *The Collected Works of Mary Sidney Herbert, Countess of Pembroke*, ed. Margaret P. Hannay, Noel J. Kinnamon and Michael G. Brennan (Oxford: Clarendon Press, 1998), I, 139–207.
Simmons, J. L. *Shakespeare's Pagan World: The Roman Tragedies* (Charlottesville, VA: University Press of Virginia, 1973).
Simonds, Peggy Munoz. '"To the Very Heart of Loss": Renaissance Iconography in Shakespeare's *Antony and Cleopatra*', *Shakespeare Studies*, 22 (1994): 220–76.

Singh, Jyotsna G. '"Come, Eros, Eros!" Rereading Emotion and Affect in Shakespeare's *Antony and Cleopatra*', in Ronda Arab, Michelle M. Dowd and Adam Zucker (eds.), *Historical Affects and the Early Modern Theater* (London and New York: Routledge, 2015), 96–108.

Singh, Jyotsna G. 'The Politics of Empathy in *Antony and Cleopatra*: A View from Below', in Richard Dutton and Jean E. Howard (eds.), *A Companion to Shakespeare's Works: The Tragedies* (Malden, MA: Blackwell, 2003), 410–29.

Singh, Jyotsna G. 'Renaissance Anti-theatricality, Anti-feminism, and Shakespeare's *Antony and Cleopatra*', in John Drakakis (ed.), *Antony and Cleopatra: Contemporary Critical Essays* (Basingstoke: Macmillan, 1994), 308–28.

Smith, Bruce. *The Acoustic World of Early Modern England* (Chicago, IL: University of Chicago Press, 1999).

Starks, Lisa S. 'Immortal Longings: The Erotics of Death in Shakespeare's *Antony and Cleopatra*', in Sara Munson Deats (ed.), *Antony and Cleopatra: New Critical Essays* (London and New York: Routledge, 2005), 243–58.

Starks-Estes, Lisa S. *Violence, Trauma and* Virtus *in Shakespeare's Roman Poems and Plays: Transforming Ovid* (Basingstoke: Palgrave Macmillan, 2014).

Steel, C. E. W. *Cicero, Rhetoric, and Empire* (Oxford: Oxford University Press, 2001).

Sternfeld, F. W. *Music in Shakespearean Tragedy* (London: Routledge & Kegan Paul, 1963).

Stewart, Alan. *Shakespeare's Letters* (Oxford: Oxford University Press, 2008).

Streete, Adrian. 'The Politics of Ethical Presentism: Appropriation, Spirituality and the Case of *Antony and Cleopatra*', *Textual Practice*, 22 (2008): 405–31.

Strier, Richard. *The Unrepentant Renaissance: From Petrarch to Shakespeare to Milton* (Chicago, IL: University of Chicago Press, 2011).

Styan, J. L. *The English Stage: A History of Drama and Performance* (Cambridge: Cambridge University Press, 1996).

Styan, J. L. *The Shakespeare Revolution: Criticism and Performance in the Twentieth Century* (Cambridge: Cambridge University Press, 1977).

Suetonius. *The Deified Augustus*, in *The Lives of the Caesars*, trans. J. C. Rolfe (Cambridge, MA: Harvard University Press, 1989).
Sumi, Geoffrey S. *Ceremony and Power: Performing Politics in Rome between Republic and Empire* (Ann Arbor, MI: University of Michigan Press, 2005).
Taylor, Gary. 'Divine [ ]sences', *Shakespeare Survey* 54 (2001): 13–30.
Tennenhouse, Leonard. *Power on Display: The Politics of Shakespeare's Genres* (New York: Methuen, 1986).
Thomas, Vivian. *Shakespeare's Roman Worlds* (London and New York: Routledge, 1989).
Tillyard, E. M. W. *The Elizabethan World Picture* (New York: Random House, 1942).
Traversi, Derek. *Shakespeare: The Roman Plays* (London: Hollis & Carter, 1963).
Vanhoutte, Jacqueline. 'Antony's "Secret House of Death": Suicide and Sovereignty in *Antony and Cleopatra*', *Philological Quarterly*, 79 (2000): 153–75.
Vickers, Brian (ed.). *William Shakespeare: The Critical Heritage*, 6 vols (London: Routledge & Kegan Paul, 1974–81).
Whittington, Leah. *Renaissance Suppliants: Poetry, Antiquity, Reconciliation* (Oxford: Oxford University Press, 2016).
Whittington, Leah. 'Shakespeare's Virgil: Empathy and *The Tempest*', in John Cox and Patrick Gray, *Shakespeare and Renaissance Ethics* (Cambridge: Cambridge University Press, 2014), 98–120.
Wilders, John. 'Introduction', in William Shakespeare, *Antony and Cleopatra* (London and New York: Routledge for Arden Shakespeare, 1995), 1–84.
Williamson, Marilyn L. *Infinite Variety: Antony and Cleopatra in Renaissance and Earlier Tradition* (Mystic, CT: Lawrence Verry, 1974).
Wills, Gary. 'Shakespeare and Verdi in the Theater', *New York Review of Books*, 24 November 2011. Available at https://www.nybooks.com/articles/2011/11/24/shakespeare-and-verdi-theater/ (accessed 19 July 2018).
Wofford, Susanne. 'Antony's Egyptian Bacchanals: Heroic and Divine Impersonation in Shakespeare's Plutarch and *Antony and Cleopatra*', *Poetica: An International Journal of Linguistic-Literary Studies*, 48 (1997): 33–67.

Worthen, W. B. 'The Weight of Antony: Staging "Character" in *Antony and Cleopatra*', *Studies in English Literature, 1500–1900*, 26 (1986): 295–308.

Wyke, Maria. *The Roman Mistress: Ancient and Modern Representations* (Oxford: Oxford University Press, 2002).

INDEX

abjection 128–9
absolutism 103, 127, 128–9
action
  dramatic 39
  military 58–9, 66, 144–5
  versus reaction 135, 138–40
  unity of 61–2
Actium, Battle of xii, xiv, 79, 144–5
  staging of xvii, 66, 74, 85
actor-managers 66
actors/actresses
  black xvi, xvii, 72, 86
  boys 32, 74
  male, as Cleopatra xvi, 32, 74, 75
  women 60–1
  see also Antony (played by); Cleopatra (played by)
Actors Touring Company xvi, 72
acts and scenes, division into 60, 68
Adelman, Janet 222
  The Common Liar 39–40, 50, 53, 249 n.9
  Suffocating Mothers 50–1
Aebischer, Pascale 98
Aeneid (Virgil) 169, 216
age/ageing 161–2
agency 93–4, 96, 97, 134, 153–4, 182–3, 184
Aida (opera, Verdi) 190–5

alcohol 141
Alexander Helos (son of Anthony and Cleopatra) xi
alienation 38
Allen, Ben 86
All for Love (play, Dryden) xiii, xiv, 24, 25, 61–3, 66, 170–1, 262 n.30
all-male casts xvi, 75
allusions 8–9, 102, 109, 136–7, 173
ambassadors 107
ambiguity 46, 120–1, 158–60, 172, 260 n.10, 262 n.31
Amyot, Jacques, *Les Vies illustres* 156–7, 158, 162–3, 175
anachronism 26, 109, 217, 263 n.39
animal imagery 95–6, 171–2
Antonius (play, Sidney) xii, 6, 96, 98, 146, 151
Antony (dramatic character)
  agency of 134–5
  and Cleopatra
    first meeting with 91–2
    quarrels with 158–62, 188–9
    similarity to 31, 35
  comparison anxiety 4, 7, 8–9, 136–8, 139
  death of 92–4, 97, 151

displacement of 53
Egyptianization of 37, 42, 118–19
emasculation 8, 49, 79
and Enobarbus 148
in film 184
focus on 97
and fortune 145–6
and gender 8, 49, 79, 95, 99–100
and Hercules 146, 147, 166–7
and heroism 139, 146–8
heroism, as anti-hero 66
and heroism, lack of 5–6, 147, 152–4
and Julius Caesar 4–5, 8–9, 136–8, 139
in *Julius Caesar* 6–7
masculinity of 8, 49, 79, 95
midlife crisis of 94–5
military strategy 163–4
as non-reactor 144–6
and Octavia 142–4
and Octavius 2, 32, 52, 137–8, 142–4, 162–5
in other texts 6, 122, 194–5
passion of 104–5
and Rome–Egypt opposition 48, 53
self-performance 124–5, 138, 148–50, 213
as tragic hero 44, 207–8, 209, 218–19
virtù of (Machiavelli) 105–6
virtus (manly courage) of 45–6
Antony (historical character) xi, xii

Antony (played by)
 Betterton, Thomas 63
 Bilginer, Haluk 76
 Burbage, Richard 1–2
 Burton, Richard xv
 Byrne, Antony xvii, 85
 Fiennes, Ralph xvii, 86
 Gielgud, John xv, 69
 Heston, Charlton xvi, 79
 Hopkins, Anthony 86
 Johnson, Richard 71, 80
 Jones, Nicholas 75
 Michell, Keith xv, 80
 Novelli, Amleto 77
 Olivier, Laurence xv, 70
 Redgrave, Michael xv, 70
 Stewart, Patrick xvi–xvii, 73
 Wood, Clive xvii, 76
Antony and Cleopatra (film, Heston, 1972) xv, 78–9
Antony and Cleopatra (film, Kent, 1908) xiv, 77
apocalypse 109–10
Aristotelian unities 24–5, 61–2
Ashcroft, Peggy xv, 70
asps 151, 171–2, 174–5
Astington, John H. 91
Atkins, Robert xiv, 69
audience 38, 39, 62–3, 64–5, 75, 82–3, 114
authenticity
 historical 25–6, 30–2, 42–3
 of self 117–18, 128, 139–40, 196–7
autocracy 103, 127, 128–9
Aydoğan, Kemal 76

Bacchus (Dionysus) 165–6
Ball, Robert 78

Barber, Frances 75
Barbican theatre xvii, 72, 84–6
Barbour, Richmond 100–1
'Bardolatry' 26
Barnes, Barnabe, *The Devil's Charter* 59
Barrie, Amanda 184
Barroll, J. Leeds 44
Barry, Mrs 63
Bartsch, Shadi 117–18
BBC (British Broadcasting Corporation) xvi, 80–1
beauty 180, 182–4
Belsey, Catherine 91–2
Benthal, Michael xv, 70
Best, Eve xvii, 76
Betterton, Thomas 63
Bevington, David 94–5, 204
Bible 109
Bilginer, Haluk 76
biographical drama 57–9
Black, Pauline xvi, 72
Blackfriars theatre (London) xiii, 61
Block, Giles xvi, 75
Blount, Edward 60
bodies 46–7, 51, 94, 95, 123–4, 196–7, 221
Book of Cleopatra 108–9
Book of Revelation 109
box office success 66, 69, 77
boy actors 32, 74
Bradley, A. C., *Shakespearean Tragedy* 29–30, 32
Bradley, David 79
Brandon, Samuel, *The Virtuous Octavia* xiii
Bridges-Adams, William xiv, 69
British Broadcasting Corporation *see* BBC

Brook, Peter xvi, 72–3
Bruno, Giordano, *De l'infinito universo* 109
Brutus (Marcus Brutus) xi, 2, 116–17, 118
Bunn, Alfred 66
Burbage, Richard 1–2
Burge, Stuart 79
Burrow, Colin, *Shakespeare and Classical Antiquity* 225–6
Burton, Richard xv
Butler, Judith 75
Byam Shaw, Glen xv, 70
Byrne, Antony xvii, 85

Cadman, Daniel 96
Caesar, Augustus *see* Octavius Caesar
Caesar, Julius *see* Julius Caesar
Caesarion (Ptolemy Caesar) xi, 14
Caesar's Revenge (play, anonymous) 6
Cantor, Paul A. 100
  Shakespeare's Roman Trilogy 210
  Shakespeare's Rome: Republic and Empire 39, 114, 208–10
Capell, Edward 63
Caporicci, Camilla 105
Carolis, Adolfo de 84
Carry on Cleo (film, Thomas, 1964) 184
Cassius (Caius Cassius) xi, 2, 116–17, 118
casting 60
  of black actors xvi, xvii, 72, 86
  cross-gender xvi, 74, 75

Castro, Diego López de, *Marco Antonio y Cleopatra* xii
'Catalogue of the Several Comedies, Histories and Tragedies' 1
celebrity 57–9, 86
Cesari, Cesare de, *Cleopatra* xii
challenges (to combat) 141–2, 162–5
character 135, 136–8
characterization 28, 32–3, 59
Charmian (Charmion) 9–10, 14, 153, 170–1, 184
Charnes, Linda, *Notorious Identity* 52–3
Charney, Maurice, *Shakespeare's Roman Plays* 37
Chernaik, Warren, *The Myth of Rome in Shakespeare and his Contemporaries* 97, 211–12
Christianity 38–9, 93, 109–10, 134
Christian IV of Denmark 47
Cicero, Marcus Tullius 122–3
  and decorum 117–18, 120, 123–4
  De officiis 117–18, 122, 123–4, 139–40, 249 n.8
  De re publica 118
  Verrine Orations 122
cinema-theatre productions 83–4, 241 n.74
Cines Film Company 77–8
Cinthio, Giovan Battista Giraldi, *Cleopatra* xii
class 102–3, 117–18, 120, 124, 127
clemency 14–15, 126–7

Cleopatra (dramatic character)
  as actor 150–4
  and ageing 161–2
  agency of 134–5, 153–4, 182–3, 184
  and Antony 35
    first meeting 91–2
    heroism, lack of 5–6, 147, 152–4
    quarrels with 158–62, 188–9
    self-performance of 149–50
    similarity to 31
  appearance of 72, 161–2, 182–4, 195–7
  beauty of 182–4
  birthday scene (3.13) 158–62
  body of 196–7
  characterization 32–3
  and comedy 97
  and costume 73, 75, 78, 86
  courage of 161
  criticism and scholarship on 26–9
  death of 26, 93–4
    in *Cleopatra* (Haggard) 183–4
    eroticism 97
    and grandeur 28, 34, 151–2
    in *Marcantonio e Cleopatra* (film) 78
    as marriage 106
    as triumph 44, 48–9, 50
  death scene (5.2) 63, 169–72, 174–5
  Egypt, identification with 53, 206–7

Elizabeth I, associated with
102, 103
and Enobarbus 8, 143–4
femininity of 26, 28–9,
32–3, 34, 51, 58
and fortune 150–1
and Julius Caesar 7–8, 9–11
'low' character of 26–7
luxury, embodiment of
97–8
national identity 216
nature, association with 105
and Octavius 14–15, 16,
93–4, 102
performances
by black actors, first xvi,
xvii, 72, 86
by male actors xvi, 32,
74, 75
by women, first 60–1
see also Cleopatra
(played by)
performativity of 58
political power of 58, 93–4
in popular culture 180, 181,
182–95
and race 72, 98, 251 n.23
representations of 185–90,
195–7
reputation 185–90
and Roman values 206–7
as ruler 48–9
self-performance 125–6,
127–30, 150
and sex/sexuality 7–8, 67,
177–9, 182–4, 185–7,
197, 198
silence of 96–7
suffering 178–9, 185–90
theatricality of 75

as tragic hero/protagonist
44, 96–7, 211
whore/prostitute,
represented as 9, 186,
187, 188–9
Cleopatra (film, Mankiewicz,
1963) xv, 78–9, 183, 184
Cleopatra (historical character)
xi, xii, 108–9, 197, 224
Cleopatra (played by)
Ashcroft, Peggy xv, 70
Barber, Frances 75
Barrie, Amanda 184
Barry, Mrs. 63
Benison, Ishia 72
Best, Eve xvii, 76
Black, Pauline xvi, 72
Croll, Dona 72
Dench, Judi 86
Glyn, Isabella xiv, 66
Green, Dorothy xv, 69
Jackson, Glenda xvi, 72–3
Kalukango, Joaquina xvii, 72
Langtry, Lily xiv, 66–7
Lapotaire, Jane 81
Leigh, Vivien xv, 70
Mirren, Helen xvi, 73
Morris, Mary xv, 80
Neil, Hildegarde xvi, 79
Okonedo, Sophie xvii, 86
Rylance, Mark xvi, 75
Shay, Michele xvi, 72
Simon, Josette xvii, 72, 86
Suzman, Janet xv, 71, 72, 80
Taylor, Elizabeth xv
Tekindor, Zerry 76
Terribili-Gonzales, Gianna
77, 78
Tyson, Cathy 72
Walter, Harriet xvi, 73

Cleopatra Selene (daughter of Anthony and Cleopatra) xi
Cléopâtre (film, Méliès, 1899) 77
Cléopâtre captive (play, Jodelle) xii, 98, 170
Coleridge, Samuel Taylor 27
colonialism *see* empire/imperialism; globalization
colour 73–4
combat, single 141–2, 162–3, 164–5
comedy 75, 76, 97, 106, 151–2
commerce 100–1
communication 106–7
comparison anxiety 3, 4, 7, 8–9, 136–8
Condell, Henry 56
conflict 32
constancy 43, 120, 148
consumption 97–8, 108
contamination, fears of 121–2, 123
continuous staging 68–9, 69–70
contrasts, Rome–Egypt 32, 35, 36, 48, 53, 58
  and commerce 101
  communication 106–7
  critique of 37, 42, 43, 121–2, 208, 212–14, 216–17
  and film techniques 79
  gender 206–7, 219–20
  and identity 53
  philosophy 99
  set design 71, 73–4, 84–5, 227
Coriolanus xv, xvii, 39, 208
cosmology 109
Cossa, Pietro, *Cleopatra* (poem) 78

costume xv, 69, 71, 82
  of Cleopatra 73, 75, 78, 86
courage 161–2
Crane, Mary Thomas 99
criticism and scholarship 21–53
  18th century 25–7
  19th century 27–9
  20th century 29–53
  21st century 89–111
  and Cleopatra (dramatic character) 26–9
  and commerce 100–1
  and construction, dramatic 30
  Cultural Materialism 45
  and death 92–4
  edited collections 221–4
  and empire/imperialism 98–102
  and ethics 104–6
  feminist 47–9, 211–14, 223
  fictocritical 179
  and food 108–9
  formalist 33–4
  and gender 34, 47–9, 99–100, 212–13, 219–20
  genre 106
  hermeneutics 105
  and identity 47–52
  journal articles 224–5
  and messengers/messages 106–7
  monographs 205–21
  'New' criticism 33–4, 36
  New Historicism 45, 46–7
  oppositional 222–3
  and passion 94–6
  patriarchal 26–7
  and politics 102–4
  and popular culture 198–9

predecessor texts 96–8
and race 47–9, 98–102
and religion 109–10
Restoration period 22–5
scholarly editions 64, 203–5
source material 91–2, 225–6
topical readings 47, 65, 100, 102–4
on tragedy 44, 46–7, 218–19
Croll, Dona 72
cross-dressing 49, 75, 79
Cultural Materialism 45
cuts/editing 63, 64, 66
Cymbeline 172–3, 175, 176

Danby, John 222
dancing 85, 86
Daniel, Samuel, *Cleopatra* xiii, 59, 96, 97, 98, 128–9, 254 n.39
D'Avenant, William 23, 60
Davies, H. Neville, 'Jacobean *Antony and Cleopatra*' 47, 222
Davis, Lloyd 107
death 92–4
 of Antony 92–4, 97, 151
 of Cleopatra 26, 93–4, 169–72, 174–5
 in *Cleopatra* (Haggard) 183–4
 eroticism 97
 and grandeur 28, 34, 151–2
 in *Marcantonio e Cleopatra* (film) 78
 as marriage 106
 staging of 63
 as triumph 44, 48–9, 50
 of Enobarbus 91–2, 93

and eroticism 35, 97
and gender 92–3
suicide 26, 28, 44, 50, 93–4, 106
decorum 116, 117–18, 119–20, 123–4, 139–40, 249 n.8
Dench, Judi 86
desire 124–5, 197, 215
Devereux, Robert (2nd Earl of Essex) xiii
Dews, Peter, *The Spread of the Eagle* xv, 79–80
Dionysus (Bacchus) 165–6
diplomacy 107
display 108
Dixon, Mimi Still 96–7, 223–4
Dodd, William, *The Beauties of Shakespeare* 25
Dolabella 153
Dollimore, Jonathan, *Radical Tragedy* 45–6, 218–19
domestication 61–3
Doran, Gregory xvi–xvii, 73–4
Dowden, Edward, *Shakspere: A Critical Study of his Mind and Art* 28–9, 187
Drakakis, John, Antony and Cleopatra: *Contemporary Critical Essays* 222–3
drama, biographical 57–9
drama, Jacobean 46
dramatic action 39
dramatic structure 30
 problem plays 35
 scene division 60, 68
 unity of 36
Dromgoole, Dominic xvi, 75
drugs 106
drunkenness 141

Drury Lane Theatre xiii, xiv, 63, 64–5
Dryden, John, *All for Love* xiii, xiv, 24, 25, 61–3, 66, 170–1, 262 n.30
Duff, William 26–7
Duke's Men (theatre company) xiii, 60, 63

editing/cuts 63, 64, 66
egalitarianism 127
Egypt xi
  Cleopatra as personification of 53, 206–7
  and costume 73, 75, 78, 86
  exoticism of 37, 67, 121–2
  and film 67, 76–9, 84, 183–4
  and luxury 97–8
  in popular culture 190–6
  as 'private' space 43, 46, 48–9, 208–9
  and set design 71, 84–5, 227
  values of 35, 37, 97–8
Egypt and Rome
  binary opposition, critique of 37, 42, 43, 58, 121–2, 208, 212–14, 216–17
  contrasts 32, 35, 36, 48, 53
    commerce 101
    communication 106–7
    film techniques 79
    gender 206–7, 219–20
    philosophy 99
    set design 71, 73–4, 84–5, 227
Egyptology 179–80, 191, 196
Eld, George xiii
Eliot, T. S. 130, 171, 262 n.30
Elizabethan Stage Society 68

Elizabeth I (Queen of England) xii, xiii, 96, 102, 103
emasculation 8, 49, 79
emotion 15, 31, 36, 94–6, 109–10
  and Antony 104–5
  and Cleopatra 27, 182–4
empire/imperialism 42, 65, 67, 98–102, 121–2, 187, 210
  and absolutism 128–9
  and corruption 122, 123
  and public/private space 48–9
  and sex/sexuality 99
  and women 99
  see also globalization
English Stage Company 72
Enobarbus 7, 14, 83, 141–2
  and Antony 148
  barge speech (2.2) 25, 64, 91, 156–7, 168, 173–4
  and Cleopatra 8, 143–4
  death of 91–2, 93
epistemology 99
eroticism 35, 93, 97, 173
Essex, 2nd Earl of *see* Devereux, Robert
ethics 104–6, 253 n.35 *see also* values
exemplarity 114, 115, 116
exoticism 37, 67, 121–2
experimentalism 115–16
eyes 119, 250 n.12

False One, The (play, Fletcher and Massinger) xiii, 6, 8, 138, 150, 152
feeling 15, 31, 36, 94–6, 109–10
  and Antony 104–5

and Cleopatra 27, 182–4
femininity 26, 28–9, 32–3, 34, 51, 58, 92–3
feminism 179, 183, 211–14, 223
fictocritical writing 179
Fiennes, Ralph xvii, 86
film adaptations 76–9, 196
   1899 *Cléopâtre* (Méliès) 77
   1908 *Antony and Cleopatra* (Kent) xiv, 77
   1913 *Marcantonio e Cleopatra* (Guazzoni) xiv, 77–8
   1963 *Cleopatra* (Mankiewicz) xv, 78–9, 183, 184
   1964 *Carry on Cleo* (Thomas) 184
   1970 *Kureopatora* (Osama Tezuka) 183, 184
   1972 *Antony and Cleopatra* (Heston) xv, 78–9
First Folio xiii, 1, 56, 60
Fletcher, John, *The False One* xiii, 6, 8, 138, 150, 152
flutes 168–9
food 108–9
form 23, 56–7, 62, 115, 115–16
formalist criticism 33–4
fortune 15, 105–6, 134–5, 145–6, 148, 150–1
framing devices 56–7, 62
Fulvia xi, 143–4

Garnier, Robert, *Antoine* xii, 97, 98
Garrick, David xiii, 25, 26, 63–4
gazing 118–19

gender 85, 95, 171–2, 223–4
   and casting xvi, 74, 75
   criticism and scholarship on 34, 47–9, 99–100, 212–13, 219–20
   and Egypt–Rome relationship 206–7, 219–20
   emasculation 8, 49, 79
   femininity 26, 28–9, 32–3, 34, 51, 58, 92–3
   and power 34, 46–7
   and Rome 51–2, 58
   see also masculinity
genre
   comedy 75, 76, 97, 106, 151–2
   horror 28, 179
   problem plays 34–5
   tragedy 29–30, 34, 37–8, 93, 106, 128–9, 129–30
   criticism and scholarship on 44, 46–7, 218–19
Gentili, Alberico, *De Legationibus Libri Tres* 107
Gielgud, John xv, 69
globalization 100, 122, 210 *see also* empire/imperialism
Glyn, Isabella xiv, 66
Gnaeus Pompeius (Pompey the Younger) 9, 11
gods 105, 109, 165–7, 169
Godwin, Simon xvii, 86–7
Goldsworthy, Adrian, *Antony and Cleopatra* 225
gossip 107
grandeur 28, 34, 151–2
Granville-Barker, Harley xv, 32–3, 68–9, 74
greed 108

Green, David 161
Green, Dorothy xv, 69
Greville, Fulke, *Antony and Cleopatra* xiii
Grimald, Nicholas 118, 120
Guazzoni, Enrico
   Marcantonio e Cleopatra (film) xiv, 77–8
   Quo Vadis (film) 67

Hadfield, Andrew 103–4
Hall, John 25–6
Hall, Peter 70, 71, 86
Hatchuel, Sarah 2, 114
Hatts, Clifford 80
hautboy (musical instrument) 167–9, 261 n.20, 261 n.23
Hawkes, Terence 222
Hazlitt, William 27–8, 29, 30
Heinemann, Margot 222
Heminges, John 56
Hercules 146, 147, 166–7, 169
heroism 135, 138–40, 141–2, 146–8, 152–4
   anti-hero 66
   tragic hero 96–7, 207–8, 209, 218–19, 223–4
      Cleopatra as 44, 96–7, 211
Heston, Charlton xv, 78–9
Hiscock, Andrew 101
His Majesty's Theatre xiv, 67
historiography 101–2, 106–7, 185–7
history
   anachronism 26, 109, 217, 263 n.39
   authenticity 25–6, 30–2, 42–3
   context 39, 47, 109–10, 115–16, 126, 225–7
homosociality 52
Hopkins, Anthony 86
Hopkins, Lisa 102–3
Hopkins, Robert Innes xvii, 84
Horrible, Cruel and Bloody Murder, A (broadside) xiii
horror 28, 179
Hotman, Jean, *The Ambassador* 107

Iachimo (*Cymbeline*) 172–3, 175, 176
identity 47–52, 99, 214–15
   instability of 49, 120
   masculine 49–51
   national 102–3, 187, 192, 216
   and notoriety 52–3
   public 118, 128, 148–9, 250 n.12
   Roman 100, 115–16, 118–20, 122–3, 128, 249 n.9
illusionism 64, 67
imagery 37, 93, 95–6, 171–2
   metaphor 33–4, 106, 139–40
imperialism/empire *see* empire/imperialism
inconstancy 43
Independent Television *see* ITV
infamy 52–3
inferiority complex 3, 4, 7, 8–9, 136–8
inhumanity 119, 250 n.12
Innes, Paul, *Shakespeare's Roman Plays* 216–17

instability
  of geographical space 48, 49
  of identity 49, 120
  political 115–16
interiority 97, 118
intermedial performances 81–7
  2007 Toneelgroep Amsterdam (Hove) 82–3
  2017 Royal Shakespeare Theatre/Barbican (Khan) xvii, 72, 84–6
intimacy, theatrical 65, 73, 80
Ireland 100
ITV (Independent Television) xvi, 80

Jackson, Angus xvii, 84
Jackson, Glenda xvi, 72–3
Jacobean drama 46
Jacobs, Salley 73
Jaggard, Isaac 60
James I (King of England) xiii, 47, 96, 102, 103
Jodelle, Etienne, *Cléopâtre captive* xii, 98, 170
John of Salisbury, *Policraticus* 140
Johnson, Richard 71, 80
Johnson, Samuel 26–7
Jones, Emrys 204
Jones, Inigo 75
Jones, Nicholas 75
Julius Caesar (dramatic character) 2–3, 13–16, 138
  allusions to 8–9
  Antony, comparison anxiety with 4, 7, 8–9, 136–8
  and Cleopatra 7–8, 9–11

Julius Caesar (historical character) xi, 4–5, 14, 138–9
Julius Caesar (play) xv, xvii, 3–4, 6–7, 116–17
  Antony and Cleopatra, comparison with 28, 37
  Antony and Cleopatra as sequel to 1–2, 114
  film adaptations 79
Junker, William 101–2

Kahn, Coppélia, *Roman Shakespeare: Warriors, Wounds and Women* 51–2, 212–14, 217
Kalukango, Joaquina xvii, 72
Kemble, John Philip xiv, 64–5
Kent, Charles xiv, 77
Khan, Iqbal xvii, 72, 84–6
Kiernan, Pauline, *Shakespeare's Theory of Drama* 220–1
Killigrew, Thomas 60, 61
King's Men (theatre company) xiii, 8, 60, 61
Knight, G. Wilson 33–4, 36, 37
Kott, Ian 73
Kureopatora (film, Osama Tezuka, 1970) 183, 184
Kusunoki, Akiko 105

Langley, Eric 93
Langtry, Lily xiv, 66–7
language 8, 10
  ambiguous 120–1, 158–60, 172, 260 n.10, 262 n.31
Lapotaire, Jane 81
Latinate language 8
Leigh, Vivien xv, 70
Lenard, Hester 78

Lepidus (Marcus Aemilius
    Lepidus) xi, 16
Levine, Laura, *Men in Women's
    Clothing* 49–50
Liebler, Naomi Conn, *The
    Female Tragic Hero in
    English Renaissance
    Drama* 223–4
Life of Antony (Plutarch) 78,
    173, 252 n.25
    adherence to 31, 57, 122,
        125, 174
    translations 156, 158–62,
        258 n.2, 260 n.10
lighting 65, 73, 74, 85
Lindley, Arthur 101
Little, Arthur L., Jr 99–100, 130
*Lives of the Noble Grecians
    and Romanes* (North)
    xii, xiii, 156–7, 162–3,
    165–6, 167–9, 170–2,
    175–6
Livia 15
Logan, Robert A. 92
Loomba, Ania 98–9, 204–5
    *Gender, Race, Renaissance
        Drama* 47–9, 219–20
Lord Chamberlain xiii
love story 31, 80, 95, 208–10,
    211–12
luck 15, 105–6, 134–5, 137–8,
    145–6, 148, 150–1
luxury 97–8
Lyric Studios, Hammersmith
    xvi, 72

MacCallum, Mungo William,
    *Shakespeare's Roman
    Plays and Their
    Background* 30–2

Macready, John xiv
Mankiewicz, Joseph,
    Cleopatra (film) xv,
    78–9, 183, 184
Marcantonio e Cleopatra (film,
    Guazzoni, 1913) xiv, 77–8
Marcus Aemilius Lepidus *see*
    Lepidus
Marcus Brutus *see* Brutus
Marcus Lurius xii
Mark Antony *see* Antony
Marlowe, Christopher, *Dido,
    Queen of Carthage* 92–3
marriage 106
masculinity 49–51, 92–3, 95,
    99, 207, 213
    emasculation 8, 49, 79
    virtus (manly courage) 45–6,
        128, 218–19
masks 85
Massinger, Philip, *The False
    One* xiii, 6, 8, 138, 150,
    152
May, Thomas, *Cleopatra* xiii
McCraney, Tarell Alvin xvii
McIntyre, Blanche 84
Melanchthon, Philip 138–9
Méliès, Georges, *Cléopâtre;
    or, Robbing Cleopatra's
    Tomb* (film) 77
memory 173–4
men
    emasculation 8, 49, 79
    playing Cleopatra xvi, 32,
        74, 75
    and *virtus* (manly courage)
        45–6, 128, 218–19
    see also masculinity
Menas xii, 13, 103–4
mercy 126–7

Messenger (dramatic character) 13
messengers/messages 35, 57, 106–7
Messina, Cedric 81
metafiction 193–4, 198–9
metaphor 33–4, 106, 139–40
Metastasio, Pietro, *La Nitteti* (opera) 191
meta-theatricality 56–7, 96, 115, 153–4
Michell, Keith xv, 80
Miles, Geoffrey 121–2
  Shakespeare and the Constant Romans 43
military action 58–9, 66, 144–5
military strategy 13, 163–4
Miller, Jonathan xvi, 80–1
minimalism 73
Minis, Hadewych 83
Miola, Robert S., *Shakespeare's Rome* 41–2, 205–7
Mirren, Helen xvi, 73
mirrors 116–18
Misenum xiv, 13, 66
misreadings 158–60, 162–3, 192
monarchy 103
monologue 96–7
Montreux, Nicolas de, *Cléopâtre* xii
monument scenes (4.15, 5.2) 74, 80, 96, 125–6, 151–2
Morris, Mary xv, 80
mothers/motherhood 50–1, 194
Mummy, The (novel, Rice) 177–80, 187, 192–5, 198–9

Munby, Jonathan xvii, 75–6
music xvii, 85, 86, 165–6, 167–9, 190–5
musical instruments 167–9, 261 n.20, 261 n.23
Mvula, Laura xvii, 85

narrators 92
National Theatre xvii, 83–4
Neil, Hildegarde xvi, 79
New Covent Garden theatre xiv, 64–5
'New' criticism 33–4, 36
New Historicism 45, 46–7
Nicoll, Allardyce, *History of Restoration Drama* 60–1
Nile, Battle of the xi
Noble, Adrian xvi, 73, 86
North, Sir Thomas 156–7, 259 n.3
  Lives of the Noble Grecians and Romanes xii, xiii, 156–7, 162–3, 165–6, 167–9, 170–2, 175–6
Northern Broadsides (theatre company) 72
notoriety 52–3
Novelli, Amleto 77
Nunn, Trevor xv–xvi, 70, 227

Oakley, Stephen 165
observers 57, 118–19
Octavia xi, 15, 43, 78, 142–4
Octavius Caesar (dramatic character) 4, 7, 86, 94, 101–2, 130, 133–4
  and Antony 2, 32, 52, 137–8, 142–4, 162–5
  autocracy of 127
  clemency of 14–15, 126–7

and Cleopatra 16, 126–7
and fortune 15
and Julius Caesar 13–16
performances 83
as reactor 140–4
self-performance 134, 141
topical reading of 47
virtù of (Machiavelli) 106
and women 15–16
Octavius Caesar (Octavian, Augustus) (historic character) xi, xii, 15
Okonedo, Sophie xvii, 86
Old Vic (London) xv, 69
Olivier, Laurence xv, 70
opera 190–5
oppositions, Rome–Egypt 32, 35, 36, 48, 53, 58
and commerce 101
communication 106–7
and costume 73
critique of 37, 42, 43, 121–2, 208, 212–14, 216–17
and film techniques 79
gender 206–7, 219–20
and identity 53
philosophy 99
and set design 71, 73–4, 84–5, 227
oral culture 106–7
Orientalism 194
Osamu Tezuka, *Kureopatora* (animated film) 183, 184
Other Place theatre xvi, 73
Oyun Atölyesi Theatre Company (Istanbul) 76

Pact of Misenum xii, 13
paganism 37–9
Park, Jennifer 108–9

Parker, Barbara L. 15, 93–4, 103
Parolin, Peter A. 108
passion 15, 31, 36, 94–6
of Antony 104–5
of Cleopatra 27, 182–4
Paster, Gail Kern 95–6
Pastrone, Giovanni, *Cabiria* (film) 67, 84
patriarchy 46
pax romana 14, 126, 134
Pembroke, Countess of *see* Sidney, Mary
perfection 104–5
performance
    18th century 63–4
    19th century 64–7
    20th century 67–74, 75, 79–81
    21st century 73–6, 81–7
    and criticism and scholarship 217, 220–1
    debut xiii, 59
    and gender xvi, 32, 60–1, 74, 75, 223–4
    Jacobean period 59–60
    and race xvi, xvii, 72, 86
    Restoration period 60–1
    see also screen adaptations; self-performance; stage productions
performativity 58, 128, 130, 135
Perrin, Bernadotte 175
personas 118, 128, 148–9, 250 n.12
personification 206–7
Pharsalus, Battle of xi, 4
Phelps, Samuel xiv, 66
Philippi, Battle of xi
philosophy, Stoic 43, 93, 127–9, 253 n.35

physicality 221
pictorialism 64, 67
Pistorelli, Don Celso,
    *Marc'Antonio e
    Cleopatra* xii
pity 62–3
Platt, Michael 103
pleasure 27–8, 94–5, 97, 123–4
plot 107
Plutarch 42–3, 155–7, 225,
    226
  and Cleopatra's reputation
    185–8, 189–90
  Life of Antony 78, 173, 252
    n.25
    adherence to 31, 57, 122,
      125, 174
    translations of 156, 158–62,
      258 n.2, 260 n.10
Poel, William 68, 69, 74
poetry 33–4, 37
poison 106, 151, 153–4, 171–2,
    174–5
politics 58–9, 102–4, 107,
    115–16, 141, 210–12
  autocratic 103, 127, 128–9
  and power 58, 93–4, 101–2,
    113–14
Pollard, Tanya 106
Pompey, Sextus xii, 7, 12–13,
    103–4
Pompey the Great xi, 11–12,
    13, 14–15
Pompey the Younger 9, 11
popular culture xiii, 76–9,
    177–8
  Cleopatra in 180, 181,
    182–95
  Egypt in 190–6
postmodernism 114–15

power 45–6, 96, 100, 218–19
  of Cleopatra 58, 93–4
  and the female body 46–7
  and gender 34, 46–7
  military 101–2
  political 58, 93–4, 101–2,
    113–14
  and sex/sexuality 7–8, 46–7
  and women 34, 46–7
predecessor texts 96–8
Presentism 109
Princess's Theatre xiv, 66–7
problem plays 34–5
Proculeius (dramatic character)
    127
productions *see* film
    adaptations; screen
    adaptations; stage
    productions; television
    productions
proscenium arch stage 60, 69–70
Ptolemy Caesar (Caesarion)
    xi, 14
Ptolemy Philadelphus xii
Ptolemy XIII xi
publication xiii, 1, 56, 60
public identity 118, 128, 148–9,
    250 n.12
public/private space 43, 208–9,
    250 n.12

race 47–9, 98–102, 192, 219–20
  and casting xvi, xvii, 72, 86
  and Cleopatra 72, 98, 251
    n.23
Rackin, Phyllis 222
Ramses The Damned (novel,
    Rice and Rice) 177–9,
    180–1, 185–6, 193–4,
    198–9

reacting (versus acting) 135, 138–40, 140–6
Read, David 93
readers 39, 114
realism 34, 83
Redgrave, Corin 71
Redgrave, Michael xv, 70
reflection 116–18
reincarnation 197–8
religion 37–9, 100, 105, 109–10
  Christianity 38–9, 93, 109, 109–10, 134
  gods 105, 109, 165–7, 169
  paganism 37–9
remediation 83
remembering 173–4
representation 21, 117, 185–90, 195–7
reputation 23, 27–8, 185–90
Restoration period 22–5
resurrection 179–80, 185–90, 197–8
revolving stages 70
rewritings 23–4
Rice, Anne
  The Mummy 177–80, 187, 192–5, 198–9
  Ramses The Damned 177–9, 180–1, 185–6, 193–4, 198–9
Rice, Christopher, *Ramses The Damned* 177–9, 180–1, 185–6, 193–4, 198–9
Richardson, John 122
Rider Haggard, H. (Sir Henry), *Cleopatra* 183–4
rivalry 13, 32, 52
Roe, John 105–6
Roman plays 30–3, 37, 114–15, 205–17

Rome
  and Cleopatra 188–9
  and costume 73
  epistemology of 99
  ethics 253 n.35
  exemplarity 114, 115, 116
  and gender 51–2, 58
  homosociality 52
  and identity 100, 115–16, 118–20, 122–3, 128, 249 n.9
  imperial 48–9, 121, 122, 123, 210
  pax romana 14, 126, 134
  as 'public' space 46, 48–9, 208–9
  Republican period 12, 39, 100, 103–4, 115–18, 120, 122–7, 210
  and selfhood 118
  Senate xii
  and set design 71, 84–5, 227
  Stoicism 43, 93, 127–9, 253 n.35
  triumviral period xi, xii, 12, 115–16, 126, 249 n.9
  values of 41–3, 97, 123–5, 127
    decorum 116, 117–18, 119–20, 123–4, 139–40, 249 n.8
    virtus (manly courage) 45–6, 128, 218–19
  and women 105
Rome and Egypt
  binary opposition, critique of 37, 42, 43, 58, 121–2, 208, 212–14, 216–17
  contrasts 32, 35, 36, 48, 53
  commerce 101
  communication 106–7
  film techniques 79

gender 206–7, 219–20
philosophy 99
set design 71, 73–4, 84–5, 227
Rowe, Nicholas 24–5, 64
Royal Shakespeare Company (RSC) xv–xvii, 70–4, 76, 83–4, 84
Royal Shakespeare Theatre (RST, Stratford-upon-Avon) xv–xvii, 70–1, 72–3
Rutter, Carol Chillington 107
Rylance, Mark xvi, 75

Sacerdoti, Gilberto 109
Sadler's Wells Theatre xiv, 66
scenery xiv, 64, 66, 68–9
scenes and acts, division into 60, 68
scenography 71, 73–4
 illusionist 64, 67
 lighting 65, 73, 74, 85
 and Rome-Egypt opposition 71, 73–4, 84–5, 227
 scenery xiv, 64, 66, 68–9
 screens 82
 for television 80
Schalkwyk, David 95
Schanzer, Ernest, *The Problem Plays of Shakespeare* 34–5, 37
scholarly editions 64, 203–5
Schoolmaster (dramatic character) 107
Scoffield, Jon 80
Scott, Alison V. 97–8
screen adaptations 76–81, 227
 film
  1899 *Cléopâtre* (Méliès) 77

  1908 *Antony and Cleopatra* (Kent) xvi, 77
  1913 *Marcantonio e Cleopatra* (Guazzoni) xiv, 77–8
  1963 *Cleopatra* (Mankiewicz) xv, 78–9, 183, 184
  1964 *Carry on Cleo* (Thomas) 184
  1970 *Kureopatora* (Osama Tezuka) 183, 184
  1972 *Antony and Cleopatra* (Heston) xv, 78–9
 intermedial 81–7
  2007 Toneelgroep Amsterdam (Hove) 82–3
  2017 Royal Shakespeare Theatre/Barbican (Khan) xvii, 72, 84–6
 television
  1974 Nunn xvi, 80, 227
  1981 Miller xvi, 80–1
  The Spread of the Eagle (Dews) xv, 79–80
Second Triumvirate xi, xii, 12, 115–16, 126, 249 n.9
Sedley, Sir Charles, *Antony and Cleopatra* 24
selfhood 97, 99, 214–15
self-performance 113–14, 116, 130–1
 of Antony 124–5, 138, 148–50, 213
 of Cleopatra 125–6, 127–30, 150
 and fortune 135, 139–40
 of Octavius 134, 141

and political change
115–16
and reflection 116–18
Seneca (the Younger, Lucius
Annaeus Seneca) 129–30
De clementia 126
Hercules plays 146
serialization 79–80
set design
illusionist 64, 67
lighting 65, 73, 74, 85
and Rome–Egypt opposition
71, 73–4, 84–5, 227
scenery xiv, 64, 66, 68–9
screens 82
for television 80
sex/sexuality 16, 173
of Cleopatra 7–8, 177–9,
182–4, 185–7, 197,
198
and empire/imperialism 99
and power 7–8, 46–7
of women 26–7
Sextus Pompey xii, 7, 12–13,
103–4
Shakespeare, William xii, xiii,
23, 27–8, 94–5
Shakespeare and Company,
Lenox, Massachusetts
xvi, 72
Shakespeare Jubilee (1769)
63–4
Shakespeare Memorial Theatre
xv, 69, 70
Shakespeare's Globe theatre
xvi, 74–6, 83–4
shame 93
Shapiro, Michael 128–9
Shaw, George Bernard, *Caesar
and Cleopatra* 70

Shay, Michele xvi, 72
Sidney, Mary, *Antonius* xii, 6,
96, 98, 146, 151
silence 96–7
Simmons, J. L., *Shakespeare's
Pagan World* 37–9
Simon, Josette xvii, 72, 86
Simonds, Peggy Muñoz 143
Singh, Jyotsna G. 49
sleeping potions 106
Smith, Peter J. 107
soliloquy 96–7
Soothsayer (dramatic character)
136–7, 138
sound 74, 85, 165–6, 167–9
source material 41, 91–2,
155–76, 225–6
Amyot, Jacques 156–7, 158,
159–60, 162–3
Cossa, Pietro 78
Marlowe, Christopher 92
misreadings 158–60, 162–3
North, Sir Thomas xii,
156–7, 158–9, 162–3,
165–6, 170–2, 259 n.4
Plutarch 31, 42–3, 78, 91,
122, 125, 156, 158
translation of 156–7,
159–60, 162–3, 169, 258
n.2, 260 n.10
The Triumph of Venus
(tapestry) 91
Veronese, Paolo, *Alexander
and the Wife and
Daughter of Darius*
(painting) xv, 69
space, geographical 32, 48–9,
58, 68–9, 125–6, 207, 209
space, public/private 43, 46,
48–9

space, theatrical 48, 73
spectacle 64, 65, 67, 72–3, 118–20, 140
spectators 57, 114, 118–19, 140, 172–3
spies 107
Spinello, Alessandro, *Cleopatra* xii
Spread of the Eagle, The (TV programme) xv, 79–80
stage
  machinery 65, 70, 71
  proscenium arch 60, 69–70
  revolving 70
  spectators on 57, 118–19
  thrust 73
stage productions 55–76, 81–7
  1759 Drury Lane (Garrick) xiii, 25, 63
  1769 Shakespeare Jubilee, Stratford-upon-Avon 63–4
  1813 New Covent Garden (Kemble) xiv, 64–5
  1833 Drury Lane (Macready) xiv, 64–5
  1849 Sadler's Wells (Phelps) xiv, 66
  1890 Princess's Theatre (Langtry) xiv, 66–7
  1906 His Majesty's Theatre (Tree) xiv, 67
  1921–2 Old Vic (Atkins) xiv, 69
  1921–2 Shakespeare Memorial Theatre (Bridges-Adams) xv, 69
  1930 Old Vic (Williams) xiv–xv
  1951 St James's Theatre (Benthal) xv, 70
  1953 Shakespeare Memorial Theatre (Byam Shaw) xv, 70
  1972 Royal Shakespeare Theatre (Nunn) xv–xvi, 71
  1978 Royal Shakespeare Theatre (Brook) xvi
  1982 The Other Place (Noble) xvi, 73, 86
  1986 National Theatre (Hall) 86
  1986 Shakespeare and Company, Lenox, Massachusetts xvi, 72
  1989 Lyric Studios, Hammersmith xvi, 72
  1991 Northern Broadsides (theatre company) 72
  1995 English Stage Company 72
  1998 Talawa (theatre company) 72
  1999 Shakespeare's Globe (Block) xvi, 75
  2006 Shakespeare's Globe (Dromgoole) xvi, 75
  2006 Swan Theatre (Doran) xvi–xvii, 73–4
  2007 Toneelgroep Amsterdam (Hove) xvii, 82–3
  2012 Oyun Atölyesi Theatre Company (Aydoğan) 76
  2013 Swan Theatre (McCraney) xvii, 72
  2014 Shakespeare's Globe (Munby) xvii, 75–6
  2017 Royal Shakespeare Theatre/Barbican (Khan) xvii, 72, 84–6

2018 National Theatre
(Godwin) xvii, 86–7
staging
of Cleopatra's death 63
continuous 68–9
Elizabethan 67–8
Jacobean 67–8
military action 66
monument scenes (4.15, 5.2) 74, 80
Stanfield, Clarkson xiv, 66
Stanton, Kay 224
Starks, Lisa S. 92–3
Starks-Estes, Lisa S., *Plays, Violence, Trauma and Virtus in Shakespeare's Roman Poems and* 214–15
Stationers' Register 59–60
Steel, C. E. W. 122–3
Stewart, Alan 106–7
Stewart, Patrick xvi–xvii, 71, 73
St James's Theatre xv, 70
Stoicism 43, 93, 127–9, 253 n.35
strategy, military 13, 163–4
Stratford-upon-Avon
Other Place theatre xvi, 73
Royal Shakespeare Theatre (RST) xv–xvii, 70–1, 72–3
Shakespeare Jubilee (1769) 63–4
Shakespeare Memorial Theatre xv, 69, 70
Swan Theatre xvii, 68, 73
Streete, Adrian 109–10
Strier, Richard 104–5
structure, dramatic 30
problem plays 35
scene division 60, 68
unity of 36
style 24, 27, 33–4, 37, 92, 125–6, 163
subjectivity 38, 97, 99, 214–15
see also agency; self-performance
Suetonius 141
suffering 178–9, 185–90
suicide 26, 28, 44, 50, 93–4, 106
Suzman, Janet xv, 71, 72, 80
Swan Theatre xvii, 68, 73

Talawa (theatre company) 72
taste, literary 23–5
Tate, Nahum 23
Taylor, Elizabeth xv, 183
Tekindor, Zerry 76
television productions 79–81
1974 Nunn xvi, 80, 227
1981 Miller xvi, 80–1
The Spread of the Eagle (Dews) xv, 79–80
Tennenhouse, Leonard, *Power on Display: The Politics of Shakespeare's Genres* 46–7
Terribili-Gonzales, Gianna 77, 78
Tezuka, Osamu, *Kureopatora* (animated film) 183, 184
theatre companies
Actors Touring Company xvi, 72
Duke's Men xiii, 60, 63
English Stage Company 72
King's Men xiii, 8, 60, 61
National Theatre xvii, 83–4
Northern Broadsides 72
Oyun Atölyesi Theatre Company (Istanbul) 76

Royal Shakespeare
  Company (RSC) xv–xvii,
  70–4, 76, 83–4, 84
Shakespeare and Company,
  Lenox, Massachusetts
  xvi, 72
Talawa 72
Toneelgroep Amsterdam
  xvii, 82–3
Theatre Regulation Act
  (Theatres Act) (1843) 66
theatres 48, 64–5, 66, 72–3
  see also set design;
  stage; staging; *individual
  theatres*
theatricality 32, 49–50, 75, 116,
  130, 140, 148
  meta-theatricality 56–7, 96,
  115, 153–4
theatrum mundi tradition 96
Thidias (Thyrsus, Thyreus) 107,
  158–60
Thomas, Gerald, *Carry on Cleo*
  (film) 184
Thomas, Vivian, *Shakespeare's
  Roman Worlds* 42–3
thrust stage 73
Thyreus/Thyrsus (dramatic
  character) *see* Thidias
Tillyard, E. M. W., *The
  Elizabethan World
  Picture* 45
Tiramani, Jenny 75
Toneelgroep Amsterdam
  (theatre company) xvii,
  82–3
topical readings 47, 65, 86–7,
  100, 102–4
tragedy 29–30, 34, 37, 37–8,
  93, 106, 128–9, 129–30

criticism and scholarship on
  44, 46–7, 218–19
Tragedy of Caesar's Revenge
  (anonymous) xiii
tragic flaw 218
tragic hero 96–7, 207–8, 209,
  218–19, 223–4
  Cleopatra as 44, 96–7, 211
transcendence 33–4, 36, 38–9
translation 156–7, 159–60, 162–3,
  169, 258 n.2, 260 n.10
transvestism 49, 75, 79
trauma 28, 35, 141–2, 214–15
Traversi, Derek, *Shakespeare:
  The Roman Plays* 35–6
Tree, Herbert Beerbohm xiv, 67
triumph 44, 48–9, 50, 102, 130,
  153–4
Triumph of Venus, The
  (tapestry) 91
trumpets 167–9, 261 n.20
Twyne, Thomas 169
tyranny 103, 127, 128–9

unities, Aristotelian 24–5, 61–2
unreliable narrators 92

values
  of Egypt 35, 37, 97–8
  of Rome 41–3, 97, 123–5,
    127
    decorum 116, 117–18,
      119–20, 123–4,
      139–40, 249 n.8
    virtus (manly courage)
      45–6, 128, 218–19
van Hove, Ivo xvii, 82–3
Ventidius 62, 85
Verdi, Giuseppe, *Aida* (opera)
  190–5

Veronese, Paolo, *Alexander and the Wife and Daughter of Darius* (painting) xv, 69
Verres, Gaius 122, 123
violence 28, 35, 141–2, 214–15
Virgil, *Aeneid* 169, 216
virtù (Machiavelli) 105–6
virtus (manly courage) 45–6, 128, 218–19
visual culture 91
Vitagraph (film company) 77
voyeurism 172–3

Walker, Greg 107
Walter, Harriet xvi, 73
watching 262 n.33
weddings 106
Weis, René 204
'whitewashing' 192

Wilders, John 205
Williams, Harcourt xv, 69
Wofford, Susanne 166
women 15–16, 105
    actors 60–1
    agency of 182–3, 184
    bodies of 46–7, 51
    and empire/imperialism 99
    and masculinity, construction of 50–2
    and power 34, 46–7, 182–3
    sex/sexuality of 26–7
    as tragic hero 128–9
Wood, Clive xvii, 76
World Shakespeare Festival (2012) 76
Wright, John xiii
written culture 106–7

xenophobia 121–2, 123, 187

www.ingramcontent.com/pod-product-compliance
Lightning Source LLC
Chambersburg PA
CBHW052148300426
44115CB00011B/1575